The Self-Reliant Homestead

THE Self-Reliant Homestead

CHARLES A. SANDERS

 BURFORD BOOKS

Printed in the United States of America.

10 9

Library of Congress Cataloging-in-Publication Data

Sanders, Charles A., 1954-
     The self-reliant homestead : a guide for country living / Charles A. Sanders.
          p. cm.
     ISBN 978-1-58080-114-0
     ISBN 1-58080-114-5 (pbk.)

1. Home economics, Rural. I. Title.
     TX147.S3415 2003
     640'.9173'4—dc21

                                        2003012665

CONTENTS

I

MOVING TO THE COUNTRY

Location, Location, Location

Size and Price

Lay of the Land

Economy of the Area

Legalities—Liens, Titles, Deeds

Taxes

Land Measurements

Making a Living in the Country

Country Auctions

The Sale Barn

At one time or another, nearly everyone dreams of owning a piece of land on which to live and raise a family. This desire is one that helped fuel the great westward push in America. It still exists today in many people, male and female, young and old. Although the days of settling a wild and young country are long since gone, thousands of people still leave the push and shove of the cities each year to look for that special place, their piece of land.

Our country has ended up with huge populations concentrated in our cities and has had to artificially support them ever since. At the same time, small farms and homesteads have fallen by the wayside, victims of artificial price supports, government subsidies, and other economic crutches. Most of these programs the small homesteader did and does not qualify to participate in. More importantly, and to their credit, many homesteaders deliberately choose not to participate in the government-sponsored giveaways, choosing rather to remain independent producers who are not required to conform to the rules of production required by such a program.

Regardless, homesteaders do need a parcel of land from which to re-create their lives. But by concentrating activities and better managing them on a smaller scale, the land requirements are less, as a rule, than for a typical general farm.

In rural America, there are literally tens of thousands of small farms, homesteads, and other tracts of land available for the aspiring homesteader. Perhaps you're looking for a couple of acres. Maybe you want to relocate to one of the small villages or towns that pepper our maps. You could be looking for a remote tract of wilderness land in the mountains. Whatever your wishes, these places are available for those who really want to make the break. There are, however, many things to consider when looking for your little piece of heaven in the hinterlands.

Location, Location, Location

First consideration must, of course, be given to the location of your desired homestead. You must determine generally where you wish to relocate. For many folks, this means a location nearby or within a one- or two-hour drive of where they currently live. Such a reasonable distance from the current residence can provide the best of both worlds. It provides the opportunity for you to retreat to your property on weekends, holidays, or vacations to build, work, and develop the homestead.

At the same time, you can retain your residence and maintain employment. In reality, most homesteaders will be required to obtain or retain some type of outside employment or income, exclusive of the homestead. This is especially true during the start-up phase of your place.

Perhaps, though, you are looking for a place quite a distance from where you currently live. In this case, you will need to narrow down the choices to one or two general areas where you propose to relocate. Next, obtain a few of the newspapers serving that area. Your public library should have an index of newspapers published throughout the United States. The listing includes addresses, telephone numbers, and prices for the publications. Once you get some of these papers, look through the classified sections listing real estate for sale. These listings may be by an individual or under a certified Realtor's advertisement. Realtors regularly have listings of properties ranging from raw land to complete working farms. They know all the regulations and rules in making land purchases and should be able to be quite helpful. If they do not have listed the type of parcel you are looking for, let them know what it is you are interested in. Good Realtors work hard to locate what their customers or potential customers want. Search the Internet for real estate in the area you are interested in. Many Realtors have gone "high tech" and have a Web presence. I'm certain that you will find a Realtor's Web site for your area of interest.

Contact any friends or relatives who might live in the area. Ask them if they know of any properties for sale. At least, you may be able to visit them and use that for a base to do some scouting on your own.

Get out and look around. Often people wishing to sell properties may just post a sign offering it for sale, without formally listing it with a Realtor or advertising it in a newspaper. In fact, I was fortunate enough to spot a 40-acre tract that the owner had posted a FOR SALE sign on just hours before. I bought that piece of land for a very low per-acre price.

Size and Price

Land prices just about everywhere have increased markedly in recent years. There are a variety of reasons for this, but this latest up cycle in land prices seems to have began with a scurry of buyers prior to Y2K. Then, as now, many people began looking for a piece of land as their "refuge" from the uncertainties of city life. In my own area, many tracts of land are being bought up by sportsmen to ensure that they will have a place to hunt. While the motives of these buyers are generally good, the effect has been to drive land prices up. Property that sold for a few hundred dollars per acre 10 years ago is now selling for $1,000 to $1,500 per acre. In many areas of the country, land is selling for upward of twice that amount. In a few areas, you may find a backwoods tract to suit you for less.

Your homestead needn't be a quarter-section farm for you to make or supplement a good living from it. An acre or two may be well suited to your plans for a garden, an orchard, and some rabbits. If you want to raise a large garden and some livestock such as goats, sheep, or cattle, then you will need a bit more land. If you wish to have a woodland to manage and harvest firewood and timber from, your requirements will be greater still. Only you can be the judge. The classic book *The Have-More Plan*, by Ed and Carolyn Robinson, discusses different-sized homesteads and offers sound suggestions for each. I'd recommend it. It's available from Storey Publications in Pownal, Vermont.

Another thing to consider is this: The per-acre price is generally higher on smaller tracts than for larger parcels of land. For example, you may pay anywhere from $1,000 to $3,000 per acre for, say, a 1- to 10-acre tract of land. Similar land in the same area might sell for as little as $500 to $800 per acre in a 40-acre tract. Of course, you still need to take into account other factors such as access, lay of the land, water, general area costs, and so on, but the general rule still applies: The smaller the tract, the higher the per-acre price. I have a couple of friends who solved the problem by purchasing a large tract, then splitting it. This was done on record at the courthouse, so everything was deeded and legal. Both friends are happy with the arrangement. Even with the best of friends, I'd be sure to handle such an arrangement in the same way. Instead of just going into a land purchase with a friend as a joint venture, sit down and decide how the property is to be divided. Do the necessary work to have the property legally divided and recorded. It's neither a lot of trouble nor very expensive, and it could save many headaches and even your friendship later on.

Lay of the Land

The orientation and topography of the land is very important. How does the land lie? Is it on a ridgetop? Perhaps it lies on level ground or is gently rolling. How about future homesites? Are there handy spots for a garden, an orchard, and outbuildings? Is there a good pond site on the land? What are the soil types generally? Is there any swampy ground?

How is the air drainage? Yes, air does drain and is an important factor in locating your homestead. Cool-air pools in low-lying areas or areas where there is a blockage of good movement or drainage of air (such as steep hills or even woodlands). They can be frost pockets and difficult to utilize for certain activities, such as fruit production.

How is the tract oriented? A general southern exposure is good. These areas warm more quickly in spring and will maximize the solar benefits of the shorter winter days. It is amazing just how much heat can be gathered in through south-facing windows during the winter.

How is the soil? You can get an idea of the soil type and condition by the types of plants growing on the property. Compare it with nearby parcels. Talk with some of the locals. What was the land used for prior to your purchase? Was it a general residence with pastureland? Was it in rowcrops? Or timber? Was it used as a landfill or hazardous waste disposal site? Check into it a bit, for it is something you should know. Check the easy things, too, like whether the land lies within a floodplain. If so, it will affect your insurability. The local soil conservation service office serving the area can tell you.

In selecting your property, consider the amenities that are available. Do electric service lines run on, along, or near the land? The costs for running electrical service to properties can be very high, and they're increasing all the time. However, unless you are specifically attempting to become detached from the power utility umbilical cord, it is pretty hard to beat the cost of on-the-grid electrical power in most areas. As a general rule of thumb, if you are a mile or more from existing electrical lines, you might effectively consider utilizing some type of solar power to supply your electricity. Any less distance, and running the electrical lines is usually more cost-effective.

If your area receives enough overall constant wind, you may have a good site for a wind-powered electric plant. Your site will require a minimum of 8-miles-per-hour average annual windspeed for a wind-powered system to be practical. Even then, an annual average of 13 mph is considered only moderately adequate.

If you are fortunate to have a suitable year-round stream on the property, you may be able to install a small hydroelectric power plant to serve your needs.

Is water available on the property? If it's a spring, does it run year-round? Will it supply sufficient quantities of water during late summer or during dry spells? Are wells common and feasible, or is the water supply in the vicinity provided by a large rural water system serving a county or region? These systems are becoming more common and deserve consideration.

How are roads in the area? Being able to tell friends and relatives back in the rat race that you live on a quiet dirt or gravel road in the sticks is great, but during a wet spring or winter of heavy snows, these same quaint roadways can become an impassable hell if you need to get out. In addition, in rural areas, the farther the road is from developed areas, the less likely it is to receive prompt attention for maintenance, snow clearing, and the like.

How about the property itself? What kind of access does it have? Does an access lane exist or will you be required to have a road built into the property? Road building is expensive.

Economy of the Area

What is the overall economy of the area to which you are planning to relocate? Chances are, you will need some way in which to support yourself and your family on your new place, at least for a while. Is there a demand in the area for your particular skills or profession?

Legalities—Liens, Titles, Deeds

One thing that must be touched on in making your land purchase is this: Be absolutely sure that the property you have selected has a deed that is free and clear of any liens. A while back, our area was plagued by an unscrupulous company that operated a lucrative scam until it was caught. These folks would buy up timberlands and have a heavy timber harvest on the tract. They would then borrow all the money they could against the value of the remaining land. At the same time, they would advertise the land for sale and, upon sale, would attest that the land was free and clear of any liens. The illusion of a clear deed was aided by the fact that the papers certifying that title insurance on the property did in fact exist were falsified. One unsuspecting couple who thought the land they had bought from this company was truly theirs were shocked to learn that a local bank held a lien against it for an amount much greater than the total amount they had paid for the property! Who knows how many purchasers were duped by this company?

The point is, be sure you have a clear title to the property you are purchasing. If this requires a title search by an attorney, do that. If you are financing your purchase, title insurance is normally a requirement, so this potential problem is taken care of.

Taxes

Local taxes usually vary widely from place to place and state to state. In many cases, taxes in rural, sparsely populated areas are comparatively high. There are a couple of basic reasons for this. First, people today generally want the amenities and services that their neighbors in more populated areas enjoy—things like paved roads, police and fire protection, and so on. Other costs handed down by state and federal mandates add to the tax burden, whether they are paying for things we want or not. Second, rural and more sparsely populated areas feature a much smaller tax base. That is, there are fewer taxpayers from whom to extract the money needed to fund the various county services, whatever they are.

It could once be said that living in the country was much cheaper, generally, than living in the cities and towns. However, much of that has changed over the years. Formerly, many rural areas in the country could offer lower taxes to landowners—although there were trade-offs. Those same rural areas could not offer the same wide range of services as did the more populated and higher-taxed areas. Roads were gravel and otherwise unimproved. Police and fire protection was usually just somewhat more than minimal. Schools were smaller and did not offer the wide assortment of class curricula, sports, and extracurricular activities that their big-town counterparts could.

The point is to check out what your property tax rate is prior to purchasing your homestead. The rural area where we live has a low tax base—there are relatively few taxpayers upon whom to spread the tax burden to run and maintain the county. This causes higher property tax rates as local governments struggle to comply with mandates from higher government sources as well as maintain the basic county infrastructure.

Many folks cringe at the thought of their peaceful, pastoral area becoming just another patchwork area of hobby farms and commuter homes. Many of these folks consider higher taxes as just part of the price they have to pay to live on their own little piece of paradise!

All of the above is certainly not meant to discourage or frighten the prospective land buyer. To the contrary, it is written to give you a good arsenal with which to go hunting for that special place in the hinterlands. You are hopefully planning to spend a good, long time on your new homestead, so it pays to be patient and locate the best one for your purposes, that you can afford, in an area you like.

Land Measurements

Historically, and not all that long ago, the job of determining boundary lines and proper fences was relegated to the elected official known as the fence-viewer. Fence-viewers settled boundary disputes between landowners and were responsible for the neglect of fences within their jurisdictions.

Fence-viewers and their deputies used a simple device known as a Gunter's Chain for measuring acreage and fence mileage. The Gunter's Chain was a linked measuring device 66 feet long, including handles on each end. It was invented in 1620 by Edmund Gunter, an English mathematician. This invention soon became the established basis for all road and land measurement.

To this day, historical researchers will come upon the number 66 or denotations of that number in survey or real estate records. It may be the measurement of a city block (normally 3 chains to a city block, 1 to a street), the distance between telegraph poles (1 and 2 chains apart), the width of a canalway (1 chain), or the width of a highway grant (1 chain, with the roadbed centered in the middle). The early "Broadways" were of dimensions such as those of Duke of Gloucester Street in Williamsburg, Virginia, laid out in 1699 as a "great noble street of six poles" or one and a half chains.

The standard length of a rail or section of rail fence was 11 feet, so that fence-viewers could walk along a fence and, by apportioning six rails to the chain, tell at a glance the size of any field. If they wanted to measure out exact chain-lengths, they could use any 11-foot rail as a measuring stick.

Shorter distances were measured in rods, also known as "poles" or "perches." Why a rod should be 16½ feet has mystified most students. But 16½ feet happens to be just one-fourth of a chain; the rod was once known as a "quarter-chain." Few know why a mile should be 5,280 feet long, but if you multiply a chain by 80, you will soon find out (80 x 66 = 5,280). Even the mystic 43,560 square feet of an acre is found to be the sum of 10 square chains (66 x 66 x 10 = 43,560). Soon it becomes obvious that most of our present land and survey measurements hark back to Gunter and his nearly obsolete chain.

As a young man, I worked for one of our state forest properties and had occasion to serve as a surveyor's assistant while measuring and marking the property's boundary lines. We used a Gunter's Chain, although I recall it being merely called "a chain."

By examining the accompanying illustration, you can see how this measuring device has carried over to today and remains the base for all surveys in the country.

Section of Land/Measurements

MAP OF SECTION OF LAND SHOWING ACREAGE AND DISTANCE

1 Section = 1 Square Mile = 640 Acres

4 furlongs 40 chains 160 rods 2,640 feet	2 furlongs	20 chains
4 furlongs **NW 1/4** 160 acres	160 rods **NE 1/4** 80 acres	**1/4** 80 acres 2,840 feet
160 rods	80 rods	1,320 feet
2 furlongs — 20 acres — 1,320 feet 10 chains	660 feet — 20 acres	40 rods — 20 acres	20 chains — 40 acres	80 rods — 40 acres
20 chains — 20 acres — 80 rods 1 furlong **SW 1/4**	20 chains — 80 rods	N.W.S.E. **SE 1/4**	N.E.S.E. 20 chains
40 rods — 5 acres / 660 feet — 5 acres	20 rods / 5 A. — 330 feet / 5 A.	1 furlong — 10 acres	10 chains — 10 acres	20 chains	1,320 feet
10 acres	10 acres	10 acres	10 acres	S.W.S.E.	S.E.S.E.
1 furlong	10 chains	40 rods	660 feet	1,320 feet 40 acres	2 furlongs 40 acres

Below, a handy chart lists common linear distances used around the farm.

These can be useful when measuring for fencing projects, laying off pastures or paddocks, and so on.

USEFUL DISTANCES AND MEASUREMENTS
WHEN DEALING WITH PARCELS OF LAND

1 mile = 8 furlongs	1 square foot = 144 sq. inches
1 link = 7.92 inches	1 square yard = 9 sq. feet
1 foot = 12 inches	
1 yard = 36 inches	1 square rod = 272.25 sq. feet
= 3 feet	= 30.25 sq. yards
1 rod or pole = 16.5 feet	1 acre = 43,560 sq. feet
or perch = 5.5 yards	= 160 sq. rods
= 25 links	= 10 sq. chains
1 chain = 66 feet	1 acre is about 208.7 ft. sq.
= 100 links	or 8 rods wide by 20 rods long
= 4 rods	or any two numbers of rods
1 furlong = 40 rods	whose product is 160
= 660 feet	(25 x 125 ft.) = .0717 acre
1 mile = 5,280 feet	1 square mile or 1 section equals
= 320 rods	640 acres
= 80 chains	
= 8 furlongs	1 township = 36 sq. miles
320 rods = 5,280 feet	= 36 sections
	= 6 miles square

6	5	4	3	2	1
7	8	9	10	11	12
18	17	16	15	14	13
19	20	21	22	23	24
30	29	28	27	26	25
31	32	33	34	35	36

This is a depiction of one legal township. A legal township is made up of 36 square miles. Notice that the section numbering begins in the northeasternmost corner and proceeds downward back and forth to Section 36. Each numbered section is made up of 640 acres and is 1 mile square.

Below is an illustration of how a section would generally be divided and described in a legal property description. Refer to the first chart on land and acreage divisions, the township chart, and the picture to help give you an idea of how tracts or parcels of land are described on deeds and in platbooks.

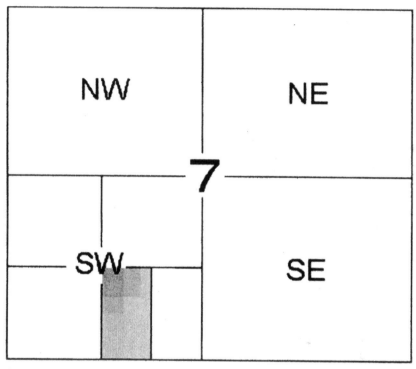

A parcel of land (shaded area) is divided from a section of land, which in turn is divided from a legal township. The shaded tract of land would be designated as the W ½ SE ¼ SW ¼ Sec. 7; that is, it is located in the western one-half of the southeastern one-quarter of the southwestern one-quarter of section seven. A parcel of land (shaded area) is divided from a section of land, which in turn is divided from a legal township.

Making a Living in the Country

When I sat down and really began to think about the theme for this section—making a living in the country—I began to think about all people who live around me and what they do to earn a living.

Sometimes prospective "homesteaders" are lured to the country by the thoughts of living a simple life and making a living solely from their small farm. If you are hoping to make a living strictly off your homestead in the traditional agricultural sense, then you are likely to be in for some big disappointments.

For many reasons, in today's economy it is difficult for one wage earner to make enough to support a family. Similarly, it can be tough to live in the country and support a family on a rural income.

In the "old days," farmers held what you might call "diversified stock portfolios." That is, every well-rounded homestead had a variety of stock: cattle, hogs, chickens, horses, and maybe sheep, rabbits, and fowl. They knew that diversification was the key to maintaining a profitable farm. Each type of livestock contributed its own important part to the whole of the farm income. I believe that a modern-day small farmer-homesteader would do well to imitate these predecessors. Often we seem to be looking for that magical moneymaker that we can concentrate our efforts on. More realistically, diversification is the better answer.

In the classic book *Five Acres and Independence*, author M. G. Kains presents a pretty thorough account of a good, well-rounded, productive homestead. Throughout this venerable old text, the author stresses the importance of having several sources of income on the place. The wisdom contained in the pages of this old handbook holds true yet today. Having something to sell at different times throughout the year is an admirable—and essential—goal.

With that all said, I'll add this: If you're relocating to the backwoods, you will very likely have to give some thought to generating income—that is, making a living. Hopefully, the topic is one you've prepared for prior to making the jump—getting the cart and horse in the proper order, you know.

Most of us want a lifestyle for ourselves and our families that a small homestead can simply not support. Outside expenses that frequently present themselves, and even the most self-sufficient homesteader requires some items that cannot be produced on the place. To be able to buy, build, maintain, and keep our place in the country, most of us are required to seek outside "gainful employment." If you fall into this category, don't get discouraged. Simply make the most of where you are. It is no crime to work away from home to be able to keep your place in the country.

I don't need to tell you that making a living anywhere these days is tough. Making a go of it out on a homestead or small place is even tougher without some outside source of income. There are exceptions, but most of us need some source of steady—or at least semiregular—income. Living in the backwoods is the dream of countless people. Not only do you still need a way to support yourself and your family, however, but you will also find that in remote and rural areas jobs are harder to come by, and they often pay less than in the city.

Some of the people described in this section have more than one pursuit that contributes to their income. Some couples pursue their work independently; others team up. Many of the folks I mention here have expanded upon something they already enjoy doing. Others have recognized the need for a product or service and used that to form the basis of a supplemental income. Basically, they created their own second job.

The people below are the friends and neighbors among whom I live here in my southern Indiana county. They are not listed here in any particular order. Despite the diversity in job interests, all these people share a common bond: the desire to live in our small rural county. Let's take a look.

MAKING AND SELLING FIGURES, DRIED WREATHS, SWAGS, AND OTHER CRAFTS. If you have an eye for color and design, this may offer possibilities. Consider wholesale and retail sales for your works. If you decide to sell to retail shops and stores, plan to visit them during the off season, when many shops like to pick up original crafts items.

SELLING WOOL TO SPECIALTY MARKETS. Sell cleaned and combed wool by the pound to spinners and other craftspeople.

RAISING LAMBS FOR SLAUGHTER. Particularly in areas with a large multicultural population, lamb is a

My wife created dozens of these charming Santa figures to sell. Locally bought wool, real fur, and fine fabrics were used in creating the figures.

very popular meat. You can easily get a good price for your lambs with a simple advertisement in the local paper, or at a food co-op or organic grocery. College towns and larger cities are especially good areas to target.

RAISING HOGS AND BEEF FOR LOCAL SALE. If you raise a few hogs to butchering size—200 to 250 pounds—you can provide your own meat as well as find a market locally with folks who want meat that they know was raised close to home. Beef steers raised to about 800 to 1,100 pounds will sell well. You should be able to easily sell halves or whole steers, especially if you can offer hauling to the custom slaughterhouse.

GARDEN PRODUCE AND PLANTS. Timing is important when producing plants. Plan to have your prime and healthy plants ready when they are most wanted by the buyers. Market them from home, or from local grocers or other retail outlets. Grow varieties that are popular locally.

HOME-RAISED BERRIES AND ORCHARD FRUIT. Sell surplus strawberries, raspberries, blackberries, apples, cherries, peaches, and other fruits with a simple advertisement in your local newspaper, an ad tacked up at a local store, or just by word of mouth. Consider marketing these items at a farmer's market to get better prices.

HOME-GROWN HERBS. Fresh and dried herbs can be a moneymaker for you. Some folks are having good success marketing specialty herbs directly to restaurants. Others sell to supermarkets, food co-ops, and organic groceries.

FURNITURE MAKING. Make solid, functional furniture and, if you are talented, you will find no shortage of buyers for your work.

PHOTOGRAPHY STUDIO. Portrait photography, high school senior class photos, wedding pictures, Christmas portraits, and other special-occasion and holiday photos can keep a photographer busy.

My neighbor works on a piece of solid oak furniture. He makes many pieces each year and restores others. If you have woodworking skills, you, too, can make money in this way.

PRINTING SHOP. Modern computer software and printing equipment make this a real possibility. Design, lay out, and print booklets, brochures, pamphlets, magazines, books, and magazines.

WILDCRAFTING. Gather roots such as goldenseal, ginseng, may-apple, bloodroot, wild ginger, and other botanicals. There is a ready market for blackberries, raspberries, persimmons, mushrooms, and other wild foods. Even sassafras root and bark have a market.

Ginseng is always in demand. Many folks make money selling dried ginseng roots.

CUTTING FIREWOOD. Tops left from logging operations usually provide plenty in the way of cordwood. Some woodcutters obtain slabs and other leftovers from area sawmills. With a good chain saw and a sturdy pickup truck, you'll be in business.

HARVESTING STONE. Picking rock from some streams, dry branches, and rocky hillsides can earn you $30 to $90 a ton, depending on the type and shape of the stone. The rock may end up as veneer on a basement or house, as a hearth and chimney in a city dweller's "country" home, or as a plain old rock wall.

HUNTING OR FISHING GUIDE. In some states, guides are required for nonresidents hunting big game. Even in areas where they are not required, hunters are often willing to pay good money for the chance to bag game or catch a stringer of fish. Hunting and fishing guides are licensed in some states, so check with your state fish and wildlife agency for more information.

DAY LABOR. Hire out by the day to do general labor, whether it's cutting brush, building fence, painting barns, mowing, rough carpentry, or just about anything else that needs doing. Laborers are normally paid at an hourly rate ranging from minimum wage to a dollar or two above that, although some jobs may pay more.

PAINTING, WRITING, AND PHOTOGRAPHY. A friend of mine has painted a mural in the lobby of our post office and has had showings of his paintings in several area galleries. His most recent successes have included four books about the local area. The first book highlighted local folk artists from the county. The second chronicled, in word and pictures, the daily life in our rural county. His third book was an ambitious—and successful—photographic history of the county. His fourth project was a collection of folktales and stories of growing up told by dozens of old-timers in the area. His most recent project involved traveling around the southern half of the state, recording and documenting the last of the small-town country stores, drive-in restaurants and theaters, and similar businesses. This gentleman has done a lot for preserving the rich history of our area, and has made a decent living as well.

SKETCH AND PEN-AND-INK DRAWINGS of area landmarks. Hand-watercolor some prints and offer them for sale at crafts fairs, festivals, and local shops.

WILDLAND FIREFIGHTER. Contact your local state or national forest office for more information in getting the necessary training and certification for this work. Firefighting is not easy work. It is dirty, often dangerous, and physically demanding—a lot of "grunt" work. It is also satisfying, exciting, interesting, and offers an opportunity to see places you might not otherwise get to.

WOODCARVING. Wildlife art is booming. Lifelike carvings of fish, waterfowl, and wildlife can earn you big bucks. If you have a knack for carving, there is a demand for good work.

WELDING. Good welders are hard to find. With a home-based welding shop and a portable, truck-mounted welder, you can keep busy. In fact, one old boy I know could be retiring in a few years, and I don't know of anyone planning to take his place.

TAX PREPARATION. If you have skills in this area, add some of the quality computer software available, and this could be a promising home-based business.

GUN SHOP AND GUNSMITHING. Sell firearms, ammunition, and related equipment; do simple, minor repairs, fit scopes and accessories, and sight-in firearms for customers. You will develop a steady line of customers and a lot of regulars.

SELLING AND SETTING UP COMPUTER SYSTEMS. A fellow I know recently quit his factory job after 20-some years and went full time into this business. He did not simply plunge into the new venture, but eased into it gradually, doing it as a part-time endeavor for several years. He knows his business and is swamped with customers.

COMPUTER-BASED SALES. Sell individual items over the Internet, notably by using the popular eBay. It is simple to become a registered seller on this Web-based market. Rules and conditions are spelled out at the Web site.

AUTOMOBILE BODY REPAIR SHOPS. These shops are required to work with several insurance companies when doing most accident repairs, but this helps to ensure prompt payment. They are all kept busy and are making decent money.

AUTOMOBILE MECHANIC. Branch out and obtain the diagnostic equipment needed to work on late-model computer-laden vehicles. Furthermore, in rural areas such as ours, there are plenty of (t)rusty older vehicles to work on as well. In both these areas of work, it seems that people are more than willing to compete with the overpriced work done in the major dealerships.

WOODCRAFTS. If you can do scrollwork, create jewelry boxes, clocks, miniature houses, inlaid wooden chessboards, or even handmade cigar humidors, you can keep busy filling orders for your work. Concentrate on what is popular at the time and fill the niche.

FLOWER SHOP. Supply cut and dried flowers, plants, special-occasion balloons, and similar gift items.

GROW FRESH AND DRIED FLOWERS. Flower shops and craftspeople use both and usually jump at the chance to get good locally grown stock that has not had to travel over hundreds of miles.

LEGAL RECORDER. Record legal proceedings, meeting minutes, depositions, and other official records. Transcribe them at home and provide clients with neat, bound copies of the records. A good word processor and good dictation skills are musts for this work.

SCHOOL BUS ROUTE. These routes are let for bid every couple of years. Driving a bus is usually used to supplement some other employment. Check with your local school administrators for details about your area.

BULLDOZING AND BACKHOE SERVICES. Skill with this equipment can keep you busy building ponds, digging ditches, installing septic systems, building roads, and so on.

HAUL GRAVEL AND FILL DIRT. A good dump truck can get you plenty of business in this area.

SMALL DITCHER. Lay water and electrical lines, put in drain tiles, and the like. Jobs are usually charged per foot of installation.

ELECTRICIANS can keep busy doing both residential and commercial work.

HEATING AND COOLING. Installation and repair are always needed in any small community.

RESIDENTIAL AND COMMERCIAL PAINTING, from painting windows to entire buildings. Be versatile and do good work at a reasonable price.

OFFICE CLEANING. This work is performed mostly after hours, and the whole family pitches in.

CLEANING RESIDENCES. If you are trustworthy and do good work, you can stay as busy as you want.

CARPENTRY AND BUILDING LOG HOMES. Not only do our local carpenters build the log homes, but they also cut the logs for the structure themselves on their band saw mill. When they are not putting up a cabin, they are kept busy with general carpentry jobs. They can also move their mill right onto a property and custom-cut lumber for the landowner at competitive prices.

MOWING LAWNS. Invest in a commercial-grade riding mower and some solid push mowers and weed whackers.

TREE TRIMMING. Keep busy doing home improvement work, clearing storm damage, and the like.

LANDSCAPING. This lucrative type of work does require a bit of traveling to larger population centers, because landscaping opportunities in rural areas are pretty limited.

AUCTIONEERING. Estate and farm auctions are held throughout the year. Auctioneers are usually paid on a percentage basis.

TIMBER SALES. The demand for good-quality hardwood is high. Consult with your state department of forestry to learn more about properly managing your woodlands for maximum value.

RAISING CHRISTMAS TREES. Cut-your-own operations work well for many folks, especially when coupled with displays of other home-raised products and items. Consider spruces or pines adapted to your area.

As I stated at the beginning of this section, making a living anywhere is not easy. If you can make a go of it solely on your homestead, you are to be commended. If you need to get out and seek employment, then follow some of the tips given here. You do not need to give up on living in the backwoods, though. Use your imagination, interests, perseverance, talent, and skills. Find what is needed in your area and pursue it. Don't give up. Living in the sticks is worth it.

Country Auctions

When folks set out to equip their homestead with the tools, livestock, machinery, and other things essential in their effort toward self-sufficiency, they are usually limited by the amount of working capital on hand. The cost of new tractors and implements, registered breeds of livestock, or fine new tools is usually high enough to keep these items well out of the reach of most of us. As a part of the self-reliant homesteader's country economy, public auctions and estate sales can prove valuable in helping equip the farm and home. From tractors, implements, and livestock to pots, pans, appliances, and home furnishings, country auctions can be a great asset to the homesteader. I have made some really good buys at auctions, and enjoy going to them. If you keep your eyes open and use your head, then you, too, can haul away some great deals and some badly needed items for your own place. Here are some tips on making you a successful auctiongoer.

First, you need to locate a good sale to attend. To find country auctions in your area, pick up a copy of the local or area newspaper, especially a Sunday or late-weekday edition—say, a Thursday issue. These are most likely to have advertisements for upcoming auctions. Look, too, for handbills posted in or near places of business such as feed stores, groceries, or the like. Once you've spotted a sale that interests you, plan to arrive at the site half an hour or so before the scheduled starting time. This will allow you plenty of time to look over the items listed. You can better check the make, condition, and suitability of an item before the bidding starts.

Auctioneers operate on a percentage basis. That is, they normally get a certain percent of the total amount of money brought in at the sale. In my area, auctioneers usually get from 3 to 5 percent on real estate sales, 10 to 15 percent on household auctions, and only around 5 or 6 percent on farm sales. (As one auctioneer told me, "It takes only about as long to sell a $5,000 to $6,000 tractor as it does a $100 table." Hence the lower rate charged on farm sales.) As a rule, the seller foots the bill for any advertising and for paying the clerks and ringmen, which around here pays about six dollars an hour.

Country auctions are busy places, often quite informal as to bidding and generally a pleasant atmosphere for all. Often the auctioneer knows

The auctioneer works the crowd trying to get the highest bid possible.

many of the "regulars" on a first-name basis, and even knows what items they will be interested in. When you get to the sale site, you will need to pick up a bidder's number, usually a card with an assigned number. This is done at a table or other spot where the bookkeeper is located. Identification such as a driver's license is usually sufficient to get a buyer's number. However, when particularly valuable items are being sold, a letter of credit or a reference from your bank is sometimes required. With approved identification or letter of credit, a personal check is usually acceptable for payment.

Once the bidding starts, your bid is usually acknowledged by ringmen—spotters working with the auctioneer—who scan the crowd for willing bidders such as yourself. Raising a hand or a nod of the head is usually sufficient to get noticed, but in some cases you may have to speak out with your initial bid. Don't be bashful; get in there and make a bid. From there, the ringman will watch for your bid and perhaps—no, usually(!)—urge you to go a bit higher if you stop bidding. Once you get your sought-after item, the auctioneer or the spotter will ask for your number, which the recorder will write down along with the name of the item bought and the selling price. As the recorder's sheets are filled up, they are relayed to the payment counter, usually the same place where you picked up your number. It's a good idea, especially if you are buying several items, to jot down the name and the price you paid for each one. Often the back of your bidder's card is printed with lines and columns just for this purpose. This will help prevent mistakes and being charged for items that you did not purchase. Too, at most sales you can merely put all of your booty in one spot until the sale is over. Theft is generally—and I say *generally*—not a problem. Of course, if you have a small and particularly valuable item, I recommend either carrying it with you or locking it up in the truck until the sale is over. A few other things should be remembered when visiting an auction. First, almost every auction is conducted on the basis that buyers know what they're buying and that each item is sold "as is." The old phrase *"Caveat emptor"* definitely applies here—*Let the buyer beware.* Second, know what item you are bidding on at a given time. Now, this may seem rather basic, but many are the folks who were caught not paying attention and ended up buying an item when they thought they were bidding on something else. Often one of the ringmen may hold an item up for the crowd to see, but once the sale really gets rolling, items, especially small ones, sell fast, and you may find yourself bidding on an item that just sold or on an item that is not up yet. If you do this once, you'll generally break yourself of the habit! There is little harm done if it is an item costing only a dollar or two, but even these mistakes can add up.

Third, know the name, quality, and condition of the item you are bidding on, as well as you can, of course. Just about all auctiongoers have gotten skinned once or twice in their careers. Just learn from the experience. There are usually plenty of folks who are willing to help you evaluate an item prior to bidding. Too, don't be afraid to bid a dollar (or sometimes even less!) for a box of "junk." Many are the times I have bought a box of junk bolts, nails, or whatever, and have been pleasantly surprised to find an unexpected item of much greater worth. Once I bought a box of old bolts, nuts, washers, and other assorted hardware for about a dollar. I had looked briefly through the box and was sure that I had more than gotten my money's worth. I was very pleasantly surprised to find, amid the rusty pieces, a clevis to fit my tractor drawbar— one that I'd been needing. And that box of bolts and fasteners has been a great help around the 'stead. I haven't even tried to figure up the savings that this purchase has made for me.

Fourth, have a limit on the amount that you are willing to pay for an item. This can be one of the most important rules of auctiongoing. Again, at one time or another most of us have gone above and beyond our limit on an item in our bidding, and kicked ourselves in the posterior later. Almost any country auctioneer will try to get you to go just a little higher, then a little higher! It's all done in good spirit, and any higher bid means more income for the seller—and ultimately for the auctioneer, as well. Watch, however, for the unethical auctioneer who will use someone in the crowd to help run up the price on an item. I once witnessed just such an incident at an otherwise good farm sale. The farm owner had a really nice old Ferguson tractor that was selling. A young man and his wife were bidding on the tractor, along with a couple of other folks. As the bidding dropped down to two participants, including the young man, I noticed the auctioneer give a wink to the other bidder, and the price of the tractor ended up several hundred dollars more than it should have been. This second bidder was across the crowd from the first, so it was easy for the auctioneer to swing toward him, leaving his gestures invisible to the young man. I left that sale soon afterward, and to this date I do not attend sales conducted by this auctioneer. I figure if he cheated that fellow, he'd take me if he had the chance.

The Auctiongoer's Survival Kit

Here are some tips to keep in mind when heading to an auction:

☞ Look over local newspapers and the like to spot upcoming sales.

☞ Arrive early to look over the merchandise. See if it is what you need and check its condition. *Caveat emptor* applies.

☞ Know what you are willing to pay for an item and stick with that amount.

☞ Know what similar items are selling for generally. Don't end up paying more than it'd cost to buy it new!

☞ When buying several items, jot down the name of the item purchased along with the price paid.

The Sale Barn

Another type of auction is the auction house, often known locally as the "sale barn." This type of sale is usually held regularly, often weekly, and in the same location. The sale is conducted on a consignment basis, which means that items are brought by the seller and sold via bidding, with the auctioneer or auction house getting a percentage of the selling price. These can be general item sales, or be specifically held for horses and tack, feeder cattle, and so on. As an example, one such sale held near our place is a combination of general sale and livestock sale. The general sale begins at 6:00 P.M., and the livestock sale promptly at 7:00. If the general sale is not completed by that time, it moves outside. These livestock sales include everything but horses and tack (they are held on alternate weekends). It is not uncommon to see goats, sheep, pigs, and cattle all run through the ring in an evening. The smaller animals such as fowl and rabbits are sold during the regular 6:00 sale. Everything from welding rods and hardware to sacks of apples, pears, and even persimmons is available at this sale. Country folks often use these sales as an outlet for surplus or otherwise unwanted produce and small livestock. It's a good place to pick up some chickens for a dollar each or a sack of home-grown apples for a couple of bucks.

These sales are often attended by regulars, both sellers and buyers. The same rules apply here as with other auctions, but I want to reinforce one of them: Know what you are buying, *especially* when it comes to livestock. Some small-scale stock raisers bring their surplus to these sales to be sold, and you can often pick up some nice animals. The prices will be competitive with going market prices, so the seller comes out well. But watch out for "junk" animals being run through the ring. Get to the sales early and look the "merchandise" over. Check for symptoms of illness or disease and for deformities. If you are not knowledgeable about these defects in animals, bring along a friend who can help guide you toward or away from bidding on a particular animal. Keep your eyes open and you can get some good deals here, just as with other auctions. I know several folks who have bought some older cows or ewes at these sales and, by hanging on to the female offspring produced, have built up some pretty nice little herds. Just as often, though, I've heard of friends who have picked up sick, foundered, injured, or otherwise unhealthy stock. These animals soon died shortly afterward or had to be put down. Again, it is "Buyer beware." It is a good idea to have your newly purchased critters checked out by a veterinarian after you get them home.

Over in our neighboring Amish settlement, a huge sale is held every Friday night. It attracts folks from a three-state area; there are usually five or six auction rings going at one time. Here again, you can bid on cattle, chickens, goats, sheep, furniture, fruits and vegetables, tools, building materials, hay, and just about anything else you can think of. It is fun and interesting to go to this enormous weekly sale, but in trying to keep track of an item in one area that you want to bid on, you may lose out on another item at another ring!

Country auctions and sales can be a valuable asset to the homesteader. They can certainly help stretch the dollars that we never seem to have enough of. Watch what you are doing and you can come away with needed items and equipment for your homestead at some real savings. Glance through the local paper this week and find a good sale to go to. But be warned: They could be habit forming!

2

EQUIPMENT, TOOLS, & HOMESTEAD HELPERS

Wheels (Trucks, Tractors and
Implements, and All-Terrain Vehicles)

The Homestead Workbench

Gardening Tools

Homestead Hints and Helpers

Selecting a Homestead Firearm
(Rifles, Handguns, and Shotguns)

Wheels

If you are a new homesteader, you may need to give some thought to the topic of transportation. In most of the rural countryside with which I'm familiar, the typical "town" car doesn't last very long. In a few places in my area, bridges are still forsaken in favor of an old-fashioned ford across the creek. Even the "good" county roads are not good. In addition, you are going to need a way to get the gardens plowed, pastures mowed, hay cut, firewood hauled, and so on. Rugged vehicles are a must.

TRUCKS

To most of us living in the country, a work vehicle is, out of necessity, a pickup truck. A serious homesteader will soon learn that some sort of truck is virtually indispensable around the place. It's hard to haul a cow or pig or load of lumber on a bicycle or motorcycle—or in the back of a car, for that matter! You will soon learn that a truck is needed.

Pickup trucks seem to be the vehicle of choice these days, and resale prices—as well as new sticker prices—are high. There are several manufacturers of quality pickup trucks, including Chevrolet, Dodge, Ford, Mazda, Nissan, and Toyota. There are standard-sized trucks, as well as smaller and intermediate-sized ones to fill the gaps. Your choice of manufacturer is pretty much a personal matter, since—in my opinion—all the models are well made and dependable. I believe that more depends upon the way the vehicle is maintained and used.

Four-wheel-drive pickups are very useful around a farm or homestead. However, you must consider the extra initial cost as well as the cost of repairs and maintenance. Although they are very versatile, four-wheel-drive trucks are not unstoppable. As a friend once told me, "A four-wheel drive only lets you get stuck farther off the road." Indeed, even these tough trucks can be stuck, hung up, dented, bent, and broken.

With fuel and vehicle costs both at all-time highs, you may consider a diesel engine in your vehicle. With ordinary maintenance, these vehicles should last for hundreds of thousands of miles. Longevity is the diesel's trademark.

With the same factor in mind—high fuel costs—the small and midsized trucks are very popular. They offer the same features as their big brothers, are tough, and can still haul a respectable load.

For my uses, a standard-sized, four-wheel-drive pickup truck with an average-sized V-8 engine and automatic transmission fills the bill.

TRACTORS AND IMPLEMENTS

If your homestead is more than 10 acres or so, chances are that you are going to find a real need for some extra horsepower to help get the work done.

For most of us, horsepower on the homestead is going to be restricted to the mechanical type. Indeed, a tractor in the 25- to 50-horsepower range will find nearly unlimited uses as you go about building and maintaining your farm.

There are many makes and models of these small to medium-sized tractors. For the homesteader, price restrictions will probably require that the search be limited to older models, however.

It is not difficult to locate used tractors for sale. Advertisements listing them can be found in the local newspapers, in trading papers, and posted at feed stores. What is difficult is believing the prices that many of these old workhorses are going for. Some of the more popular models of tractors regularly sell for two to three times as much as their original price!

There are many sources for locating old tractors. Let's look at a few of them. First, farm and estate auctions are always a good place to locate

A tractor is a useful piece of equipment to have, especially on the larger homestead.

tractors as well as needed implements. These sales are not without risk, however; see chapter 1.

Areawide publications devoted to advertisements of all types regularly carry several columns of farm tractors and implements. These are not only good for locating tractors and other items of interest to you, but can also help you get a good idea of what various makes, models, and sizes of tractors are selling for. These "trading papers" usually cover a pretty wide geographic area, roughly a 100- to 150-mile radius.

Classified advertisements in local or area newspapers normally have some tractors and equipment listed in the "farm equipment" columns.

Many folks merely advertise their tractors by setting them in the front yard and sticking a FOR SALE sign on them. It seems to work and is low-budget advertising. If you have a limited knowledge of tractors, enlist the help of a friend who is more mechanically inclined to help give your prospective purchase a good looking-over.

Since you have decided that you need a tractor, you need to familiarize yourself with some of the different types and features generally found on the small to medium homestead sized tractors—say, the 20- to 40-horsepower range.

Several makes of older tractors are common. Ford, Ferguson, John Deere, Massey-Ferguson, Allis-Chalmers, International, and Case are among the more widely recognized names.

Newer makes include some foreign-made models such as Yanmar, Belarus, Kubota, and several others. If you are a stickler for buying American, you should note that most of the smaller tractors of the major brands such as Ford and John Deere are now also made overseas.

If you are not familiar with the various models of each particular brand of tractor, spend some time as you search to learn a bit about each one. Each model of tractor has a few features unique to that particular make.

Basic to this is learning the general horsepower rating of the various tractors. You don't need to know how to spout off horsepower ratings for every model, but try to have an idea of what the horsepower is for the tractor you are looking at. This will help when you're trying to match implements later on.

Another basic distinction you will quickly learn is whether the tractor has a wide front or a "tricycle" front. Now, this may seem unimportant, but let me tell you, if your homestead or farm is on hilly ground, you will *definitely* want to look for a tractor with a wide front end. The added stability and safety of these tractors is invaluable when working on hills and slopes. I know of several farmers who have been severely

injured or killed while working on hilly ground with tricycle-front tractors. If I may put it in a nutshell: *Do not* buy a tricycle-type tractor if you
are going to be working hilly ground.

Another seemingly obvious feature is how the tractor accommodates
hooking up to the various implements you will need. You'll find a bit of
variety here, because there are three or four attachment methods,
depending upon the make of the tractor. The simplest is merely the use
of a drawbar. This is pretty well universal; almost every tractor has such
an attachment point. Years ago, before hydraulic lift systems were common, many farmers made the transition from horse-drawn implements
to the newfangled tractor by merely cutting down the implement
tongues on their machinery with a saw, then adding a metal strap or two
to attach the implement to the tractor drawbar. The drawbar remains
the most common way to hook up trailers, manure spreaders, and many
other wheeled implements.

Nowadays most tractors have some type of hydraulic lift method for
raising implements when moving to and from the fields, or when turning around or backing up. While some lift systems are unique to the
make of tractor, I recommend looking for a tractor with the "three-point
hitch" lift system. This system is almost universal, and used implements
are much more easily found for these types of tractors.

TRACTOR IMPLEMENTS

Tractors are versatile. You will likely find yourself finding new ways to
utilize these labor-saving machines. Below are listed a variety of attachments and common implements that you may find useful on your place.

TRAILER. A good two-wheel trailer is handy for all sorts of things on
the farm.

WAGON. Good for hauling hay or wood or other loads. Be sure your tractor has enough horsepower to handle the wagon and load.

SICKLE-BAR MOWER. These old-style mowers are handy for clipping the
pastures in late summer.

ROTARY MOWER. Rugged cutters, these mowers can cut heavy grass,
brush, and even small saplings.

ROTARY FINISH MOWER. Handy for giving a manicured look to large
areas.

THREE-POINT LIFT BOOM. Very useful for moving heavy loads such as stones, or even hoisting a beef or hog for skinning.

STONE BOAT. These are often made from an old car hood. The sled is pulled behind the tractor and the stones merely tossed or rolled onto it. This is much easier than hefting them onto a wagon or trailer.

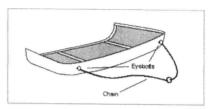

A stone boat is used to haul large stones, which can be rolled onto the sled and do not have to be lifted as they would with a wagon or cart. You can make one from an old truck hood. Use heavy eyebolts and a stout section of chain. An ordinary clevis attaches it to your tractor.

HAY RAKE. A good five-bar rake is handy and generally does a better job than the older wheel rakes.

HAY TEDDER. Used to fluff cut hay to quicken curing.

HAY BALER. Available to make large round bales or the easily handled small square bales.

This big bale is ready to put into the feeder ring. The protective net covering will be cut and removed before the hay is fed.

BALE SPIKE. Needed to move large round hay bales for feeding.

POSTHOLE DIGGER. Very useful for digging a large number of postholes. Mine has augers for 8- and 12-inch holes.

The bale spike on the rear of the tractor is needed to move the large round bales of hay for feeding.

GRADER BLADE. Great for dragging your lane, moving snow, gravel, dirt, or whatever.

FRONT-END LOADER. A valuable tool for your tractor. Very handy for loading and moving all sorts of materials.

MANURE SPREADER. Used to apply manure to the hay fields and pastures.

Simple implements, such as this adjustable grader blade, are helpful in moving dirt, grading the land, and other tasks.

SEEDER. A handy device that will help you cover ground quickly.

SPREADER. Great for applying granular fertilizer or lime.

PLOW. A basic cultivation tool. Be sure to get one of a size that your tractor can handle.

DISK. Used after plowing, it breaks the soil down into finer chunks.

TWO-ROW PLANTER. Handy for seeding a larger area than you would care to do by hand.

A handy three-point seeder is useful in reseeding pastures, seeding new areas, and even spreading small batches of fertilizer.

CULTIVATOR. Allows you to mechanically weed your crop fields or patches.

SPIKE-TOOTHED HARROW. An older version of the tool used to smooth and break up the disked field.

SPRING-TOOTHED HARROW. A modern version of the spike-toothed harrow.

BOOM SPRAYER. Needed for applying chemicals to large fields.

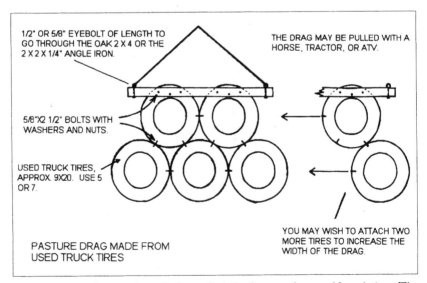

1/2" OR 5/8" EYEBOLT OF LENGTH TO GO THROUGH THE OAK 2 X 4 OR THE 2 X 2 X 1/4" ANGLE IRON.

THE DRAG MAY BE PULLED WITH A HORSE, TRACTOR, OR ATV.

5/8"X2 1/2" BOLTS WITH WASHERS AND NUTS.

USED TRUCK TIRES, APPROX. 9X20. USE 5 OR 7.

PASTURE DRAG MADE FROM USED TRUCK TIRES

YOU MAY WISH TO ATTACH TWO MORE TIRES TO INCREASE THE WIDTH OF THE DRAG.

A handy pasture drag can be made from a little hardware and some old truck tires. The drag is used to spread the cowflops that accumulate in a well-used pasture.

WOOD SPLITTER. Utilizes the tractor's hydraulics for its wood-splitting power.

ELECTRIC GENERATOR. Runs off the tractor's power takeoff (PTO). Best used with the more economical diesel tractors.

CEMENT MIXER. Uses the PTO to provide portable cement-mixing capability.

ALL-TERRAIN VEHICLES

A relative newcomer to the farm and homestead is the four-wheel all-terrain vehicle (ATV). An ATV can literally do much of the work of a small tractor. Various small implements such as mowers, cultivators, sprayers, spreaders, and blades are available for many of these vehicles. Needless to say, they can tow a small trailer and a haul respectable pay-load. With their good ground clearance and available four-wheel drive, they can get you to just about anywhere on your place.

I use my ATV just as much as I do my tractor. It is handy, gets around all over my property, and is versatile. I have a cargo box mounted on it that I can use to carry the chain saw, fencing tools, ax, and other tools.

Another very useful piece of equipment on the place is our all-terrain vehicle (ATV). We use it for all sorts of jobs. The box mounted on the front is used to carry fencing tools, the chain saw, or other tools and supplies.

Many of the implements listed in the above section for tractors can also be purchased in a size suitable for your ATV. Below is a list of some of the farm-related implements you might consider.

- Trailer.
- Wagon.
- Rotary mower.
- Grader blade.
- Manure spreader.
- Seeder.
- Spreader.
- Spike-toothed harrow.
- Spring-toothed harrow.
- Boom sprayer.

The Homestead Workbench

One of the great satisfactions of living in the country is working with materials and tools to make your small place as productive as possible. The workbench is one of the most occupied spots on most homesteads. If you are just starting out, however, it can be difficult to know just what tools you are going to need.

Here is a list of some of the more commonly used tools that I recommend you include in your homesteader's toolbox. If you are unsure about the terminology used here, the folks at the local hardware emporium will know what you're looking for.

- Workbench with sturdy vise.
- Hand saw—crosscut, 10 point.
- Framing square.
- Files—one rasp, one large flat, one medium three-corner, one half-round.
- Yardstick and rulers.
- 25-foot tape measure.
- 100-foot tape measure.
- Claw hammer—16 ounce.
- Ball peen hammer—12 ounce.
- Drill bits—$1/16$- to $1/4$-inch assorted machine bits, $1/4$- to $1\frac{1}{2}$-inch spade bits.
- Wood chisels— $1/4$ inch to 1 foot.
- Side-cut pliers—6 and 12 inches.
- Needlenose (longnose) pliers.
- Diagonal-cut pliers.
- Slip joint pliers.
- Adjustable wrenches—6, 8, and 12 inches.

☞ Screwdrivers—straight and Phillips, assorted sizes. I am also seeing a growing number of screws and bolts that accept only Torx drivers. Get a set of T6 through T30 to start out.

☞ Tin snips.

☞ Hacksaw.

☞ Socket sets. Start out with a good general set of ½-inch-drive sockets and ratchet set. You will likely decide that you also need ¼-inch and ⅜-inch-drive sets as well. I recommend getting standard SAE sets. I do not use metric sockets much at all.

☞ Variety of screws, nails, bolts, nuts, and washers—you *will* accumulate these as you go along!

I also recommend a few power tools. They will certainly make your projects go a lot more smoothly. Consider these tools:

☞ Circular saw with carbide-tipped blade and a finer-toothed blade for plywood, and the like.

☞ Saber saw for cutting shapes and holes.

☞ Drill. I recommend a 12-volt or greater cordless, rechargeable, and versatile model. You can use machine bits or wood bits in these.

☞ Drill press. Get the small, tabletop type to set on your workbench. One of my most used tools.

Gardening Tools

The list below gives you a good idea of the basic tools for your garden shed. You will have a need for each of these tools at one time or another.

☞ Bow saw—for heavy pruning.

☞ Folding pruning saw.

☞ Pruning shears (hand shears).

☞ Lopping shears—larger, with about 24-inch handles.

☞ Digging fork for digging potatoes, turning the compost pile, and so on.

☞ Hoe—the best weeder. I like one with a long handle.

☞ Garden rake.

☞ Leaf rake.

☞ Shovel. Look for a round point and long handle.

☞ Spade for turning earth, digging a trench, and so on.

☞ Ax.

☞ Hatchet.

☞ Wheelbarrow.

☞ Pitchfork for moving straw, hay, and the like.

☞ Pump-type hand sprayer.

As you become involved in various projects and gain expertise, you will want and need to add to your collection of tools. Those mentioned above will get you well on your way to completing jobs on your place.

ROTOTILLER

For almost every gardener who grows more than a postage-stamp-sized garden, a good rototiller is a valuable tool. These labor- and time-saving machines will earn their keep in preparing seedbeds, laying off rows, cultivating crops, mixing in garden debris, and other chores. There are numerous models available at nearly every garden and discount store across the country. Select the best one you can afford. For most gardeners, a 3- to 5-horsepower model will more than suffice. If you really do a lot of growing—say, a 50- by 100-foot plot or so—then consider one of the heavier, more powerful models. This will pay off by being better able to handle the magnified beating that the larger plots of ground will give it over time. When using a tiller, the vibration and lurching around of the machine is telegraphed directly to the user who is hanging on to it.

Front-tined tillers are good basic machines for the smaller garden. They are usually a bit lighter and easier to handle.

Gaining in popularity are the rear-tined machines. I am currently using a rear-tined tiller that I bought used. It is a very good machine and a great asset to our gardening. Although they are generally bulkier and heavier than their front-tined counterparts, they make up for it in soil-chomping ability. If you have a garden of about 500 square feet or more, I would consider one of these types of soil churners.

Homestead Hints and Helpers

Every day around the home place brings with it many new experiences. The numbers of projects, chores, repairs, and other tasks are often seemingly endless. With these jobs come little problems or inconveniences that homesteaders often take delight in solving, working out, or working around.

In fact, homesteaders are notorious for coming up with innovative ideas for making the workload easier. A bit of time spent in the workshop can result in a lot of time saved. Little conveniences and contrivances here and there go a log way toward increasing productivity and enjoyment on the small farm and homestead. Here are a few simple projects that I have found to be very helpful on our own place.

FENCING BOX

If you have fence around or on your property, then you need some type of toolbox for toting all the necessary fencing tools needed to do construction or make repairs. In the photograph, my own fencing toolbox is shown. It seems that every such tool-toter I've seen is of a different size, different materials, or different style. What that says to me is that the makers simply used what they had on hand and on their minds to make the box that would best suit their own purposes.

I made the box here simply of scrap plywood. The handle came from a broken rake. The box was loosely designed to hold containers and tools needed for fencing jobs around our place. I chose measurements that would allow some common containers to fit in the box. On one end, you can see the bottom two-thirds or so of a plastic antifreeze jug. It's handy for holding spike nails, balls of string, spools of wire, and so on. In the center and opposite end of the box, I partitioned off the main compart-

A homemade toolbox for fencing tools. Plastic oil bottles were cut to hold different sizes of nails and fence staples. Other storage areas were made for chisels, measuring tapes, wire, and other necessities.

ment to accommodate the cutoff sections of plastic oil bottles. They are very handy for holding various lengths of fence staples, nails, pencils, small tools, and what have you. The containers were created very quickly and easily by clamping a guide board to the table of my band saw and cutting off the top quarter or so of each bottle. The resulting containers were cut cleanly and uniformly.

A guide board clamped to the table of your saw helps to make straight cuts for your parts bins.

PARTS CONTAINERS

Incidentally, I have constructed shelves in my workshop, and filled them with several of the plastic containers described above. They hold nuts, bolts, screws, and nails of various or graduated sizes as well as other hardware. These particular containers are made from the white or gray plastic oil bottles and labeled with a black permanent marker to easily identify the contents. They have greatly helped to organize my workshop collection of hardware and fasteners. Consider asking your friends to save their oil bottles for a while; you will soon have a good supply to work with. For larger parts, consider used antifreeze jugs. They come in

Here is a shelf full of homemade parts bins. Each was made from a plastic oil bottle. A permanent marker was used to label the bins.

the similar shape as the oil bottles, only larger. They may be cut in the same manner as the oil bottles and labeled to indicate the contents.

TOOLSHED STORAGE CONTAINER

In our toolshed, we needed a place to secure some medications, fluids, wasp spray, and the few toxic chemicals that we use around the place. That was easily accomplished by using some scrap 1 x 4s and creating some shelves between the studs of the building. Next, I added a door made from a piece of plywood, attaching it with some used hinges. A hasp completed the project and provided some security from inquiring young minds.

GARDEN TOOLBOX

In the garden, we often find a few odd minutes to do some weeding here or there. What we couldn't always find were the hand tools. That problem was remedied by recycling an old mailbox and resulted in a convenient and dry spot to store garden hand tools. A coat of paint and some lettering, and the box was put in place. Since we pass the box whenever we enter or leave the garden, it's a simple matter to keep the tools where they belong and find them there when we need them.

IN THE CHICKEN HOUSE

Over in the chicken house, recycling again came in handy. When the structure was built, I used a door I had gotten free from an old house that was being demolished. As is often the case when using any old or recycled materials, measurements were odd and unique. The door was not a standard size—therefore, I simply constructed the door opening to fit the door. With a saber saw, I removed the door's plywood panel (saving it for later projects) and added chicken wire in its place. This provided added ventilation in summer. The opening is covered with clear plastic during the cold winter months.

Visible in the photograph through the chicken wire are 5-gallon buckets, which we made into good nest boxes. I traced the inside bucket edge onto a scrap board and cut the crescent shape with the saber saw. It was added to the bucket with small nails and helps keep straw and eggs in the nest box. A friend did the same thing more simply by merely cut-

Five-gallon buckets make handy nests for laying hens. You can add a crescent-shaped piece of wood, as seen here, or merely cut down a bucket lid in the same shape and snap it in place.

ting off the suitable portion of the bucket lid and using the remainder in the same way I did the wooden wedge.

BOTTLE-CALF FEEDER

In our area, and most areas where dairy operations exist, the seasonal abundance of male dairy calves creates a good opportunity for the homesteader or small farmer to acquire some good animals at very reasonable prices. This past season, some of the neighboring Amish farmers were virtually giving calves away. It was common to pick up calves less than a week old for $10 to $30. Regardless of how you end up with your animals, the feeding of more than a couple of calves is quite a chore!

Another project that came from the scrap pile helped us solve the problem of feeding four hungry and lively bottle-calves at the same time. As you can see in the photograph shown later in chapter 4, the bottle holder allows one person to feed all four calves at once. Again, the project depends upon the materials you have on hand, but do try to get at least a foot or so between the bottles. In our experience, the top board is necessary to hold the bottles in place. Hungry calves can get pretty aggressive as they empty the bottles! The board is just a scrap 1 x 4 and is attached with an old hinge on one end and a spring-loaded hook and eye on the other. The kids really enjoyed feeding those calves and rapidly became a help at feeding time.

HEATED PAINT STORAGE

I needed a way to keep paints, stains, caulking, and other compounds from freezing during the cold of winter. After experimenting by trying to add rigid foam insulation to a wooden cabinet, I was left scratching my head in frustration. Then I decided that I could solve the problem by recycling an old refrigerator into a heated storage cabinet. After all, it was large enough to hold just about all of my paints and such, it already had electrical power, and best of all, it was already insulated.

The wiring was pretty simple for this project. After removing the necessary panels, the socket holding the little appliance bulb was wired directly to the power cord. This made the light socket "hot" all the time. Basically, I just removed the switch from the circuit. I soon found that an appliance bulb crated far too much heat in the cabinet. So I journeyed the local hardware emporium and purchased a screw-in device that creates a standard plug-in receptacle from a lightbulb socket. Then I plugged in an ordinary night-light. With a standard 7-watt bulb, the heat generated is sufficient to keep the paints and fluids from freezing. Experiment with your own to see what works for you. Something in the 7 to 25-watt range should be sufficient. If you are uncomfortable working with electrical appliances, try to bribe, coerce, or otherwise enlist the help of a knowledgeable friend. The main shelves should provide plenty of room for your freezable fluids, and spray paint cans fit nicely in the door shelves. A friend who does some welding says that the heated cabinet should work well to store welding rods in, providing uniform heat and a good dry environment.

CHEST FREEZER FEED BIN

Once those calves we were bottle-feeding got big enough to go on grain, we needed a good, dry, critter-proof place to store feed. After thinking about it for a bit, I decided that an old "dead" chest freezer would fill the bill. I merely removed the light bin dividers and any hardware that might snag on a feed sack, then set the new feed bin in place. It has been serving nicely now for several years and can keep about 500 pounds of feed clean, dry, and vermin-free.

BUILD A HOMESTEAD COPY CART

I don't know too many homesteaders, gardeners, or small farmers who haven't at one time or another wished for one of those fancy big-wheel garden carts. It seems that there is always something that needs to be toted around the place, be it hay or straw, rocks, firewood, garden tools, plants, compost, or whatever. Think about it for a bit, and the need for a handcart on your own place will probably become evident. Well, being the basic cheapskate that I am, when I finally decided that I was going to have one of these carts, I figured I could save some money if I built it myself.

I have a friend who had taken the plunge and bought one of the carts from a commercial outlet, so I took the liberty of snapping a few photographs of some of the structural details that I wanted to replicate. Afterward, I spent half an hour or so with a pencil, paper, and ruler to come up with the rest of the plans, as well as the measurements for making the cuts for the cart body from a single sheet of ½-

My homemade Copy Cart. It is oversized and can haul a great deal of straw, compost, leaves, and even firewood.

inch plywood. So with a good fire going in the stove in the workshop, I set about to come up with my own version of the garden cart, the Copy Cart.

I purchased the wheels for the cart from Northern Hydraulics in Burnsville, Minnesota. This firm has a big mail-order business for all sorts of tools, parts, and equipment. (If you don't receive the almost-too-frequent catalogs from Northern Hydraulics, phone 1-800-533-5545 to get on the list.) I selected the 26-inch pneumatic-tired wheels for use on my cart. They are on roller bearings and made to take a ¾-inch axle. For the axle, I purchased an ordinary ¾-inch iron rod from a buggy factory in the nearby Amish settlement.

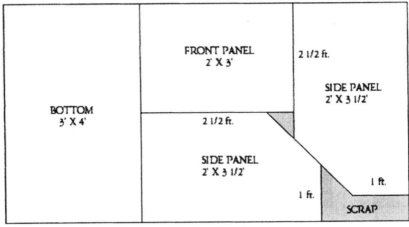

All the pieces for the Copy Cart can be cut from a single sheet of plywood.

I planned to cover the edges of the plywood pieces with metal to prevent splintering and to prolong the life of the panels. For the metal sheathing, I again journeyed over to the Amish settlement, this time to a business specializing in post building and metal construction. There I had the metal shop do a little custom bending on some seconds and left-over pieces of heavy-gauge roofing metal they had available. Soon they fashioned the metal into pieces of angle-stock 2 inches by 2 inches by 8 feet, and some into U-channel 1 by ½ by 1 inch by 8 feet. The 2 x 2s were used on the corners for strength and durability, and the U-channel was used to cover the cut edges of the plywood. All the metal was secured with either long-shanked pop rivets or small carriage bolts.

I attached the axle by cutting ¾-inch holes into two pieces of an old bed rail. The heavy metal added strength to the cart bottom, and the precut holes where the bedsprings had once been attached provided ready-made holes for attaching the rails to the cart bottom with short ¼-inch carriage bolts. The axle is positioned so that the leading edge of the wheel is only a couple of inches from the front edge of the cart itself. This provides a very good balance for hauling and is handy for tipping the cart up to load bulky articles such as barrels or large boxes.

The cart handle and stands were made from ¾-inch electrical conduit bent with a conduit bender. I admit, it took some head scratching for me to figure out how to make two pieces with the conduit bender that needed to be nearly identical. But with some measuring, checking, eyeballing, remeasuring, and rechecking, the stands, as well as the cross-brace, came out really well. I wanted to duplicate the general style of the opening system on the front gate found on my friend's cart, but lacked the hardware used on the store-bought version. So to the junk boxes I went. I came up with two ordinary door slip-bolts. As you can see from the photograph, I attached one to each side of the end gate near the top. When each bolt is set to protrude, they are situated in reinforced holes near the top front corner of the side panels. I drilled a small hole near the end of each bolt and used a small clip pin to hold them secure. This prevents the side panels from splaying outward and allows the end gate to swing from the top, enabling compost, dirt, or whatever to be dumped out the front, similar to the way a dump truck works. If I want the end gate secured at the bottom, two more of the slip-bolts will hold it in place. As soon as I scrounge up a couple, I'll add them.

The tool loops are another addition to the cart. I added these to the outside of the cart for carrying pruners, trowels, and other hand tools. It keeps them visible and in one spot until needed. A scrap of nylon webbing was secured to one of the side panels using small bolts. Washers keep the webbing from pulling off the bolt heads. A piece of an old leather belt should work just as well.

Most of the bolts, screws, and assorted small hardware bits were scrounged from my own collection or from my dad's gigantic accumulated hardware collection. I had some red paint left from repainting my barn, so the cart was given a good coat of the preservative. By buying new plywood, wheels, and conduit, as well as the axle, sheet metal, and long-shanked pop rivets, I ran the cost of my cart up to around $80. Still, that is considerably less than a similar new commercial version would cost. This custom version is also about 6 inches wider than the commercial model, and has side panels about 6 to 8 inches taller as well. For those, I just used what I had. The diagram, however, shows how every piece of wood needed for the cart can be cut from one 4- by 8-foot sheet of plywood.

Our homemade Copy Cart has proven to be one of the handiest and most useful tools that I have on the place. In fact, we were using it to haul bales of straw in before it was completely finished. Since its completion, I've hauled concrete blocks, some split firewood, old bedding from the chicken house, and some hay bales. Of course, the kids had to have a ride in it as well.

BOTTOMLESS APPLE PICKER

When it comes time to pick apples, I use a handy device I made in the workshop. For want of a better name, I'll call it a bottomless apple picker.

This handy helper was modeled after some commercially available ones I had seen advertised, only with an improvement. It is basically a little wire basket on a stick and is used to reach up among the limbs of the apple tree and gently pluck the fruit into the basket; you then bring it down to retrieve the fruit. These store-bought pickers are mounted on the end of a long pole, and require you to bring the pole down with every apple or two and empty them into your basket or bucket. The picker I made differed in that the wire basket has no bottom. Instead, a long sleeve sewn from an old bedsheet allows the picked fruit to drop down into the picker's basket.

To make this handy harvester, I made a small cylinder of 1 x 2 welded wire. The cylinder was made to be about 5 or 6 inches across and about 8 to 10 inches tall. Cut the wire to be long, because about half the wires on one end will be cut to form the "fingers" that will help grab the fruit from the limb. To do this, take some good pliers and bend the wire end back on itself to make a rounded tip that will not pierce the fruit. Bend the fingers inward slightly toward the center of the cylinder to assist in grasping the fruit. This will make it easer to pluck from the limb. Attach the wire cylinder to a long piece of ½-inch metal conduit or similar material of a length that will allow you to reach the hard-to-get-to areas on your fruit trees. Attach the basket with regular metal hose clamps. At the bottom of the wire cylinder, use some heavy thread to lace the cotton sleeve onto the wire cylinder. Make the cylinder in a length handy to hang on to as you hold the handle of the picker.

To use the picker, I loosely wrap the sleeve around the handle a few times and grip it right along with the pole. Loosely twisting the sleeve around the pole allows the picked fruit to slow down as it drops through the wire basket and downward. To pick the fruit, merely position the basket around an apple with the stem between a pair of the protruding fingers. Give the pole a twist or two, and the fruit drops through the wire basket and down through the sleeve. Once you have half a dozen or so apples in the sleeve, just hold the end over your basket and allow the fruit to gently drop in.

This is one of the handier devices that I have whipped up in the workshop. I have used it a lot and loaned it to friends and family to help them with their apple harvest.

TAKING CARE OF HAND TOOLS

Even with all of the modern machinery, gasoline engines, and assorted techno-gadgets available today, a great deal of work around the homestead is still done with hand tools.

All the assorted rakes, hoes, cultivators, axes, mauls, shovels, sledges, and other human-powered tools get put to the test—if not daily—seasonally.

Once the garden's done, the woodpile is stacked, and the haymow is full, plan to spend a rainy day putting your hand tools in order.

It's much easier to prepare your tools for winter storage if you have kept them in good working order all summer. Here are a few easy ways to do just that.

First, keep a small mason's trowel hanging in your toolshed. I keep mine just inside the doorway. When you are finished using a tool such as a hoe, spade, or shovel, give the metal a quick going-over with the trowel to scrape off deposits of dirt. It doesn't have to be squeaky clean; that comes next.

Just inside doorway of the toolshed, have yourself a wooden box or foot tub full of clean mason's sand that has been saturated with used motor oil. After you have

A box containing oily sand makes cleaning and maintaining tools easy.

gotten most of the dirt off the tool with the trowel, plunge the cutting edge of the tool into your sandbox several times. The scouring action of the sand will remove any remaining dirt, and the oil will leave a protective coating on the metal.

Now that the metal surfaces are cleaned and oiled, it's time to turn to the handles; new or old, these will likely need some attention. If the tools are new or nearly so, give the handles a light sanding to remove any shellac left on them from the manufacturer. Sand over any rough or potentially splintery spots as well. Go over the wood, checking for cracks or breaks. If one is present, replace the handle. It's better to do it now than to put it off and cuss later when you need the tool.

Now it's time for a good coating or two of linseed oil. You may find linseed oil available either raw or boiled. Many folks consider the boiled oil to be best for our purpose here, but I don't know that using one over the other makes much of a difference. Do not, however, try to make your own boiled linseed oil by actually boiling it! Trust me on this one; I tried it years ago as a youngster when I was trying to prepare a finish for a rifle stock. The term *boiled* is industry lingo and has to do with the refining process.

A handy method for applying linseed oil to a wooden handle of a tool is to use an ordinary old jersey glove. Just don the glove, pour a "handful" of oil into the palm, and work it into the wood of the handle. An old saying for applying linseed oil to wooden tool handles goes something like this: "Once a day for a week; once a week for a month; and once a month thereafter." While I admit that I don't quite meet this mark, I can tell you that oiled tool handles will keep out moisture and rot and will preserve the handle for generations.

A TIRED PLANTING BED

As winter's icy grasp finally begins to slip, the homesteader who has not kept a little something growing all winter is surely thinking about getting a few seeds stuck into the ground. After a long winter of dried, canned, frozen, or store-bought fresh vegetables, a mess of fresh ones would taste mighty good. One of the easiest and earliest ways to get those first lettuce and spinach salads growing is to use an old method that has been common practice around these parts for generations.

Folks around here often get those first salad greens going in a planter made from an old tire. For my own planter, I utilized the old tread from a log skidder to give me plenty of size and depth. Stop by your local service station, recycling center, or tire retailer and ask the folks there to save a tire or two suitable for your purpose. I'd recommend a fairly large one, such as a rear tire off a farm tractor or log skidder (like I used).

After laying the tire at the spot where I wanted it, I used a utility knife to cut the sidewall completely out of the upper side. This was fairly easy to do, and nearly doubled the planting area available. Next, I filled the tire with a good compost-and-manure mixture and seeded my lettuce and spinach. The whole thing was covered with some old storm windows obtained for the purpose by some creative scrounging. The result is a fine, durable hot bed, and the only cost involved was for . . . the seed!

BEDSPRINGS AND GARDEN GATES

A simple, sturdy, and effective gate can be made simply from the old metal frame off an old bed.

To make your gate, take the heavy angle iron frame and attach a couple of hinges. This can be done by either drilling holes in the frame and attaching the hinges with bolts, or welding the hinges to the frame. Then just hang the gate on your gatepost.

You can use the existing springs and wire mesh on the frame. It is suitable for the garden or for small livestock. You might want to add something sturdier by attaching a piece of woven fence wire. For a really sturdy gate, consider welding in place a section of heavy livestock panel.

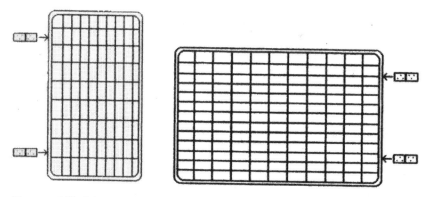

Even an old bed frame can be used to make a gate. A smaller bunkbed-sized frame can easily become a vertical walk-through gate. A larger, full-sized frame can become a horizontal gate that is wide enough to allow a garden tractor or similar-sized equipment to pass through. Attach hinges by bolting or welding. Use the existing wire springs and mesh, or attach woven fence wire or weld a piece of heavy metal livestock panel onto the frame.

More Hints

In this section, you will find an assortment of hints for making life around the homestead easier. These ideas will help make your place more self-sufficient and secure. You are likely to develop your own variations or improvements on these methods as you adapt them to your own situation.

MAKING CORNERS IN WIRE OR METAL

Here is a helpful method of making clean, sharp corners for light metalworking projects. The method uses no fancy tools and produces a neat "factory"-looking corner for all kinds of light-gauge materials such as hardware cloth or metal flashing. I have used it when applying metal flashing to the tops of beehive covers.

To make these custom corners, take the material that you want to bend and place it on your workbench or other solid straight-edged form. Align the mark on your material where you want the bend to be with the edge of the form. If necessary, clamp the stock to the form. Get the bend started by tapping the material with a hammer along the length of the bend, or by bending the stock by hand.

Now for the "magic"! Take a piece of scrap angle iron and place it over the new bend along its length. Hold it firmly in place and give it several good whacks with a hammer along its length. The material will be shaped between the inside angle of the iron and the outside angle of the form. Remove the angle iron and *Voilà!* You should have a clean sharp corner in your stock. If you need a bit of a rounded corner, placing the stock material over a form that has just a bit of a radiused edge should give you a suitable bend.

USING WATER HEATER TANKS FOR WATER STORAGE

Many of us who are otherwise well prepared for weather-related emergencies, power outages, or other disasters are put to scratching our heads when we try to figure out a good method of storing water for emergency use. It's easy to have a couple of 5-gallon jugs of water stored away, but the storage of a larger quantity of clean, usable water is a more difficult task. Not all of us have bubbling springs or deep, clear wells on our property. In some instances, without electricity even these water sources can be inaccessible.

It is commonly known that under extreme emergency circumstances, a person can get by for quite a while without food, but only for a short time without water. Under normal conditions in moderate weather, an adult needs about 2 to 3 quarts of water each day. That amount would naturally be increased if you were engaged in heavy physical labor or any hard physical activity. Therefore, a minimum of about 4 to 5 gallons would needed to be stored for each person for one week's needs. The problem, then, is to come up with a plan to supply the needed water for your family for an extended period of time.

One method I have come up with is quite simple, inexpensive, and effective. It is made up of materials that are obtainable at no cost or at low cost. It can add an additional 125 to 150 gallons of water to your storage supplies.

The system consists of connecting three used water heater tanks in series to your existing water supply to provide a battery of water storage tanks. The number of tanks is arbitrary. Theoretically, you can plumb in a tank for each member of your household. This method will maintain up to 150 gallons of consistently fresh water as a backup to the quantity already contained in the existing water heater. An added benefit of this method is that until it is needed in an emergency, it allows incoming water to warm to room temperature before entering the water heater, thereby reducing the amount of electricity or gas required to heat your normal household water supply.

To obtain the parts and materials necessary for your water storage battery, you'll need to hit up a local plumber or appliance dealer. These folks usually have old water heating units around, and can easily be persuaded to let you have a couple of them just for hauling them off.

It may require a bit of diligence in searching for the tanks to use in your system. Most water heaters are not discarded unless the tank has developed a leak somewhere. Stay with it, and you should be able to locate the needed tanks.

To set up the water storage battery, you'll first need to remove the outer jacket and insulation from each unit. Start by removing any panels or covers attached with screws. With a hacksaw-type blade in your saber saw, cut down the length of the metal cabinet near the seam. By carefully removing this metal cabinet, you can end up with some good heavy-gauge sheet metal to be used for a variety of projects around the homestead.

Once the tank has been removed from the water heater jacket, it would be a good idea to clean it out a bit. To do this, you can remove the heater elements and flush out the inside. This should remove most of any buildup of lime or other deposits that may be inside the tank. If you live in an area of heavy mineral deposits, such as limestone, this may take a bit of effort. Once the tank is flushed out, you may wish to go a step farther and wash out the inside with a bleach solution. Rinse well and reinstall the elements, tightening them well to make a tight, leak-proof seal. Instead of replacing the elements, you may install threaded plugs in their place.

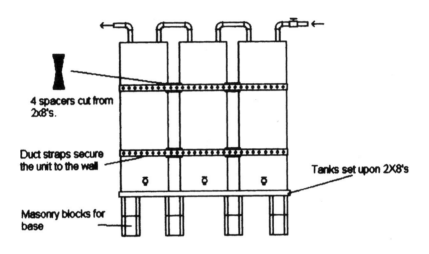

4 spacers cut from 2x8's.

Duct straps secure the unit to the wall

Masonry blocks for base

Tanks set upon 2X8's

An emergency water supply, constructed from discarded water heater tanks, can supply needed water for a family.

Placement of the tanks will have to be customized to your particular location. Remember that each of the tanks weighs in the neighborhood of 50 pounds, and 50 gallons of water weighs an additional 417 pounds or so. This will make the weight of a three-tank battery about 1,400 pounds. A good solid floor will be required to support a load of this size. As a base for the units, you can easily place concrete blocks atop each other or on end and place them over them a couple of 2 x 8s. While the raised tanks are not absolutely necessary, they are helpful, if for no other reason than to make withdrawing water from the tanks easier through the drain valves located near the bottom. And consider using a metal strap to secure the units to the wall for protection against upsets during an earthquake or other disaster. Ordinary furnace duct straps work well for this. They are available at most hardware stores.

Plumbing in the tanks is an easy-enough matter. Simply connect the tanks so that the incoming household water enters the first tank, leaves it and enters the second tank, exits its and enters the third tank, then reconnects to the existing household supply line. The fittings you'll need for these connections are easily obtainable at your local hardware store.

If or when the emergency supply of water is needed, you must first immediately shut off the main water supply valve to your water line. This would be especially critical in the event that you suspect your main water supply has been contaminated.

Once the water main has been shut off, you can easily draw off needed water from the tank drain valves located near the bottom of each tank. For good water flow, you may have to open a faucet of two in your household system to allow air to flow into the pipe system.

The beauty of this setup is that it is adaptable to nearly any water system and can be sized from a single tank to as many as you need and have room for. It can help you to be better prepared for an unexpected "long dry spell."

USING PVC PIPE AROUND THE HOMESTEAD

ROW HOOPS

The uses of PVC pipe are nearly countless. It seems like enterprising homesteaders are constantly coming up with new uses for the stuff. Possibly one of the best uses for joints of ¾-inch PVC pipe is to create a miniature greenhouse in your garden. This material, combined with a sheet of heavy clear plastic, can make a great growing-season extender in your own garden no matter how large a plot you have.

To construct your row covers, you will first need to cut twice as many 18-inch pieces of ⅜-inch reinforcement rod (commonly called rebar) as you have pieces of PVC pipe. Light electric fence posts, cut in half, also work well.

Drive one rebar at the proper distance where you want the end of the PVC pipe to be. Continue down along either side of the row at about 3-foot intervals. Along the top of the hoops, secure one straight length of pipe (add or cut if needed) by attaching it with the plastic strips commonly used for securing electrical wires in automobiles. These flat plastic fasteners click shut and hold securely. At each end of your row cover, you may with to further stabilize the whole structure by adding either a 30 or a 45 plastic elbow then attaching a short straight piece to run down to the ground. This will help strengthen and stabilize the whole structure.

PVC BIRDHOUSE

Excellent birdhouses can be made from scrap pieces of 4- or 6-inch plastic pipe. For example, to make fine bluebird houses, take a section of 6-inch pick pipe about 1 foot long. To one end, glue an end cap. Just below the end cap on the main tube, use a door lockset hole drill and bore the appropriate 1¼-inch hole. About ½ inch from the bottom of the open end of the tube, drill two holes about ⅛ inch in diameter and about 1½ inches apart. Directly across the diameter of the tube, repeat the procedure. You may make two or three shallow cuts with a saw directly below the entrance hole. This will permit the adult birds approaching the box to get a grip on it as they prepare to enter. Cut one deep enough that the resulting slot runs completely through the pipe about an inch long. It will be used for the next step. To provide a climbing surface for fledgling birds as they prepare to exit the box, you will need to hang a narrow strip of hardware cloth (approximately 1 inch by 10 inches) on the inside surface of the birdhouse. Insert the strip in the open end of the pipe, slip the end of the hardware cloth through the saw cut, and bend it over as snugly as possible. Cut another piece of ¼- or ½-inch hardware cloth about the same diameter as the pipe. Insert it flatly into the bottom of the tube. This will be the actual bottom of the birdhouse. Through the four ⅛-inch holes that you drilled near the bottom of the tube, insert a U-shaped piece of wire and bend the ends to secure it. This will hold the hardware cloth floor in place.

PVC STORAGE CONTAINER

Occasionally, you may be presented with the need to cache or hide items around the homestead. Perhaps you wish to hide your egg money in something other than a fruit jar. You may feel the need to put away a firearm and supply of ammunition. Or you may just have something of value that you would like to hide away securely from prying eyes. A simple and durable storage container can be made in a few minutes by using scraps of appropriate-sized PVC pipe. All it takes is a section of pipe of the proper diameter and length for the item or items you wish to store.

Glue into place an end cap on one end of the pipe. On the other end, glue into place a collar with female threads to accept the same-sized male screw-in plug. You are all set.

When using your storage container, you may need to use a desiccant to prevent damage to the stored item. This is simply and cheaply done by merely tossing into the container an old sock or other cloth bag filled with rice. The rice will serve as a very suitable moisture absorber. You can also apply a bead of silicone sealer when you thread the cap into place. This will serve as a final moisture barrier.

PVC ELECTRIC FENCE HANDLE

Electric fences are versatile, easy to put up, and effective. Often, though, the homesteader may come upon a stretch of fence where a gate is needed. A cheap and easy version of an electric fence gate handle can be made using scrap pieces of ¾- or 1-inch PVC pipe. Take a piece of pipe about 10 to 12 inches long and drill a small hole in each end. If you have a sturdy coil spring that will fit up inside the pipe, fine; if not, it will still work. Merely secure your electric fence to one end of the pipe and continue the wire up through the pipe. Attach it securely to the spring if you're using one. On the other end, bend a piece of heavy wire into a hook. Secure the end of the fence wire to the other end of the hook. This simple handle will allow you to open and close a stretch of electric fence without turning it off or jumping clear of your boots.

PVC HANGING PLANTER

An attractive hanging planter can be made from PVC pipe. To create your planter, first locate a piece of 4-inch PVC pipe as long as you want your planter; something in the area of 16 to 24 inches works well.

Next, bore 1½-inch-diameter holes in the pipe at points where you want plants in it. I spaced the holes staggered in rows up and down the piece of pipe; a row of three, turn the pipe 90 degrees, then a row of two. Add another row of three and another row of two, turning the pipe as you go.

Next, glue an end cap onto the bottom of the pipe with regular PVC cement. Near the center of the end cap, drill three or four small holes to allow for water drainage. At the top of the pipe, drill three holes about ⅛ inch in diameter at points dividing the circumference of the pipe into thirds.

To hang the planter, you can use twine, wire, chain, or whatever you have handy. I used four small S-hooks and some light chain. Equal lengths of chain (about 12 to 14 inches) were attached to the three small holes using S-hooks. The three pieces of chain were joined at the top by the fourth hook.

You can now add soil and your plants. You may also add a watering tube to the planter if you wish. Merely take a piece of ¾-inch PVC pipe about ½ to 1 inch longer than the planter and drill several small holes up and down its length. Position the small pipe in the center of the planter as you fill it with soil. You will end up with soil packed around the hollow center tube, which will permit water to evenly reach all the plants in the planter.

This planter works especially well with geraniums or other compact, bushy flowers. I suppose compact strawberries could also be planted in one of these.

SQUARING A BUILDING

When laying out the foundation or posts for a new building, it is easy to get it all square if you remember the simple "6-8-10 Rule." This rule is a practical application of the Pythagorean theorem that we learned in high school and thought we'd never use. I find that the name *6-8-10 Rule* is much more easily remembered than the "official" theorem.

Here's how it works. Start at the point where any of the four corners of your building will be and string out a line where one side will be. Measure 6 feet along the line and mark it. Next, from the same corner, run a string and, by using the framing square or by eyeballing, approximate the 90-degree angle needed. Now measure 8 feet along that line and mark it. From the two points you have marked, measure the hypotenuse of the triangle. Adjust the angle of one of the sides until it equals 10 feet precisely. Once you have the first side at 6 feet, the second side at 8 feet, and the diagonal at 10 feet, the corner will be square and you can proceed.

For those of you who doubt this rule will work, first recall that the Pythagorean theorem states that to find the length of any hypotenuse of a right triangle, we can use the formula $A^2 + B^2 = C^2$. In our practical application of this theorem, we merely insert the lengths measured along the sides of the building for the values of A^2 and B^2. It doesn't really matter which length you plug into which value. In figuring the formula, we find that $6^2 + 8^2 = 10^2$. Going farther, we get $36 + 64 = 100$. We can easily figure that the square root of 100 is 10, the length of the hypotenuse of our right triangle on the line across the corner of our building. Note the accompanying illustration if you have any questions as to how this works. If you use this simple application of the ancient theorem, you will end up with nicely laid-out building foundations, square pole buildings, and straight outbuildings every time.

WHEELS ON YOUR LADDER?

Now, why would you want to put wheels on your ladder? It seems like it would make the thing a little difficult to keep in one place, doesn't it?

The fact is, however, the wheels go onto the "upstream" end of your ladder. For example, if you have a woodburner in your home, you are faced with the periodic chore of swabbing out the flue—both for safety's sake and to keep the flue drawing well. To get a ladder up on a steep roof can be a difficult chore at best, and can damage shingles. To help out the chimney sweep in your family, try this. On the upper end of the ladder, bore a hole through each runner to accommodate the axle of an ordinary lawn mower wheel. Attaching the wheels to your ladder will make it simple to "roll" it right up the roof. Further, attach to the ladder, just a few inches back from each axle hole, a short piece of 1 x 4 lumber. Attach it so that the angle created between it and the ladder is roughly the same as the angle of the two sides of your roof. After adding these simple devices, it is an easy matter to roll the ladder up the roof, flip it over, and allow the 1 x 4s to hold the ladder in place. Then you can scamper right up to do the necessary chores.

CERAMIC DRIP FILTER

A good supply of fresh water is essential on the homestead (or anywhere else). This simply made filter will work without electrical power, in any situation—whether you're at home, camping, or anywhere else that you might need to purify water.

This filter works on the same principle as those expensive portable ceramic cartridge filters in use by many backpackers and wilderness campers. While it is not exactly portable, it does work well and will cost only a fraction of the commercial models. Variations on this system have been used for decades in some third-world countries. French troops used this system to purify their drinking water during the early days of occupation in Indochina and Southeast Asia. To make your filter, locate a source for unglazed ceramic crocks. By *crocks*, I am referring to the tall straight-sided types often associated with making sauerkraut. These should be available at crafts shops that supply ceramicware figurines and the like. To operate your filter, merely set it up so that it sits above a larger catch vessel. The catch vessel can be any clean large pan; or you may want to rig up a funnel of some type to catch the water in a vessel with a smaller opening. Regardless, just fill the ceramic crock with water and allow it to drip through into the catch vessel. The porosity of the ceramic is such that all the little creepy-crawlies and critters will be filtered out, and the result will be drinkable filtered water.

MAKE A SOLAR-LIGHT FISH FEEDER

If you have a pond where you are raising fish, you can easily augment their insect food supply by installing a solar-light fish feeder.

To do this, get a solar-powered, self-switching walkway lights. These can be picked up at a local hardware or home supply store for comparatively little. Next, attach the light to a pole or post in the water, or suspend it over the water. Just be sure to position the light so that it is just a couple of feet over the surface of the water.

Since the light is solar-powered, you will not have to supply electrical power. By being self-switching, the light will come on at dusk and switch off at dawn. During the course of a night, countless insects will be attracted to the light. Vast numbers of them will fall into the water, where they will be readily and eagerly consumed by the fish. *Voilà!* You have an automatic fish feeder at a cost of $5 or $10.

If you wish to use your existing electrical power, you can easily run a drop cord and low-wattage light out to the pole or post. Add an inexpensive timer and you're in business.

MENDING A BUCKET, TUB, OR STOCK TANK

In this day of plastic and throwaways, we are not often encouraged to make repairs to something as simple as a bucket or tub. However, an important part of homesteading is to make do with what you have—to use and reuse tools and items around the homestead to get the most out of them.

A good galvanized bucket or tub is certainly handy to have around the place, and each can end up seeing a nearly endless variety of uses. However, if your bucket gets a hole in it, it is obviously of lesser use. A good old way to repair that bucket is simple, and it works.

Merely enlarge the hole just enough to accept a small machine screw or bolt that you have handy. Put a metal washer on the bolt, then a washer made of a piece of old inner tube or a piece of leather. Slide the bolt through the hole. Put another washer of leather or rubber on the other side, followed by another flat washer, then the nut. Tighten everything down. Many old-timers prefer the leather washer because it will absorb a bit of the water and swell to firmly seal the hole. Other folks use rubber because they have it lying around the workshop. It seems to work well, too.

This simple repair method can be used to extend the life of what might first be looked at as a throwaway situation. I have used this "quick fix" on metal buckets as well as large stock watering tanks. There is no need to throw away your bucket or tub, or your money.

DRAG A CHAIN THROUGH YOUR GARDEN

Here is a simple tip whenever you are using commercial granular fertilizer while planting your garden.

Fertilizer placed directly in the row with some seeds—beans, for example—will "burn" them and they will fail to sprout. So whenever I am preparing the soil for planting my garden—regardless of the seed types—I do the following. Lay off the rows as you normally would. Scatter your fertilizer at the desired rate down the row. Next, simply drag a short piece of chain, attached to a length of binder twine or string, down the row to mix the fertilizer into the soil. I just use a short piece of an old log chain about a foot long and tie the ends together to the string. Then sow your seed and cover as you normally would. This simple procedure will help prevent the seed from getting "burned" by the fertilizer and will help ensure much better germination.

SHAKE UP YOUR INSECT PESTS

Come garden time, we occasionally have an outbreak of Mexican bean beetles or other insect pests looking for some easy meals. We usually use Sevin or Bonide in the powdered form to help rid us of the critters.

A really easy way to make a garden "bug duster" is to simply use an ordinary coffee can. In the bottom of the can, make several holes using a small nail. I've found that a #2 or #4 nail is just about right. The snap-on plastic lid makes filling the duster easy, and another lid snapped over the bottom for storage prevents spills and keeps the powder where it belongs.

CIDER VINEGAR IS GOOD FOR YOUR LIVESTOCK

Apple cider vinegar is a good vitamin-packed substance. In his fine book *Folk Medicine*, Dr. D. C. Jarvis prescribes it, in combination with honey, as a daily tonic for good health.

Cider vinegar also has benefits for your livestock. One example is that it will help remedy "stump sucking" in horses. Stump sucking occurs when horses or other livestock are not getting sufficient minerals in their diets. This may be due to overcrowding on a paddock or pasture, or to low-quality feed or hay. Regardless, this activity consists of the animal stripping and eating the bark from every tree or shrub that it can reach in an attempt to get the supplemental vitamins and minerals it craves. To prevent or cure this activity, try putting a capful of ordinary cider vinegar on the feed of each animal. You should soon see the craving for and eating of bark diminished or eliminated.

Cider vinegar can provide similar benefits for chickens as well. A couple of ounces in the chicken waterer will help keep your flock healthy. Do not, however, add cider vinegar to a galvanized waterer. The acid in the vinegar will cause a reaction in the zinc-galvanized metal and could cause adverse effects in the chickens. It is safe to use, though, in glass or plastic waterers.

FREEZE-PROOF YOUR HAND PUMP

We have an old hand pump sitting atop an old hand-dug well that we have used to water our cattle. When I installed the pump, I used ordinary 1½-inch PVC pipe. On the bottom end of the pipe, I attached an ordinary foot valve. This valve prevents water from draining out of the pipe and makes pumping water much easier, since you do not have to "prime the pump" every time you use it. This is a great setup for warm weather or in areas that don't experience freezing weather. Here in southern Indiana, however, we regularly get winter temperatures of 0 degrees, and sometimes as low as 20 to 30 below. Temperatures this cold can make quick work of cast-iron pumps and plastic pipe.

Since the foot valve prevents water from draining out of the pipe, and freezing weather can cause the pump and pipe to burst, we need to come up with a way to prevent this from occurring. That is done easily by doing the following. Pull the pump and pipe up out of the well. Drill a small hole in the PVC pipe at a point above where the normal winter water level is in the well. For normal summer operation of the pump, merely fill the hole with a snugly fitting self-tapping screw. This will allow the water to remain in the pipe and eliminate the need for priming the pump each time it is used.

Come winter, you'll need to raise the pump and pipe and remove the screw. This will allow the water to drain out of the pipe as far as the hole and eliminate the chance of the pipe and pump freezing and bursting. You will need to either keep a bucket of water at the well to use in priming the pump, or carry one with you from the house to the well.

Be sure, when drilling the hole, not to make it too large, or the pump will "suck air" and it will be difficult to draw water. Try a short #6 or #7 self-tapping screw and appropriately sized hole.

This simple alteration should help you keep your hand pump operational year-round.

Selecting a Homestead Firearm

A firearm is an important tool for your country place. Not everyone living on the land has developed a familiarity with firearms. In fact, many have never held a firearm of any type in their hands. Some have no desire to. Some homesteaders develop an interest in owning a firearm as the need presents itself. Others were raised where firearms were as accepted and as commonplace as an ax, hoe, or other tool.

Having been around firearms both privately and professionally for nearly 40 years, I can offer some recommendations on the selection of your homestead firearm.

A couple of very important points must be kept in mind when choosing your firearm, for whatever purpose. First, select a well-made firearm from a reputable manufacturer. Over the years of its use, a firearm can get bumped around a lot and receive a lot of nicks and dings. Add to that the pounding the firearm takes from the actual firing process, and it becomes evident that a durable weapon is a must. You need to have a firearm that can take such a beating. Second, select your weapon chambered in one of the more popular calibers or gauges. Then you can be more certain of being able to obtain a supply of ammunition for your weapon, especially in rural and out-of-the-way places.

A homestead firearm will most likely be used for any or all of four purposes: hunting, predator and varmint control, sport shooting, or home defense. Any prospective firearm owner who has little or no experience with a weapon should definitely, and I mean *definitely*, receive some sound training in the proper care and use of one. Every state has hunter education courses available, usually at no cost. You do not have to be a hunter to participate in these classes. The courses cover a wealth of information of interest and value to the shooter, young or old, novice or pro. These classes are taught by dedicated and certified volunteer instructors or your own state's version of a conservation officer. Check with your local fish and wildlife department to learn of a hunter education course in your area. For young people, the 4-H Shooting Sports program is another really good way to become familiar with firearms. Your local county extension agent should be able to get you started in this program.

A brief description of firearms and ammunition will be useful. Simply, a firearm consists of three major components: the action, the stock, and the barrel (hence the phrase *lock, stock, and barrel*, which indicates the entirety of a topic or object).

The firearms we will be considering can be placed into two broad groups: shoulder arms and handguns. Rifles and shotguns fall into the group of firearms called shoulder arms. Obviously, they are designed to be fired from the shoulder: You plant the stock of the firearm firmly against your shoulder to add stability when aiming or pointing it. Handguns are just that, smaller firearms designed to be held and fired while being firmly gripped in one or both hands.

Similarly, ammunition falls into different categories. When discussing firearms, the topic of "caliber" or "gauge" invariably comes up. Indeed, it is vital to the safety of both you and those around you to have some knowledge of ammunition as well as the firearm itself.

The *caliber* of a firearm refers to the size of the ammunition it uses. Caliber is usually expressed in hundredths or thousandths of inches. For example, the .22-caliber rimfire has a bullet that is .22 or $^{22}/_{100}$ inch in diameter. A bullet for the popular .308 Winchester is .308 or $^{308}/_{1,000}$ inch in diameter. Some calibers are measured in millimeters, such as the 6mm Remington. The calibers of most of our military's firearms are now given in millimeters—for example, the 5.56 NATO (.223 Remington) and the 7.62 NATO (.308 Winchester).

Shotguns, on the other hand, are referred to by *gauge*. This determination is made by the number of lead balls of the size of the gun's bore required to weigh 1 pound. For example, it would require 12 lead balls the size of a 12-gauge shotgun barrel bore to weigh 1 pound. The same method of measurement applies to the other popular gauges of shotguns such as the 20, 16, and 10 gauge. The only exception to this rule of determining shotgun gauge is with the .410 gauge. This "gauge" is actually a caliber. That is, the bore of a .410 shotgun is actually .410 or 410/1,000 inch in diameter. The thing to remember, though, is that normally rifles and pistols are referred to by caliber, while shotguns are referred to by their gauge.

RIFLES

The old .22-caliber rimfire is still one of the most popular rifle and pistol calibers in existence. The diminutive little .22 has put meat on many a farm table and routed many a chicken house raider. They are almost universally available and cheap to shoot.

They are accurate, not very loud, and have no recoil to speak of, all desirable qualities for a beginner's firearm. Further, a good homestead .22 rifle is just handy to have around. With good ammunition, an average shooter can make accurate hits on targets to 75 yards or so. There are several manufacturers of these light and versatile weapons, and they can be purchased for a nominal price. For target shooting, squirrel hunting, and short-range varmint shooting, a .22 is hard to beat. Add a 4x scope if you like and you have a handy homestead firearm, for well under $200.

HANDGUNS

For use around the home place, a .22 semiautomatic or revolver with a 6-inch barrel is very handy. It is easily carried, light, and can be used to take a wide variety of small game and varmints. Loaded with a magazine full of some of the "hotter" ammunition available, it can make a very convincing home defense weapon as well. Select one of high-quality models and you should have an heirloom weapon to pass down to your children and grandchildren.

If I were making a choice of a handgun strictly for home defense, I would give serious consideration to the .45 ACP in a semiautomatic of good manufacture. Here again is an old war veteran that is seeing duty as a civilian. The .45 ACP fires a heavy bullet at a relatively low speed. As a result, it can penetrate well with great knockdown power, yet not carry dangerously beyond its target as some of the "hotter" calibers do. Some popular pistols offered in this caliber include the Colt 1911 and its variations, the Sig-Sauer P220, the Ruger P90, and the Smith & Wesson Model 4506. All are good .45-caliber pistols.

Some shooters, particularly beginning shooters and most women (due to their physical size), find the recoil of the .45 just a little too much to enjoy. Accordingly, many in these groups find that the 9mm semiautomatics on the market offer characteristics that they like, along with manageable recoil. This caliber is one of the most popular pistol cartridges in the world today. It is offered by dozens of manufacturers in dozens of models. If you're selecting a pistol in this caliber, lean toward the major manufacturers or go with the solid recommendation of a knowledgeable friend or gun dealer.

SHOTGUNS

Now, with all this said about rifles and handguns, I am going to make the following statement: If I had to settle on just a single firearm for use on the homestead, I would probably choose neither a rifle nor a handgun. Given the "one gun" alternative, I would have to choose a shotgun. More specifically, I would select a well-made popular model of a 12-gauge pump-action shotgun. For hunting, protection of livestock and crops from predators (two- or four-legged) or varmints (two- or four-legged), a shotgun covers the spectrum well. For hunting, shotguns are adaptable for taking any species of game. Loads for the shotgun range from fine shot for taking small gamebirds such as dove or quail to single slugs heavy enough to kill a grizzly bear. They are widely used for hunting squirrels and other small game. Those of us who did not cut our hunting teeth on taking squirrels with a single-shot .22 rifle probably used an old single-shot, break-action shotgun. They are effective weapons against farmyard predators and fearsome home defense weapons.

Just as you cannot expect to raise a garden with only one hand tool, I believe that every homestead should have more than one firearm to use for different purposes. Handguns are light and handy to carry. A .22-caliber rifle is useful for plinking, short-range varmint control, and hunting. A shotgun in 12 gauge, in either a break-action single shot or a dependable pump action, has a wide range of uses on the homestead. With the right ammunition, it is suitable for hunting, varmint control, and home defense. A high-powered centerfire rifle has a place on the homestead, too. In states where they are legal, they are excellent for hunting deer, elk, and other large game. They are essential for long-range varmint control. In semiautomatic actions, they make formidable defensive weapons. If, however, you must settle on just one firearm, or are just beginning to fill your gun rack, then consider the shotgun.

Firearms Handling

Here are three rules that should be committed to memory. Practice these rules every time you handle a firearm.

☞ Treat every firearm as if it is loaded, even if you know it is not.

☞ Never point a firearm at anything you do not intend to shoot.

☞ Always be sure of your target . . . and beyond.

3

GARDENING & GROWING

The Homestead Garden

Small Fruits (Blackberries, Raspberries, Strawberries, Gooseberries, Grapes, Blueberries, and Apples)

The Homestead Greenhouse

The Homestead Garden

As a homesteader striving toward self-sufficiency, it goes without saying that gardening—probably in combination with some type of livestock production—will form the mainstay of your food-production plan. There are as many different types of gardens and gardening techniques as there are gardeners.

If you're a newcomer to gardening, you'll likely have huge ambitions when it comes to the number of varieties of vegetables and other foods you plan to grow. Even experienced gardeners fall prey to late-winter shopping trips through the green and weed-free pages of the seed catalogs. The same seasoned gardeners often end up with more varieties than they really needed . . . or wanted. It is very easy to let your plans exceed your space or your time available to work the garden. Remember that the intent and purpose of the homestead garden is to produce as much of the family food supply as practical. The gourmet vegetables and exotic varieties should wait until you're sure you have the time, space, and expertise to devote to them.

Remember that you can learn something from every gardener you talk with. In fact, do exactly that. Visit with your gardener friends and neighbors and learn from their experience, their successes and failures. Glean from them—harvest, if you will—the successful methods that they use, the seed varieties suited to your area, their methods of controlling pests (insect and animal!). Chances are, you will be benefiting from literally hundreds of years of total gardening experience.

For a basic food supply, you will probably want to concentrate on a few of the vegetables that you and your family use the most. As you gain experience, you will then be likely to want to add more varieties and perhaps dabble in some specialty crop that you particularly enjoy. In my family, green beans, corn, and tomatoes are the three "must-grows" for our yearly garden. We use tremendous quantities of tomatoes, canned whole, juiced, in sauces, and added to other canned foods. I can't imagine what a year would be like if we would be unable to grow the dozens of tomato plants that produce the hundreds of pounds of red, ripe tomatoes that we put up each summer. We try to grow a few early varieties to give that first taste of ripe tomatoes in late spring and early summer. The main crop for canning and juicing comes a bit later. Finally, a good variety of meaty paste tomato for sauces, ketchup, and salsa will save hours of cooking down.

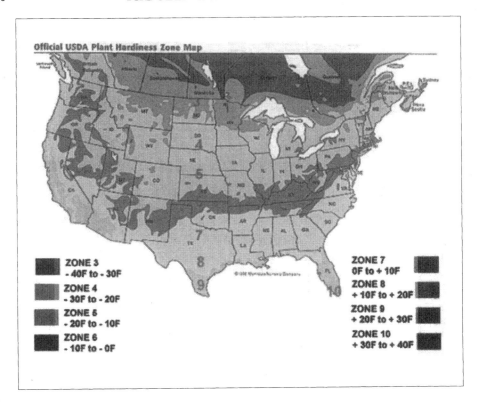

Study the plant hardiness map when planning your garden and selection of plants and seeds. Consider the length of the growing season in your area and plan and plant accordingly.

We generally use Early Girl as our first crop. It is a good dependable variety, not really large, but good for those first tomatoes of the season. We have also experimented with the variety Sub-Arctic Plenty in our little greenhouse. With this short-season variety, we picked our first ripe, albeit small tomato on June 4. We have also tried a variety called Oregon Spring, with excellent results.

Another time-tested method of getting tomato plants off to an early start is to set an ordinary round clay flue tile around each plant. The reddish color combined with the mass of the tile tends to absorb a great deal of sun-generated heat during the cool spring days. In turn, the tile holds the heat and releases it throughout the cool nights. Our Amish neighbors use this method regularly and always have an early crop of tomatoes. On some really cold nights, you might want to put a piece of glass or similar material over the top. Just be sure not to leave a covering over the tile during the day: It can heat up quickly inside and bake the tender, young plant. These red clay tiles are available at concrete supply outlets and construction materials stores.

You can also use milk jugs or 2-liter soda pop bottles to make a sort of mini greenhouse for your plants. Simply remove the cap and cut the bottom out of the jug. Set it down over the plant and anchor it with a long J-shaped wire hooked over the lip of the jug and shoved into the ground. Remove the covers on bright, sunny days. I have also seen folks who simply wrap clear plastic around tomato cages set around their plants. The plastic is taped or clothespinned into place; on really frosty nights, a piece is clipped over the top. The cages are left in place as the plants mature, and the plastic is removed once the nightly temperatures warm enough to prevent them from getting frostnipped.

One trick you might want to try is this: When setting tomato plants, I try to wait until evening. Then I give each plant a good soaking to settle the soil around its roots. If this is done in the hot afternoon sun, the soil can become very hard in the area where it has been wetted. If you wait until evening to set the plants out, however, then the watered soil will not get the chance to dry and harden.

Our early tomato plants are followed with Better Boy, Celebrity, and Rutgers or Beefsteak for the main crop. The Rutgers has one advantage in that it is not a hybrid, and some of the seed may be saved for the next year's crop. I was raised to believe that a better tomato than Better Boy simply did not exist. Perhaps back then, it didn't. However, today, the Celebrity is really hard to beat. Its large, uniform size combined with its excellent texture and taste make it a simply outstanding tomato. I must admit that we rely mainly upon Celebrity for most of our canning tomatoes.

The Supersteak and other Beefsteak-type tomatoes are excellent for kitchen use as well as for some preserving. These cover-the-bun varieties are good slicers and go well, indeed, with those burgers hot off the grill. Just be sure to use high-acid varieties if you plan on canning them.

Finally, we normally set out several paste tomato plants of the San Marzano variety. We have found them to be even meatier than Roma, another good pear-shaped paste-type tomato. Both are excellent. These pear-shaped varieties have a high meat-to-juice ratio so you will not have to cook the wallpaper off the walls to get your sauces down to a thick and usable consistency. We use the San Marzano for pizza sauce, spaghetti sauce, and my wife's own special "911 Sauce," a *hot* salsa made with Thai peppers!

One technique that we always use to increase yields is to mulch the tomato plants once they are established. After the plants have taken hold well, I go through the patch and cultivate it well, hoeing and pulling any weeds that are visible. Next, we apply one or two thicknesses of newspapers, and then add a thick mulch of straw. The covering not only keeps weeds down, but retains moisture as well, which in turn means that more remains available for the developing fruit. Here's a word of caution, though: Don't mulch too early. Let the soil warm up well before adding the thick layers of straw. Mulch can also hold in the coolness and prevent the soil from warming. We lost several tomato plants a couple of years ago that way. But once the soil is warmed and the new plant established, nothing can beat a good thick blanket of mulch. If it sounds like a lot of work to put it down, remember that it will save you hours and hours of weeding and possibly watering later on.

In fact, if there was only one single hint or idea about gardening that I could pass on to you—one single tip to ensure your gardening success— it would be just this one word: *mulch!* I don't believe there is any other gardening practice that can transform an average garden into an excellent one better than good and abundant mulching. This not only goes for tomatoes, but also for the whole garden. Best of all, it costs nothing, or at least very little. A thick blanket of mulch can make the difference between a successful garden and a parched and weed-choked one.

Finally, after mulching, we make support cages from old woven wire fencing, and stake one of the wire cylinders around each plant. The support allows the plant to grow much more upright, up off the ground. The resulting fruit develops more evenly and with fewer blemishes and bad spots. Too, the air circulates better through and around the plant and generally promotes a good, healthy plant. Oh yes, it makes it much easier to pick the ripe tomatoes as well.

As a garden crop, green beans come in a close second in importance to us. These nutritious vegetables are easy to grow, easy to preserve, and easy to prepare into delicious dishes. We usually pressure can our green beans, because we like the margin of safety that this offers over a boiling-water bath. Home extension services are beginning to recommend this method as well. We find that the flavor of canned beans is superior to that of their frozen counterparts. Varieties we have used include bush varieties like Topcrop, Tendergreen, and Bush Blue Lake. Pole bean varieties have been limited to the old Kentucky Wonder and Blue Lake, simply because I've never found any reason to try other types. Currently, we plant only Blue Lake pole beans. They are heavy producers, stringless, excellent for canning, and have a great flavor. It seems that our cellar shelves are always emptied of these long before the new crop is ready. We normally plant the beans at the rate of four or five seeds per hill. Once the new seedlings emerge, I allow them to get maybe a week's worth of growth before I hoe lightly around them and "stick" them with sassafras beanpoles. I enjoy growing, picking, and using pole beans, and our boys like to help pick the beans from the inside of the pole bean tepees.

When planting bush beans, I like to plant in double rows. When using a standard front-tined tiller, merely take the hoe and scratch in two rows in the wheel tracks. I like the distance between them—about 8 to 10 inches. It allows for a light hoeing between the two close rows before the beans grow enough to shade out weeds. Planting in this way also helps maximize the use of your garden space.

Corn is the third most important garden crop for us. There is something about sitting down at a winter supper table before a dish of steaming roasting ears that is hard to describe. It is a true taste of summer. The golden ripe ears of corn are best preserved by steam-blanching them, then freezing them in meal-sized batches in airtight plastic bags. Thawed, simmered, and smeared with butter, they are hard to beat come winter. I have probably tried more corn varieties than almost any other vegetable that we grow. In addition to our crop to put up, I often experiment with a new variety or two. The old standby in our area used to be Golden Bantam, an old open-pollinated variety from which you can save the next year's seed. It yields good-quality, fairly heavily kerneled ears and is a very good corn for freezing or canning. Several of the hybrid varieties of sweet corn are rapidly gaining in popularity. In fact, the old Golden Bantam has for some time been replaced by its hybrid Golden Cross Bantam. This variety produces a more uniform ear and is an excellent variety for preserving. Other varieties I've tried include Early Sunglow—great for those first early ears of sweet corn—Iochief, Seneca Chief, Illini Xtra-Sweet, NK-199, and one or two of the "candy corn" varieties. Of all the different varieties tried, I keep coming back to the Golden Cross Bantam, the old open-pollinated Golden Bantam, and Early Sunglow. These three are dependable, tasty, and good bearers. Another outstanding variety I have tried and will try again is called Incredible. It is one of the most consistent bearers I have seen and may replace some of my old standby varieties.

As a sensible homesteader, I assume that you utilize primarily, if not exclusively, organic gardening techniques in your food growing. Corn responds well to such treatment, and you will see good results from mulching. The old time-honored method around here is to give the corn a good hoeing when it gets about 12 to 16 inches tall. Just prior to the hoeing, I side-dress the rows with some granular fertilizer scattered along the base of the plants. The hoeing removes the weeds and mixes in the fertilizer, of course, but as I hoe, I also pull the dirt up around the growing stalks just a bit. This ridging of the corn rows helps the corn to develop a sturdier root system.

Peppers are an important item in our garden and our menu that we put up each year. California Wonder is usually our main green sweet pepper. This old variety is dependable and a good bearer. Other varieties that we have tried and like include Jupiter and Big Bertha. Green peppers are full of vitamins and very tasty additions to many dishes. They are prolific and can easily be sliced and frozen or dried. We have also preserved them stuffed with a meat-and-rice mixture and canned.

We use a lot of hot peppers in our food as well. We like jalapeños and often dry strings of them for use in chili. The seed for another type of hot pepper was received from a pen pal in Texas. These hot little rascals are yellowish orange when ripe and shaped like small acorn squash. We finally decided that they were the sizzling Scotch bonnet peppers. They bear heavily and are really hot!

Finally, we grow lots of the tiny Thai peppers for use in salsa and for drying. These fiery little peppers grow on compact, bushy plants and are, by far, the hottest peppers I've found. They grow into an attractive plant, first covered with hundreds of small white blooms, followed by the tiny bright red peppers. They look great in the garden or in a hanging basket. If you try them, don't let their small 1-inch size fool you. These things can hurt you! They are the pepper of choice for the dreaded 911 Sauce my wife makes.

Any of these varieties may be strung, dried in a dehydrator, or frozen for later use.

We have grown several hills of pumpkins and cushaws for preserving and for sale to local grocery stores and individuals. I do not have a particular favorite variety of pumpkins, so I usually just try a new variety now and then. The varieties Howden and Pankow's Field pumpkins have both done well in our patch. The green-striped cushaws are from seed given by my wife's grandfather. They are very good when made into squash pies. We save seed each year for them.

To grow pumpkins and squash, the common method around here is to hoe up an 18- to 24-inch-diameter hill of soil, mix in a little fertilizer, compost, or manure, and flatten it out. With your finger, make five or six evenly spaced holes in the hill about 1 to 1½ inches deep and drop in the seeds. Gently fill in the holes and pat everything down firmly. The plants that develop will spread out all over the place, so be sure to allow plenty of room—at least 4 to 6 feet. These vegetables take a lot of space. Their vining characteristics will send them out into adjacent rows, up nearby cornstalks, and anywhere else in a 10- to 15-foot radius.

We have also gotten a jump on the season by starting the seeds in our greenhouse and setting them out a foot or so apart in one long row. This method was used once or twice when we were growing them for sale. For most home garden use, a hill or two will provide you with more than enough fixin's for your pies!

We like the taste of homemade pumpkin and squash pies and generally steam the meat from the shells and can it in pint jars. Those pies, although a traditional holiday treat, are welcome anytime they come out of the oven.

Of course, a garden is not complete without a salad patch, and we usually try to get ours going as early as we can. Alternating rows of red and green lettuce are pretty in the garden and attractive in the salad bowl as well. Black Seeded Simpson is a good loose-leaf variety of lettuce, and Red Sails provides the color in the patch. One of our favorite ways of getting an early spinach and lettuce crop going is to plant it in an old tire. There it germinates quickly. It's always nice to get a taste of those first early-spring salads. Bloomsdale Longstanding Spinach is a variety that we enjoy. It is easy to get going in early spring, and if you harvest it regularly, it doesn't bolt or go to seed quickly. We try to keep it going late into winter and start again at the very first hint of spring. Tyee spinach is another good variety to try if you live in areas that get hot early. It is slow to bolt and produces very well. Either of these varieties will be good additions to your salad garden.

Green Comet Hybrid Broccoli is a regular in our patch. We have tried other varieties, but have come back to this one. It does well with both spring crops and later fall crops. It heads out well and doesn't go to seed too quickly. It is very good fresh and also freezes well.

I normally set my broccoli plants in two rather closely spaced rows in a zigzag fashion. In this way, I can get a few more plants into a given space. The closer spacing also helps crowd out weeds.

Cabbage is another vegetable that we grow and preserve for winter. We set out plants in both spring and fall. In my experience, I think the fall-planted cabbage actually does better for us. We like the varieties

Market Prize, Early Flat Dutch, and Stone Head Hybrid. This last variety is good for late-season planting or short growing seasons as it matures in about 55 days.

When setting the cabbage plants, we sometimes place an ordinary wooden match vertically right up against the stem of the plant and push it down into the dirt. This supposedly helps keep cabbage loopers, a variety of worm, from curling around the plant stem and chewing it through. It seems to help.

Of course, we usually have a few unanticipated varieties of vegetables that we crowd into an empty corner or odd spot in the garden. Due to their vining characteristics, cucumbers for salads and pickles are usually limited to bush varieties. We still end up with plenty to eat fresh and to pickle.

Watermelons are normally limited to the sweet and compact little Sugar Baby simply because I grew them as a kid and I like them. As for cantaloupes, we don't really have a preference. We usually just pick up a packet of seed at the hardware store. Both watermelons and cantaloupes are grown using the flat hill method described for growing pumpkins. They will take up some space, so plan for that. We space the hills about 5 or 6 feet apart in the row.

There will be no better time for you to start your food-producing garden than this year. Start small, learn from your neighbors and from your experiences, and you will soon be reaping, literally, the fruits of your labor. The feeling of accomplishment and security that accompanies the growing, harvest, and putting up of your garden produce is great indeed.

Composting

The recycling of normal everyday household scraps, lawn waste, and other organic leavings into rich compost is a must for homesteaders— and for any gardener, for that matter. No single activity is as simple, as easy, as productive, or as rewarding as turning unwanted refuse into rich planting material.

As with most of the other facets of homesteading presented so far, composting can be as simple or as elaborate as you wish to make it. Probably the easiest method of composting refuse is to simply stack the yard waste into a single pile. Grass clippings, leaves, and other fine vegetation can simply be tossed into a heap and allowed to break down at their own pace. One obvious disadvantage to this method is that the pile can tend to scatter rather easily due to wind, children, and animals.

A much neater and more efficient method of composting makes use of easily constructed bins that contain the waste material. The methods of constructing composting bins vary as widely as the people using them, and have been dealt with in nearly every gardening magazine. Personally, I have used a couple of types—one made of a section of discarded woven wire fencing, and another made of loosely stacked concrete blocks. Each worked well. The first, the wire bin, was easily made in about five minutes. I merely decided what size of hoop I wanted, measured the appropriate length of wire, and bent the ends to hook over the other end of the length of fencing to form the cylinder—a giant tomato cage of sorts. The loose hooks make it easy to open the bin when turning or using the compost. Into this cylinder went the various vegetative refuse, and out came some rich fine compost.

The second bin was made from used concrete blocks, stacked without any mortar into a three-sided bin. As illustrated, the rows were stacked on their sides to allow for the circulation of air. Note the poles placed through the openings in the front blocks to help contain the compost.

A third bin can be made from treated or other rot-resistant lumber. Using as many 8-foot 2 x 4s as needed for the height you need, cut and

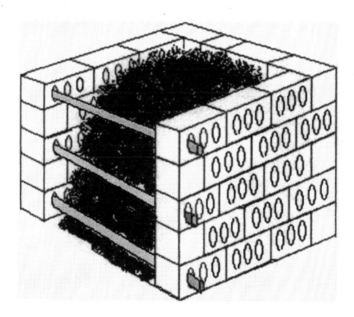

How to make a compost bin by dry stacking concrete blocks. By stacking them on their sides, air is allowed to circulate. Note the poles that are placed through holes in the front blocks to help keep the material contained.

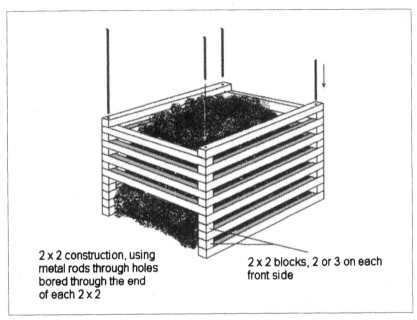

2 x 2 construction, using metal rods through holes bored through the end of each 2 x 2

2 x 2 blocks, 2 or 3 on each front side

This sample compost bin is made from 2 x 2s. Long rods are pushed through holes located near the end of each 2 x 2. Blocks are used in the front along the bottom couple of runs. This will let you easily shovel or fork the compost into your wheelbarrow.

rip the boards until you have a good stack of 2 x 2s, each 4 feet long. Into each end of each 2 x 2 and about an inch from the end, bore a ½-inch hole completely through. Next, take four ⅜-inch rods (old electric fence posts with the "fins" removed work well) and use as corners. Place two of the 2 x 2s parallel to each other on these rods. Place the next two 2 x 2s over the rods at right angles to the first. Repeat this procedure, alternating the laying of the 2 x 2s until you reach the height desired. One 2 x 4 will be needed for one course, equaling a little less than 4 inches in height. A dozen 2 x 4s should give you a finished bin just under 4 feet in height and approximately 4 feet square. Additionally, you can easily gain access to the finished compost in this type of bin. Make a few short 2 x 2 blocks, 4 to 6 inches long, with the ½-inch holes bored through them. Pull up the front two rods of the bin and replace the front three or four 2 x 2s with the spacer blocks. This arrangement will give you access to the finished compost at the bottom of the bin, making it much easier to remove with a shovel or fork.

Virtually any vegetable matter produced on the 'stead can be tossed onto the compost pile, each variety adding its own nutrients and value to the finished rich, crumbly compost. Grass clippings, shredded leaves, livestock manure, clean kitchen scraps (sans meat and fat), garden trimmings, and more can all be turned into compost.

As mentioned, the bin itself can be made from a wide variety of materials. Again, use what you have. My bins sit side by side for easy turning of the material from one bin into the next. One of the bins is made from old concrete blocks, the other from old woven fence wire. Simply put, the bin can be made from any material that will hold the heap together.

The site for your compost bin is the first important consideration, although not for the reasons you might think. A properly constructed and functioning compost pile emits little, if any, objectionable odor. The main reason for the site consideration is twofold: access to the area where the compost will be used and access to the kitchen door! It is easier to get into the habit of composting those always abundant kitchen scraps if the compost pile is handy; same with access to the garden scraps—carrot tops, stalks, and soon. Too, try to locate the heap a short wheelbarrow distance from the garden or greenhouse. In short, make it as easy as you practically can.

After you have completed your compost bin, next comes filling the bin with the future compost. First, spade over the sod in the area where you have placed your bin. Next, toss in a heapin' helpin' of grass clippings or similar material. Shovel in a layer of manure—horse manure is great, but almost any livestock manure works well. Add another layer of leaves and/or clippings. Next, shovel in a layer of ordinary garden soil. Finally, add some more leaves/grass. Remember that you will be adding your daily kitchen scraps. In a day or so, you will notice that the pile is really "cooking." The temperature will have become so hot that you will not be able to keep your hand in the pile—that's what you want; the decomposition has begun. After a couple of weeks, the process is well under way.

Now is the time to turn the pile. If you have constructed two or more bins, merely fork the pile from the first bin into the second, and the second into the third. The pile is now well mixed to assure even decomposition, and the first bin is ready to accept the fixin's of a new batch. If you have only the one bin, at least give the pile a good turning, mixing the contents well. This allows the bacteria to reach all parts of the material and speed up the decomposition.

After four or five more weeks, turn the pile again, being sure to mix the compost as best you can with the fork.

This compost should be ready to use in about 90 days. Sink a spade into the pile. You should come up with a spadeful of rich black soil, ready for use.

Before I use the compost, I run it through a simple homemade sifter. The one I made was built from some scrap 1 x 6s with half-inch hardware cloth nailed to the bottom. The size fits nicely over my wheelbarrow. Toss in a few shovelfuls of compost; give the sifter a good shaking, and the fine compost falls through the wire screen into the wheelbarrow. The larger pieces of compost and trash that do not sift through are tossed into another wheelbarrow and used to mulch around shrubs, fruit trees, and the like. The fine compost can be used immediately or stored in bags or drums for later use as planting mix, potting soil, mulch, or soil amendment.

You will find that any time in the garden is time well spent. Gardening is one of the most basic of homesteading skills and is certainly one of the most important. With some effort, you will be rewarded with shelves and bins full of preserved food that will nourish and satisfy.

Small Fruits

Small fruits play an important part in filling the homestead grocery list. Personal tastes alone pretty well set the limits for the types and varieties of fruits that can be grown on the homestead. Varieties of nearly every type of small fruit have been developed that will adapt to almost all growing regions.

Certainly, the jams, jellies, pies, cobblers, and wines influence the daydreams of many a prospective fruit grower.

Fruit bushes not only make appropriate plantings along the garden edge, but can be attractive landscape plants as well.

Blueberry bushes can become attractive border plants along the edge of the yard. A well-made arbor can allow a few grapevines to form an effective screen.

BLACKBERRIES

Blackberries are actually members of the rose family. These juicy fruits can be grown in just about every region of the United States.

Wild blackberries grow in different forms abundantly over many regions of the United States. Here in southern Indiana, old farmsteads and recently timbered areas are soon choked with wild blackberries. Old overgrown areas often offer the low-growing dewberry, a blackberry cousin. I have spent time in west-central Oregon, and I have never seen blackberries grow in such abundance. There, acres of the brambles produce more fruit than could possibly be used by human, beast, or bird. From east to west, these brambles adapt to their location and offer some high-quality fruit for the picking.

I have heard it argued that tame blackberries just do not have the flavor of their wild counterparts. From my own experience, I have to agree. However, what the tame berries lack in flavor, they make up for in size and fruiting. The thornless blackberries that I was given have developed into a nice berry patch and are heavy producers. The berries are very good, but are at their peak of flavor when they just about fall off in the hand as they are picked.

Blackberries thrive in clay loam that is moist yet well drained. They prefer soil that is enriched with humus. Leaves, weeds, straw work well. Generally, a good mulch that is added occasionally will break down and provide that healthy humus-filled soil.

Blackberry plants are aggressive. That is, they grow rapidly and propagate in a variety of ways. Seed, of course, gets many plants started, particularly in the wild. For gardening purposes, though, it is best to depend upon roots, rooted seedlings, or suckers. The easiest way to obtain new blackberry plants is merely allow the live canes to curve down to the ground. Once in contact with the soil, they will begin to put down roots. This is called tipping. Of course, you can easily increase this tendency by gently bending your longest canes over and anchoring them with a small hooked wire to ensure good contact with the soil. To use these new plants, just clip them off a few inches toward the base of the parent plant, gently dig up the new root system, and move the plant where you want it.

For larger-scale plantings, you may wish to dig into the base of the clump of the parent plant and remove a few rooted cuttings. These are usually the youngest plants that you will see coming up around the older canes. Moving a few from each existing clump does not harm the rest; in fact, this thinning will actually help the original plants to thrive. You should be able to come up with several new starts using this method.

To get started, you can often find transplants locally just by putting out the word among your gardening friends that you are in need of some. Commercial nurseries, including the mail-order houses, also offer a wide variety of plants. Transplants may be set out in either spring or fall. I prefer to get them going in spring to let them get their root systems established well.

BLACKBERRY VARIETY

VARIETY	ADAPTABLE TO NORTHERN CLIMATE	THORNLESS	DESSERT QUALITY	OTHER INFORMATION
Darrow	Yes	No	High	Fairly early bearer. Long season, very prolific. May also produce a fall crop. Very thorny.
Ranger	Yes	No	Good	Early bearer. Winter-hardy.
Eldorado	Yes	No	Good	Good for the North.
Alfred	Yes	No	Good	Recommended for coldest northern states.
Thornless	Somewhat	Yes	Good	Hardy and thorn-free.
Black Satin	No	Yes	Fair	Early bearer. Good for pies, jelly.
Thornfree	No	Yes	Fair	Tart. Large fruit. Prolific bearer. Generally, brambles can be pruned rather easily.

The diagram at right depicts how your plants might look prior to pruning and how they should be shaped after pruning.

RASPBERRIES

Raspberries are one of the jewels of a small farm's crops. All those folks with a good raspberry patch on their place will discover an eager market for any surplus berries produced—if there are any! By the time the berry crop is frozen or canned, made into jam, baked into fresh cobblers, and just eaten by the handfuls, you may find that you do not have much of a surplus to sell. Black raspberries can also be made into a truly superior wine. I have included my own recipe for this in chapter 5.

Black raspberries should definitely be considered for the family farmstead. Even in a relatively small area, you can produce a large crop of sweet, finely lobed berries. There are several varieties that can probably adapt to your area. The canes are vigorous and adapt well to many soil types. They are generally hardy to about 25 degrees below 0.

With proper care, the berry patch can produce for many years. An important step in the production of these bramble fruits is summer topping. This consists of removing, by either snapping off with the fingers or cutting with a pair of shears, the top 3 or 4 inches of the new shoots as they develop. Topping should be done with black raspberries when the shoots are about 24 inches high and with purple ones when they reach 30 inches, if they are grown without supports. With supports, the shoots may be allowed to grow 6 to 8 inches more. Plantings need to be topped a number of times as new canes arise over a period of several weeks. In most seasons, this operation will, in part, coincide with harvest.

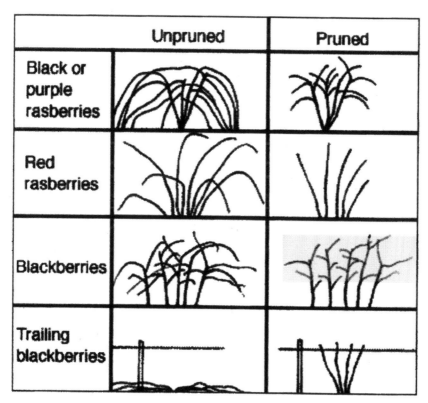

How bramble plants look before and after pruning.

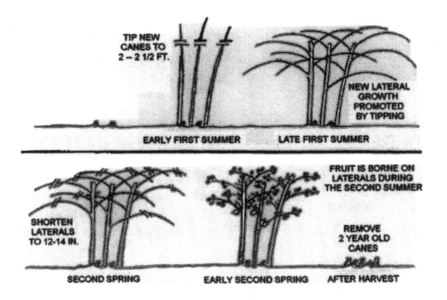

Proper pruning for black raspberries.

In your patch, you will very likely have some competition from your bird friends. After many different attempts at various deterrents, we finally settled for protective netting stretched over a simple support frame made from discarded metal tubing from an old greenhouse frame. This is simply the most effective method for preventing the loss of a considerable share of the berry crop to the winged bandits. I have also had some success with stretching a strand or two of 10- to 15-pound-test monofilament fishing line from poles set at each end of the row of bushes. It is reported that if you use a line the birds can barely see, they will not come in and try to land on the bushes.

RASPBERRY VARIETIES

VARIETY	ADAPTABLE TO NORTHERN CLIMATE	DESSERT QUALITY	OTHER INFORMATION
Jewel	Yes	Good	Midseason ripening. Good disease and virus resistance. Vigorous, erect plants. Moderately hardy.

Bristol	Yes	Good	High yielding and early, with medium-sized fruit of excellent flavor. Susceptible to anthracnose, but tolerant of powdery mildew.
Black Hawk	Yes	Good	A slightly later, moderately productive plant with large, firm fruit.
Allen	Somewhat	Good	Large and attractive berries, growing on vigorous, productive plants. Flavor is mild.

Characteristically, the canes of raspberries die shortly after they have produced a crop. These canes can be removed after the harvest season. They should be cut off immediately after harvest.

STRAWBERRIES

In my experience, strawberries are the most labor-intensive of the small fruit crops to grow. For many people, though, the amount of labor is not excessive compared to the gallons upon gallons of sweet red fruit produced by a home-sized strawberry patch.

The variety of strawberry with which I have enjoyed the most success is the popular and productive Redchief. This hardy and disease-resistant variety is well adapted to a wide area and is a tremendous producer of excellent-quality fruit. Personally, I can think of no better variety for the homestead patch.

Since we normally mulch most of our vegetable garden with straw, we found that doing the same with the strawberry patch was no great inconvenience.

Our primary difficulties in growing strawberries were animal in nature. In spring, just as soon as I had raked back the winter covering of straw, the deer located the patch and devoured nearly every young plant just as quickly as new growth appeared. Later, those berries that had managed to appear on the beleaguered vines fell victim to the local furry masked marauders—the raccoons. Between the deer and the raccoons, our patch was pretty well decimated.

STRAWBERRY VARIETIES

VARIETY	ADAPTABLE TO NORTHERN CLIMATE	DESSERT QUALITY	SEASON
Midland	Yes	Very good	Early
Redchief	Yes	Very good	Midseason
Surecrop	Yes	Good	Midseason
Tennessee Beauty	No	Very good	Late

Since then, I have tried a variety of ways to limit damage by raccoons and deer. The best method I have found is to run an extension cord out to the garden, attach a portable radio, and tune to a "lively" radio station. You can also attach a timer if you want, to allow the radio to come on and off at certain time intervals. I have learned that changing radio stations and the radio location every week or so also adds to the effectiveness.

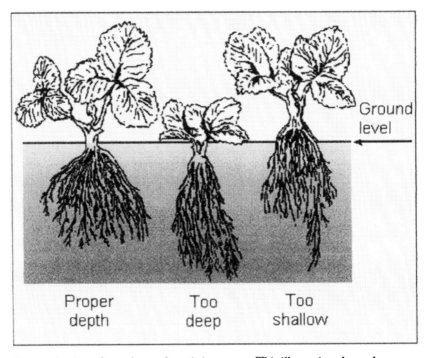

Proper planting of strawberry plants is important. This illustration shows the proper depth for setting plants. Courtesy University of Missouri.

A really good way to set strawberries is in rows about 3 to 4 feet apart. The plants themselves will take off and put out lots of runners, so they should initially be set about 2 feet apart. Strawberries are a bit particular when it comes to setting the plants. Too deep or too shallow in the soil, and the plant will not thrive. Take a look at the illustration at left to get an idea of how to set your plants.

The first plant is shown set at the proper depth. The second plant is set too deeply. The third is set to high and has roots exposed to the air. Set your plants as in the first illustration, spread the roots out nicely, and your plants should fare well.

The plants will put out much growth and, along with the runners, will soon fill in the gaps. It is recommended that you pick off the strawberry blossoms during the first year of growth to stimulate good root development and to help establish the plant. However, I couldn't resist leaving a few of the white blooms to get at least a sampling of the jeweled red fruit. It did not seem to harm the plants at all.

One thing about strawberries that I like is that the plants regenerate prolifically. They're constantly sending out runners and putting down roots wherever they take a notion. In fact, throughout the summer I'll make a pass down the rows and reposition the new plants beginning to take root from the runners. Gently lift the rooting plant from the soil and move it and its runner back into the established row. Every other year, these new plants are allowed to take root solidly and are allowed to take over the row path. These new plants become the replacement plants. In fall, after the new plants are going well, they are clipped from the old plants and the old row is tilled up. It is an efficient and inexpensive way to regenerate your bed.

Even when you are not establishing a new row, the existing patch can be renewed. Just after the harvest of berries is done, remove the old foliage. This is easily done by setting the height of your power mower deck to allow the blade to cut to within 1 to 1½ inches above the plant crown. Rake all the debris and leaves up and either burn them or throw them in the compost pile. Add a scattering of a good fertilizer (12-12-12 is good). Then go ahead and neaten up the rows, hoeing or tilling out rogue plants that might be straying into the path.

To put the strawberries to bed for the winter, add a 3- or 4-inch-thick layer of straw over the rows after you get a few frosts. Come spring, rake the straw off the plants and let it pack into the pathways. This will help keep down weeds and add tilthe to the soil as it decomposes.

GOOSEBERRIES

Gooseberries are an old homestead fruit. Most folks are not familiar with this berry, a relative to the currant. The low, thick bushes are especially easy for children to pick from, once they learn to bypass the slight prickliness of the bushes. Children relish the ripe greenish to reddish berries and seem to enjoy even the tart underripe ones.

Most American varieties of gooseberry are actually hybrids of American and European species. The plants are small, deciduous, and woody shrubs. They grow to be about 4 feet tall and are well suited to the home fruit patch.

Gooseberries make an excellent jam and can be made into a very good wine as well. They require little care beyond a bit of pruning occasionally and an annual application of an all-purpose fertilizer such as 10-10-10 or some good compost.

A couple of varieties come to mind that should do well in almost any home fruit patch. Pixwell is a popular variety and is very productive. The fruit is of average quality but bears abundantly. Poorman yields red-fruited, large, and flavorful berries. It is probably the best cultivar for the home garden.

GRAPES

Having had a bit of experience with several varieties of grapes, I have come back to the wisdom that most old-time homesteaders knew already: The old Concord grape is probably the best single homestead grape to have on the place. The several varieties of wine grapes that I had growing on the place did produce some good fruit, and had good flavor. However, I found that some of them were a bit finicky to grow. On the other hand, the old Concord has superb color and flavor, and is well

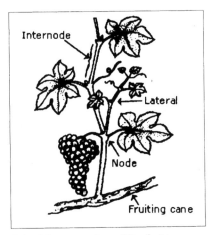

A healthy grape shoot. The fruiting cane is last year's growth. The new shoots emerge in the spring. Courtesy Oregon State University.

suited to jam, jelly, wine, or juice. It is simply a great grape.

It is important that your site have good air circulation, sun exposure, and a soil that is well drained to grow quality crops of grapes. Air circulation is best if the location has a gentle slope; avoid low, frosty pockets. Plant the vines away from trees so that they will receive full sunshine. Grapes are not as particular about soils as other fruit crops; overly rich soils will stimulate excessive vine growth at the expense of fruit quality. Grapes require a soil pH of 5.5 to 7.0.

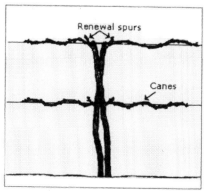

A pruned grape plant showing the Four-Cane Kniffin system. Courtesy Michigan State University.

When setting your grape plants, I'd recommend planting vigorous one-year-old plants in either late winter or early spring. Plant the vines the same depth or slightly deeper than they grew in the nursery. Keep the topsoil separate to place over and around the roots. Be sure not to place fresh manure or fertilizer in the hole. Tamp the soil firmly around the roots, and water if dry. After setting the vine, prune it to one stem and cut this stem back to two or three buds.

Some of our plants came from starts dug up from the base of existing plants. These were dug and cut, along with some soil and roots, and transplanted into prepared sites. Other grapes I have grown were started from cuttings. These were merely prunings from existing plants. The cuttings were placed in a bucket of moist sand with two or three buds below the surface and 6 to 8 inches of stem, with three or four buds protruding above. The sand was kept moist—not wet—and the cuttings soon began to establish their own new root system. Once the new plants were exhibiting some growth, they were transplanted to their permanent site.

Grapevines may be pruned anytime during the dormant season. However, it is recommended that you delay pruning until late winter or spring to offer some protection from cold stress.

Mature grapevines will produce much more wood than they can support. Consider the wild grapevine growing in the woods—it produces an enormous amount of wood just to climb to the sunlight. Your cultivated grapevines won't need to do that, but they will still produce much more wood than is necessary or desirable. Generally, about 90 percent of the new growth of a mature grapevine is removed during dormant pruning. Plan on leaving about three to four buds per foot of horizontal grape stem or trunk. Remember that grapes bear their fruit on one-year-old wood.

Grapes are, indeed, one of the staple homestead fruits. Thinking back to my parents' and grandparents' places, I recall making frequent visits to the heavily scented, fruit-laden vines and plucking the sweetest, ripest grapes. Those were good days.

BLUEBERRIES

The rich taste of blueberries is one of those special and all-too-rare garden treats. But that doesn't have to be so. Blueberries can be grown on your place in a relatively small area with good results.

Blueberries (*Vaccinium* spp.) are erect woody perennial bushes belonging to the heath family. I first became acquainted with them when I found small wild varieties growing high atop the bluffs and rocks on the sharp ridges around my home area. Later, on a canoe trip into the wilderness of Minnesota, I gathered bunches of the prolific wild fruit to go with pancakes and to snack on. Finally, I started a few of my own bushes here at home, to have my own dependable supply of the sweet dark fruit.

Here in the Midwest, there are several varieties that do well. Listed below are several adaptable and popular varieties that should do well over much of the country.

BLUEBERRY VARIETIES

VARIETY	DESSERT QUALITY	SEASON	OTHER INFORMATION
Earliblue	Good	Early	Good producer. Freezes well.
Collins	Good	Early	Attractive large berries.
Berkeley	Fair	Midseason	Large berries, productive. Cans well.
Bluecrop	Good	Midseason	Large berries. Slightly earlier than Berkeley. Both cans and freezes well.
Blueray	Good	Midseason	Large berries. Cans well.
Jersey	Fair	Midseason	Produces large crop. Freezes well.
Coville	Good	Late	Good variety to extend season. Berries tart until ripe. Cans well.

| Herbert | Very good | Late | Productive. Large fruit. |
| Lateblue | Good | Very late | Large, productive. |

Generally, blueberries can be grown if your winter temperatures are mostly above 20 below. You will also need a growing season of about 160 days or longer and at least 1,000 hours of temperatures under 45 degrees during the winter. For southern growers, some species of Rabbiteye blueberries and southern species hybrids require less winter chilling. These varieties can be grown as far south as the Gulf Coast. Blueberries are rather shallow-rooted and do best where the water table is about 14 to 22 inches below the soil surface. Don't attempt to grow blueberries unless you can supply needed water when the rainfall is not adequate.

Most of the major tree and seedling suppliers sell blueberry starts. When purchasing your plants, try to get two-year-old plants 10 to 15 inches tall. Be certain not to let the roots dry out prior to transplanting. Keep them moist and covered. Dig a hole the size of a 5-gallon bucket or larger and mix in some good organic material such as sphagnum or peat moss with the soil. (As the mail-order fruit tree suppliers used to state: "Dig a $20 hole for a $10 tree.") The same goes for blueberry bushes. Put about half the mixture in the hole, set the plant, and fill the hole with the rest of the soil mix. Blueberry plants should be spaced about 5 to 8 feet apart. If placed in rows, space the rows about 8 to 10 feet apart (or wide enough to get your particular tractor, mower, or whatever between the rows: Remember that the mature bushes themselves will get to be from 3 to 8 feet in diameter, and be sure to allow for this). Blueberry bushes can make an attractive screen when planted in a row along a roadway or property line. They are also often planted in maintained rows, as indicated above.

It will take three or four years for your transplants to begin producing fruit. It is also a good idea to remove most or all of the first-year blossoms. This will encourage vigorous plant growth instead of fruit growth during that important first year.

Blueberries are not very self-fertile. This means that two or more different varieties must be planted in the same area to ensure good pollination and good fruit crops. Blueberries require moist yet well-drained acidic soils. There are several commercially available soil amendments that can get your soil in the 4.8 to 5.2 pH range. I give my plants an annual dose of common 10-10-10 fertilizer in addition to any acidic soil amendments. With good fertilization and soil management, it is not uncommon for your cultivated bushes to reach 5 to 10 feet in height.

Blueberries require a good mulch as far out as the drip line of the plant. A thick mulch of sawdust or crushed corncobs is good. Oak leaves are also very good and help supply the acid needed by the plants. I often use plain old pine needles around my plants. They are good mulch and also supply the acid that blueberries love. I head over to the nearby state forest and use a scoop shovel to gather piles of them that accumulate along the roadway that runs through the forest property.

When it comes to blueberries, I have found that insect pests are few. However, birds can wreak havoc in your blueberry patch. Catbirds, brown thrashers, and similar songbirds love blueberries and seem to nail them just before you get out to pick them. One remedy had good success with was to purchase some simple toy pinwheels at the your local dime store or Wally World. I fastened a piece of 1½ inch PVC pipe to a nearby fence post and just dropped the pinwheel in. The loose fit enabled the pinwheel to turn into the slightest breeze. The motion created by the shiny spinning toy has worked well in keeping the berry bandits at bay. While this works well for my few bushes, you may need to consider fine net coverings if you have a row of several bushes. I have used net coverings over rows of raspberries: They are very effective in reducing bird destruction.

Blueberry bushes will need to be pruned after about their fourth year. Don't be bashful with the pruners. You will need to prune out two main types of growth to encourage prolific fruit bearing—first, the very slender stems that do not bear much, and then oldest and largest branches that are probably bearing mainly at the tips.

On a healthy, mature blueberry bush, you may expect to harvest about 12 to 14 quarts of fruit each year. With half a dozen or more bushes, this can translate into some extra money for you. Depending upon your area, you should be able to easily earn two to four dollars a quart for the fruit. However, if you only have two or three plants, you will be likely to use all the berries yourself.

APPLES

Small farm orchards, having once nearly disappeared from our countryside, are once again becoming more common as country people rediscover the value of apples. Not only are small home orchards becoming familiar sights, but small-scale commercial orchards are reappearing as well. Our awareness of good nutrition, health, and diet have no doubt contributed to the resurgence in the popularity of these small family enterprises. These small orchards provide a feeling of security and self-sufficiency to homesteaders and other landowners all over the country.

Because of its complex parentage, and the wealth of genetic material within its makeup, the apple shows more variability in its progeny than any other major fruit. No other fruit has such variability in flavor, texture, shape, color, or season. There is truly a cultivar to suit every taste.

It is important to note that apples do not grow true from seed; that is, every seedling is different. So if you plant a seed, say from a McIntosh, and it germinates, the resulting seedling will be unique, unnamed, and yours to do with as you will. I'll offer a word of caution, however, to temper any feelings of optimism about filling the world with wonderful new apple discoveries: The chances of raising a seedling better than, or even as good as, the many thousands of existing named cultivars is exceedingly remote—1 chance in 1,000, in fact. You must remember that the many varieties we enjoy today have rarely developed through chance. Most are painstakingly developed by professional geneticists based at agricultural colleges, research institutes, or experiment stations and using modern horticultural techniques. This deliberate research and breeding have resulted in the development of many of the varieties popular today. For example, the widely popular commercial variety Idared is the result of the work done by Mr. Lief Verner at the Idaho Agricultural Experiment Station in Moscow, Idaho. It resulted from crossing the varieties Jonathan and Wagener. It was developed in 1935 and formally introduced in 1942. The apple gained importance commercially due to its late-keeping qualities and the fact that it shows some resistance to scab, a common disease of apples. Also on the list of the many popular and important developed varieties we enjoy today are Liberty, Jonagold, Red Rome Beauty, Mutsu, Cortland, and many others.

Now, all this is not to say that no good new apple variety can occur outside the laboratory; for it does, albeit rarely. Many of the

Picking apples is fun. We get to eat as many as we want.

varieties known today were discovered purely by accident. Golden Delicious is the most widely planted apple in the main fruit-growing areas of the world. It was produced as a chance seedling found in 1890 by A. H. Mullins of Clay County, West Virginia. The very popular Granny Smith apple originated in Australia in about 1865, having grown entirely by chance from a seed tossed out by Mrs. Thomas Smith of Ryde, New South Wales. Another old variety, the Keswick Codlin, is recorded to have been found "growing among a quantity of rubbish behind a wall at Gleaston Castle near Ulverstone" in Lancashire, England, in 1790. It remains very popular there even today.

Amateur horticulturalists and orchardists have also contributed mightily to the numbers of apple varieties known today. One good old variety, Wealthy, was raised by Peter M. Gideon of Excelsior, Minnesota, in about 1860. The seedling originated from seed of the Cherry Crab. The popular variety Jonathan was raised by Phillip Rick and originated on a farm in Woodstock, New York, around 1825. This important commercial variety is thought to be a seedling of the old Esopus Spitzenburg open-pollinated type.

GROWING YOUR OWN

The adaptability of apples is such that just about any landowner can consider growing them. Even the smallest plot of land has room for a couple of apple cultivars. Apples are quite simply the overall most useful fruit for growing in cool and temperate climates. By having both early and late varieties, along with some long-keeping varieties, you can have prime apples nearly all year long, with perhaps only a short gap in summer.

The uses for apple are seemingly unlimited. Homemade apple pies, baked spiced apples, and apple dumplings are just a few of the traditional desserts that your orchard can provide. Apples can be canned, dried, frozen, sliced, chunked, sauced, baked, steamed, stewed, fried, or of course eaten fresh. They can be made into side dishes, pies, cobblers, cakes, jellies, breads, juice, cider, or wine. They are possibly the most versatile single food crop you can grow.

Before you head charging to the nursery catalogs to begin the search for your orchard plantings, some planning will be in order. The amount of room you have available will help determine the size and type of apple trees that you choose. Apple trees basically come in three sizes: standard, semidwarf, and dwarf. Some specially grafted miniatures are even available that are suited to growing in large tubs or half barrels.

The standard-sized trees are the largest available. They are full-sized trees and require the most space in the orchard. Standard trees should be set out about 40 to 45 feet apart. This may seem like a great distance, but it is essential to prevent crowding of branches and permit good flow of air among the trees.

Dwarf trees are simply that—small versions of the parent. Grafted onto special dwarfing rootstocks, these trees are useful for small spaces and enable easy pruning, spraying, and picking. These small trees bear fruit sooner than standard trees, but they have a shorter bearing life. When transplanting, dwarf trees should be spaced 10 to 15 feet apart.

Between the standard and dwarf trees we find the semidwarf trees. These, as you might guess, are about halfway in size between the standard and dwarf trees. These trees are quite practical in the small home orchard, offering more fruiting plant than the dwarf, yet still being fairly easy to maintain and harvest fruit from. Semidwarf trees should be planted on 20- to 25-foot centers.

The great number of apple varieties available can be somewhat overwhelming to the "budding" orchardist, and selection can be confusing if not downright difficult. With the exception of Golden Delicious, most apple varieties are self-unfruitful—that is, they do not make good pollinators of their own flowers. To ensure good pollination, and a resulting good fruit crop, it is generally best to plant at least two varieties together. Poor pollen-producing apple varieties—such as Winesap, Staymen, Gravenstein, Baldwin, and Rhode Island Greening—need to be planted with at least two other varieties to ensure pollination of all the varieties. For beginning orchardists, it's a good idea to follow the recommendations of the nursery or catalog for the more popular and easily grown varieties. There are also some good disease-resistant varieties that I plan to look into, because my area seems hard hit by fire blight. Varieties such as Jon-A-Free and Liberty are two good disease-resistant varieties that you might want to consider.

Most nursery-produced apple trees will have tops that are one to two years old. The length of time required for standard and semidwarf trees to bear fruit after planting varies, but most can be expected to begin bearing at between four and seven years. Dwarf trees can begin bearing in only a year or two, although their total life span is shorter. You may want to set out a couple of dwarf trees along with the rest of your orchard to be able to enjoy fruit much sooner than by planting the larger trees alone.

Temperature is the single most important factor limiting the cultivation of apples. A climate with some consistent cold weather is needed to ensure proper formation of fruiting buds on the tree. Additionally, in areas where late frosts are common, consider planting a late variety of apple so the delicate and critical blossom stage will likely miss the last frost. Be sure, too, to locate your prospective orchard in an area where air drainage is good, and not in a frost pocket where the cold air could pool and damage the delicate apple blossoms. Simply put, try to locate your orchard on a hilltop or hillside and not down in the bottom ground.

Some varieties such as Northern Spy will thrive and bear good crops in the Far North, and others such as Dorsett Golden or Anna will do quite well even in the southern regions of the country if they are given just a little bit of extra care. Your local agricultural extension agent can offer suggestions about which varieties are best adapted to your particular region.

Apple trees are not too finicky when it comes to soil types. Perhaps this fact helps account for their wide growing range and popularity. They like good deep loam but are tolerant of a wide range of soil types as long as it is not too wet. They don't do well on acid soil, so you might have to add some lime. The ideal soil is only slightly acidic, about pH 6.7, well drained, and a medium loam 18 inches or more in depth. *Good*

Typical pruning of an apple tree. On the left is prior to pruning; on the right, after pruning.

drainage is the operative term here, because waterlogged soil leads to all kinds of problems such as root death, poor growth, low yield, apple canker, and possibly the complete loss of the tree.

One of the main things to remember—and one of the old sayings for fruit growers—is to dig a $20 hole for a $5 tree (this may be adjusted for inflation, but you get the idea). Dig a hole that appears to be much too large for your new tree and mix in some rich compost or soil with the soil that you removed. Spread the roots out in a natural fashion—that is, don't bend and cram them to fit into the hole. Fill in the hole a little at a time, firm it by hand, and keep going until the hole is filled. Water around the new tree well to help settle the soil and remove air pockets. Some braces might be needed to hold the tree in place until it is well established.

Occasionally, apples will bear heavily one year and largely fail to bloom the following year. This condition is called biennial bearing. Since the buds of most hardy fruits that open in spring are formed during the previous summer, a very heavy crop during one year may prevent bud formation and subsequent fruiting the next season.

Biennial bearing can be difficult to change or correct. However, a return to normal yearly fruit production may be stimulated by early and heavy thinning of the fruit during the year when the trees are producing a large yield. I've talked with home apple growers who merely swat the branches with a broom to knock a lot of the young apples off the limbs. Commercial orchardists often use chemical sprays to cause some of the young fruit to drop. Sevin is one commonly used chemical. After the fruit is set, each tree is sprayed with a normal solution of the chemical. Ten days later, the procedure is repeated. The result should be a light to moderate drop of weaker fruits and a good distribution of more vigorous young apples.

Many folks who have only a few trees can pick the surplus young apples from the branches by hand. When doing so, try to leave the "king" fruit, or the one in the center of the cluster of blossoms. It is also important to check the apples as they develop. When the fruits are about half grown, search out any apples that are touching and remove one of them. Regardless of the method you select, if you do choose to thin your fruit, only about one fruit per foot of branch should be left, and the thinning should be done within 30 days of blooming.

Growing apples, from planning the orchard to finally enjoying your own home-grown fruit, is a very rewarding part of country life. Once you start your own fruit trees, you will find that time spent there will be some of your most relaxing. The rewards of having your own apple trees will be far greater than just the sweet crunchy fruit. As you gain experience and enjoyment from your own fruit trees on your own homestead, you will find that you, too, have truly put down roots. They can soon become your favorite "family tree."

APPLE RESOURCES

For more information on apples and apple culture, consider reading:

PRUNING SIMPLIFIED, by Lewis Hill, Storey Publications.

THE PRUNING BOOK, by Gustave L. Wittrock, Rodale Press.

ORGANIC ORCHARDING, by Gene Logsdon, Rodale Press.

THE APPLE BOOK, by Rosanne Sanders, Philosophical Library.

Your local agricultural extension office should also have a wide variety of information on growing apples in your particular area. A couple of the most popular nurseries offering apple trees of many popular varieties are:

J. E. MILLER NURSERIES, 5060 West Lake Road, Canandaigua, NY 14424, 1-800-685-4912, www.jemillernurseries.com.

STARK BROS. NURSERIES, Highway 54 West, Louisiana, MO 63353-0010, 1-573-754-5111, www.starkbros.com.

For those of you searching for rare or antique varieties of apples, try contacting these three sources:

LAWSON'S NURSERY, Route 1, Box 472, Yellow Creek Road, Ball Ground, GA 30107, 1-770-893-2141.

SOUTHMEADOW FRUIT GARDENS, P.O. Box 211, 10603 Cleveland Avenue, Baroda, MI 49101, 1-616-422-2411, www.southmeadowfruit-gardens.com.

ROCKY MEADOW ORCHARD AND NURSERY, 360 Rocky Meadow Road Northwest, New Salisbury, IN 47161-8335, www.rockymeadow.com.

The Homestead Greenhouse

For all of us living close to the land, the production of a dependable and healthful food supply is a primary objective. Toward that end, some consideration will likely be given at one time or another to whether to construct a small greenhouse for homestead use. A greenhouse can provide countless hours of enjoyment and a steady supply of wholesome food. The benefits of producing your own healthy plants and crops, extending the growing season, and even perhaps helping to heat your home are certainly possibilities when utilizing the homestead greenhouse. We have also been able to make several varieties of our own favorite garden plants available for sale to neighbors in the community.

The greenhouse itself comes made in as many styles and materials as there are homesteaders. All seem to build—or grow—their own personality into their greenhouse structure. From elaborate metal-and-glass premanufactured "sunrooms" for the house to inexpensive plastic film stretched over a crude frame, greenhouses run the gamut in design and construction. Yet each of them fulfills the same basic purpose of extending the growing season for those of us who depend upon producing as much of our food as we can.

Our own greenhouse is a combination of recycled and new materials. The frame was obtained from a friend who runs a commercial greenhouse. The 1-inch metal conduit had served as the ribbing for a Quonset-style greenhouse until it was replaced by a larger structure. I obtained a generous supply of precurved metal tubing and constructed the greenhouse frame, lean-to fashion, on the side of the garage-workshop.

A nice home food-production area. You can see a small greenhouse, the garden, orchard, and berries at far left.

First, I bolted a treated 2 x 4 onto the exterior wall of the garage below the eave. This would serve as the point anchoring the top of the greenhouse to the existing building. The foundation (outer wall) consisted of short 4 x 4 posts set in the ground 12 feet from the wall. Treated tongue-and-groove 2 x 6s were nailed to the posts to allow for some filling and leveling—necessary on the slight slope. Two-by-four plates were applied, and 1 ⅛" holes were bored in both the top wall plate and the base plate to accommodate the conduit. As each rib was set in place and "fine-tuned" to the correct arc, a small hole was drilled in each of the plates and through the conduit. A galvanized nail was set through the holes and used to secure the rib in the base 2 x 4 and in the 2 x 4 high on the wall.

Next, the door and window openings were framed. I used measurements to accept the used door and window frames that I had obtained for a few dollars at a recent auction. I applied caulking to the door and window trim as each was set in place to help to seal the fixture.

The greenhouse covering was a result of some experimentation. I first applied some ordinary 6-mil clear plastic film, but I found that it could not withstand the onslaught of the elements; it gave way in about eight months. I would not recommend wasting your money on this ordinary, construction-grade plastic film. There are other heavy plastic films specifically made for greenhouses. These are also the types that my friends in the greenhouse business use. Another friend, who raises herbs for drying, grows her plants in a greenhouse using this type of thick plastic film stretched over a frame made of white PVC water pipe. It works well.

The plastic currently covering our own structure is designed for greenhouse use and was obtained from a supplier of the material strictly for homestead-type greenhouses. It consists of a 7-mil woven plastic "fabric" with a 1-mil layer of solid plastic bonded to each side. The woven texture gives much resistance to ripping or tearing, and the solid layers bonded to each side help greatly in the weatherproofing. Further, the whole fabric is treated to resist ultraviolet degradation, a factor that normally contributes to the short life span of plastic films in greenhouse applications. For more information on this rugged woven plastic covering, try contacting Northern Greenhouse Sales, Box 42, Neche, ND 58265.

The plastic film was folded over, placed under treated furring strips, and nailed into place. In some spots, I used a staple gun, then applied the furring strips. These wood strips help keep the plastic edges from catching the wind and pulling loose. They also provide a good uniform surface for applying tension to tighten the plastic as it is applied. At the top of the structure, the plastic was wrapped around the strip and pulled taut. I then nailed the strip to the upper surface of the treated 2 x 4 attached to the wall of the garage.

Inside the greenhouse, I used scrap lumber to build the benches. Heavy wire shelves that had been discarded by a local grocery store were also added to hold more trays of seedlings. The germination bed was constructed by first framing up the sides with 1 x 6 lumber. A sheet of foil-backed foam insulation board was cut to fit the bed (made just slightly wider than the seed germination trays are long). Next, a ½-inch layer of sand was spread over the foam board. I arranged an electric heat cable on the sand, then covered it with about an inch more sand. The cable does a nice job of heating the seed trays, and the sand acts as a heat sink, absorbing and distributing the heat.

The thermostatically controlled heat cable maintains a good germination temperature for most varieties of vegetables we grow. Along the front wall, we placed short stacks of used tires and filled them with sand. Atop each stack was placed another tire with the sidewall removed. Cutting the sidewalls from the tires was surprisingly easy, using a utility knife. This greatly increases the amount of available planting area in each tire stack. The top tire was then filled with compost and soil, then seeded in lettuce, spinach, or whatever. This also makes a fine planter for an extra-early or late tomato plant. The dark color of the tires serves to absorb heat, and the sand contained in each stack helps to store it. We

This heated germination bed quickly produces healthy seedlings. It contains sand and thermostatically controlled heat cables.

have not made use of the greenhouse year-round, but have had great success extending the growing season. Since it is attached to my garage and shop, I utilized an existing window opening, the woodstove in the garage, a window fan, and a timer to add heat to the greenhouse. By keeping a fire going in the garage—which I often do anyway—and timing the fan to turn on as the day begins to cool, we have been able to pick the last tomato off of the vine on Christmas Eve!

For starting seeds and transplants, the greenhouse is hard to beat. We begin by gathering some of the black plastic flats that stores and nurseries display their containers of plants in. The local grocery saved a bunch of them for us. They are great for filling with planting mix and starting seeds in. I cut a piece of thick plywood to a size just slightly smaller than the tray. I attached some wooden ribs, added a handle, and now can quickly make rows in flats of soil mix. The planting board really speeds things up when planting seeds in the trays.

The seeds sprout quickly on the heated bed. I made some simple germination bed covers from scraps of treated wood and leftover pieces of the plastic greenhouse covering. They are set loosely over the beds and help hold in the heat. Once the seeds sprout, the covers are removed.

We heated our greenhouse in a couple of ways. When I designed the building, I purposely placed it over an existing window of the garage. I can slide the window open and turn on a small window fan to draw heated air from the garage into the greenhouse. Conversely, in summer I can pull heated air out of the greenhouse and route it through the garage. In fact, during some of the sunny yet cold winter months, the little greenhouse acts as a sort of solar heater and provides a lot of warm air to be blown into the garage. At times, especially during the very early and very late parts of the growing season, I simply place a small kerosene heater in the greenhouse. It does a great job in keeping the temperature favorable to growing plants.

Once the new plants grow large enough to move into separate containers, they are gently lifted, one by one, and transplanted into ordinary Styrofoam cups. I prepare the cups by poking two or three small

This handy little row maker is used when seeding trays. It is made from a piece of wood cut to the size of the tray with five wood strips added. To use it, merely press it down into the planting medium and lift it out. Five neat rows will remain.

Trays in my greenhouse. The rapidly growing seedlings are in homemade compost growing medium.

holes through the bottom to allow water to drain. This can be done, a stack at a time, by shoving a long heavy wire down through the cups. A friend saved us a large grocery sack full of used plastic yogurt cups that worked well, too. We have also used commercial-type plant containers, which held six plants each. Any of these containers will work fine, and I'm sure you can come up with ideas for other suitable plant cups as well—anything from tin cans to boxes will work. As a planting medium, I have used home-produced compost and commercially available starting mix. The compost is more labor-intensive, as it requires a good sifting to get it to the proper consistency for seed starting. I end up getting some weed seeds started as well when using it. The commercial mix is formulated for seed starting and is available in very large bags. Although we enjoy using the compost, we have come to like using the commercial product due to the volume of it needed for our use. If you think you might like to try using this type of growing medium, look for one of the Scotts products. They are good.

If you are interested in selling garden and bedding plants, you will learn that a simple, short advertisement in the local newspaper will probably get you all the customers you want and more! Additionally, after a season or two of selling, your reputation will add even more customers. The bulletin board at the local supermarket, feed store, or other public place will also bring in buyers. There is a real shortage of sturdy, home-raised garden plants and an abundance of buyers. Don't try to get too fancy at first; just have a good basic selection available. After a season or two, you will know which varieties of plants sell well and which you ended up with too many of after the season. You may, as we did, get enough requests for a particular variety of vegetable to warrant seeding a flat or two for good sales. This is a good way to discover a variety you may not have tried, as well as introducing your friends and customers to new varieties that you like.

Growing and selling garden plants is not without problems and considerations. We have found that, for right now at least, the growing of vegetable plants for sale to the public is not compatible with our plans. We realized that after a brief but busy season, we hardly broke even, if we count our labor at anything close to slave wages.

Second, the size of our greenhouse—a typical size and well suited to production for the home—was not large enough to produce plants on the scale needed even for the rural area we live in. When folks find out that you have plants, you will need every bit of space you can find to have plants growing in.

Third, and perhaps most important, we found that we neglected our own plants and garden planting while trying to keep a supply of plants available for sale. Essentially, we were too busy trying to take care of plants for everyone else, and ended up not taking care of our own. Raising our own plants is what got us into the greenhouse business in the first place. It was frustrating to watch our own gardens become less than we would have liked simply because we were busy in the greenhouse.

Fourth, although we advertised the days and hours that we were open for plant sales, people showed up at any hour and any day of the week. It seemed that most of the customers would show up at mealtime, right along with the telephone solicitors!

Fifth, I discovered that I simply didn't care for all the traffic coming in and out of our place. If you open your place up for business, you pretty well open the door to anyone who may wish to enter your property. The last two problems could be handled by selling your plants on a wholesale basis to an established business in the nearest town. The trade-off— receiving a lower price per plant versus maintaining your privacy—is something you will have to weigh.

Now, I know that all of the above problems have some type of solution. I've pointed out a couple of possibilities. But in the near future anyway, our family is going to concentrate our efforts to producing our own plants—with a few extras for family and friends—and food in the greenhouse.

All things considered, building and working in your own small greenhouse is a very rewarding way to spend some time. Remember, there are as many ways to build a greenhouse as there are homesteaders. The main thing is to use what you have or can readily obtain, adapt the structure to your own circumstances, and then use the dickens out of it! If you are working toward selling plants, you will find an eager market waiting. In any case, you will be rewarded with fresh vegetables nearly year-round, healthy and vigorous garden plants, and the satisfaction of knowing that you're another step closer to self-sufficiency.

GREENHOUSE RESOURCES

For more information, I recommend the following publications:

THE FOOD AND HEAT PRODUCING SOLAR GREENHOUSE, by Bill Yanda and Rick Fisher, John Muir Publications, Inc., P.O. Box 613, Santa Fe, NM 87501.

THE SOLAR GREENHOUSE BOOK, edited by James C. McCullagh, Rodale Press, Box 6, Emmaus, PA 18099-0006.

THE GUIDE TO SELF SUFFICIENCY, by John Seymour, Hearst Publications, New York.

4

ANIMALS & LIVESTOCK

Raising Your Own Beef
on the Homestead

Starting Your Home
Chicken Flock

Raising Rabbits

Filling the Haymow

Keeping Bees

For most homesteaders, and certainly for the vast majority of small farmers, the raising of livestock plays a crucial role in the home-based economy. The types of livestock that you choose to include on your own place may be determined by your climate, the size of the homestead, food sources available, the available market (if you choose to sell some animals), and just your personal preference. It is sometimes argued that you can buy all your meat—beef, chicken, pork, lamb, rabbit, and so on—far more cheaply than you can raise it. While this may be true when speaking in terms of money alone, other factors must be considered when referring to meat raised for homestead use.

As you might expect, the first thing to consider when comparing home-raised and store-bought meat is quality. Home-raised meat is born, raised, and processed with one thing in mind: to be used as food for the family. Generally speaking, commercially raised livestock is also raised with one thing in mind: to produce the most marketable product in the quickest time at the greatest profit. Somewhere in there, quality has to suffer. Those of us who raise our own meat know what is going into it in the way of feed and additives. While many of us occasionally must fall back on a application of medication or the like to restore or maintain the health of an animal, we know that no massive doses of hormones or steroids have been pumped into our future dinner entrées.

Another factor worth serious consideration is this: In the event of a serious emergency—economic or otherwise—the livestock raiser would have a valuable potential food source available. Obviously, we cannot place such reliance on our supermarkets or grocers. In hard times, grocery shelves and meat counters would likely be quickly depleted of their stock, leaving bewildered and dependent customers wondering what to do next.

Also, if you have children in your family, the value and importance of having livestock on the homestead cannot be underestimated. Youngsters learn much by having animals around. The responsibility of having feeding to do, hay to help get in, manure to load into the spreader, and similar chores helps young people build self-esteem and a good work ethic. Children can sense and build upon the feeling of contribution and importance in the family. They will learn that things are expected of them and that their efforts are a valuable part of the family life. In this way, we are helping shape our youngsters into productive and responsible adults who are not afraid to work. Children also learn the no-nonsense life-and-death cycle of animals that God put on earth for us to use wisely. Youngsters growing up on a farm where animals are raised for food have no doubt about where their food comes from. Unlike many of their city-raised counterparts, they will develop a direct appreciation and respect for the life cycle of meat animals. Countless numbers of young people have learned the "facts of life" while observing animals on the farm and homestead. Many have even assisted parents in helping struggling animals in the miracle of birth. These youngsters, and their adults, develop a true respect for life and better understand the God-given miracles involved.

Still, we need to look at ways to raise the best livestock that we can, without the whole endeavor becoming little more than an expensive hobby. Let's do that now.

Raising Your Own Beef on the Homestead

These days it seems that red meat in general, and beef in particular, is continually maligned as one of the greatest detriments to our health and well-being. I'm here to tell you that you can raise some mighty tasty and nutritious beef on your own place, and do so without a lot of the fat and chemicals that lace most commercially raised beef. Our own beef is raised mainly on grass and hay, with little grain or supplement. Free access to trace mineral and high-magnesium blocks, water, and pasture all help turn out fine beef, much leaner than store-bought and at a competitive cost.

This may seem sort of obvious, but when getting into the cattle business you should keep in mind the fact that these critters are *big!* An old beef cow can easily reach 1,000 to 1,200 pounds. Even the normally docile old animals can accidentally step on your foot, and if you get them excited or scared they can seriously hurt or kill a person.

Our own experience with cattle has been interesting and educational, if not extremely profitable from a dollars-and-cents point of view. Cattle on most small places can do little more than keep the place from growing up in weeds and providing butchering beef for you and for sale. Small landholders should not expect to get rich on cattle. Our veterinarian, who has told me that he doesn't see many small family herds—six or so cows with calves—make a real profit, echoes this thought. But he adds, "A small herd like this will pay the property taxes and keep the pastures trimmed down."

In fact, it is possible to sell a few fat calves, young steers, or butchering cows and make the program pay for itself—and perhaps pay the property taxes as well. In addition, they can help keep your place from growing up around your ears. Over the years, we have had cows, bulls, calves, and steers. Having raised bucket-calves and having kept cows with calves, I have developed some educated opinions about the two methods of raising beef.

CATTLE BREEDS

What type of cattle do you want? There are basically two categories: dairy and beef. Among the common dairy breeds are Jersey, Guernsey, Brown Swiss, and Holstein. Popular beef breeds include Angus, Hereford, as well as the more exotic Limousine, Semintal, Charolais, Saler, and a whole pastureful of other breeds. Dual-purpose breeds such as Milking Shorthorns exist, but are not really common anymore. They do offer possibilities for the homesteader, however.

Both beef and dairy cattle have been carefully bred over time to do the best at what they were bred to do, whether this is producing milk or meat. The dairy breeds are biologically and physically designed to produce milk. That is to say, they are bred to convert feed to milk and do not have the heavily muscled bodies of the stocky beef breeds. The beef breeds do best at converting feed into a meaty, heavily muscled carcass.

Bucket calves are a good alternative to consider. Dairies commonly get rid of the male calves produced. Prices for the animals fluctuate, but they're generally affordable. Here, my sons feed a calf with a special bucket that has a large nipple attached at the base just for this purpose.

This is not to say that dairy calves cannot and should not be raised for beef. Countless ones have. Many a Jersey bull calf has been raised to become steaks and roasts. Often, however, when homesteaders breed back the family milk cow to freshen, they choose an Angus bull or other suitable smaller beef breed. This results in a renewed milk source and a good calf more suited to raising for meat since it will exhibit many of its Angus parent's characteristics. Breeding the Jersey cow to a smaller-framed bull will help ensure that the smaller cow will have an easy birthing.

I have been around cattle for many years, but have only recently raised what we refer to as bucket-calves or bottle-calves. We started into this project by purchasing seven Holstein bottle-calves from local a local dairy-man. In a dairy operation, the male calves are removed from the herd, whereas the heifer calves are kept and raised as milking herd replacements. At the time we bought ours, the going price in our area was about $125 each. It is interesting to note that this past season, some of the neighboring dairy farmers were getting no more than $30 a head. Some were actually giving them away after not getting bids for them at the local sale barn! They are usually sold as day-olds or at a few days of age.

The folks we got ours from were very helpful and wanted to keep the calves for a full week to make sure they got off to a good start. They monitored them for scours—diarrhea that can kill a

This handy bottle holder lets you feed four calves at a time. But with four hungry calves, you really need to hang on!

new calf in a matter of 24 hours or so if not treated. The week also allowed the calves to receive some new milk from the mother cow. This colostrum, the first rich milk, is important to the calves, because it contains many of the antibodies and bacteria that the youngsters need to get off to a good start. Those same antibodies and bacteria help to prevent the scours mentioned above.

Our bull calves were raised on bottles with calf starter formula, adding some dry feed at a few weeks of age, and weaned off the formula entirely at about 10 to 12 weeks. Calf starter is available at any livestock supply store; the dry feed was custom-blended at the local mill. The formula is nothing magical, just a mix of 500 pounds of ground corn, 50 pounds of calf supplement, 25 pounds of molasses feed, and 2 pounds of salt. This is a good basic growing ration. Once the animals reach about 500 or 600 pounds, we switch from calf supplement to steer supplement; otherwise the formula is the same. Make sure that weaned calves have clean water available at all times. A large steer or cow will need about 12 gallons of fresh water per day.

Medical problems were not serious during these early weeks. A couple of the calves had a bout with scours, but with some simple medications they came out of it all right. If young calves do get scours, it is imperative to get them off the calf formula and get some fluid and electrolyte replacement into them. We did learn that in a pinch, powdered Gatorade is as good an electrolyte replacement as the stuff that comes from the vet. It is mixed with water and given just like the stuff from the vet. Your own vet can advise you on any potential problems that might be specific to your area.

Since these were Holstein calves, they began to develop horns. Once the calves had reached about 500 pounds, we called the vet to have the animals dehorned and castrated. Dehorning is briefly painful, and is somewhat bloody, but in a day or so the event is seemingly forgotten and the animals are back into their routine. If you have purchased polled or hornless breeds of cattle, then obviously you will omit the dehorning procedure. Dehorning is not actually necessary, but it does help prevent accidental injuries to the other cattle or to humans. The dehorned animals sell a little better on the market, as well.

Our veterinarian convinced us not to castrate the calves until they had reached about 500 pounds. He explained that the testes of the bull calves serve as natural hormone implants and cause the calf to grow faster during those first several months. These natural hormones also seem to help shape the calf into a huskier, more "bull-shaped" animal.

As for converting bull calves into steers, I recommend cutting as the best method. Other methods such as banding and clamping are effective if done properly, but this one is surefire.

Banding consists of applying special rubber bands over the male calf's scrotum to cut off all circulation to the testes. In a few days, the glands atrophy and drop off. Some folks do not like this method because a problem with egg-laying flies sometimes occurs after the testes drop off. Banding is done using a specially made pliers-type tool to stretch the band large enough to slip it in place over the scrotum. When using this method, you must be certain to get both testes down into the scrotum and through the band.

Clamping is done by using special pliers that crimp the blood vessels going to the testes and scrotum. By crushing the blood vessels, again the glands soon die and drop off.

As I stated above, I consider cutting the preferred method for castration of the male calves. It is quicker and cleaner with less chance of infection or attack by flies. The animal is secured by either snubbing it to a post or holding it securely in the vet's portable squeeze chute. Then the vet quickly cuts open the scrotum, pulls each of the testes down, and cuts the cord and blood vessels. After the glands are removed, a quick shot of antibiotic spray helps ensure quick healing.

Since Holstein cattle are bred to produce milk and not beef, they seem to spend the first year just developing their frame. Not until the second season do they start to bulk up much. Even then, Holsteins don't put on the muscle that the beef breeds do. They eventually do fill out well, however. On the other hand, Holstein beef is a rival to any in taste and texture. These big cattle do indeed produce some very tasty steaks, roasts, and burgers. However, remember that they seem to spend the first year of their life just building bone.

As interesting and educational as raising the bucket-calves was, I really prefer to just let the old cow raise the calf. Therefore, we currently have only beef-breed cows and calves on our place. These are good Angus-Hereford cross cows bred to an Angus-Saler bull. Some may ask about birthing or birthing problems. We have had dozens of calves born on our place, and I can think of only one loss. Just a few weeks ago, I was cutting firewood in a woodlot above one of our pastures and watched one of the old cows give birth. I have helped with a birthing or two, but even then, I don't think I was really needed. As this is written, we have four new calves and should be getting a couple more any day. Problems are normally few with an arrangement like this—in most cases, the cow is much better at raising the calf than a person is!

Cattle can be bred at any time of the year. Mature cows come into heat every 21 days. They will usually stay in heat for 12 to 24 hours. Heifer calves can sometimes breed as early as 6 months of age, but they should be allowed to reach 12 to 15 months or so (about 500 to 750 pounds) before breeding. Any smaller, and they may have some real problems calving. Heifer calves should be kept separated from any herd bull until suitable size is reached.

Cattle have a gestation period of about 270 to 285 days. Most cows need no help in delivering their calves, though occasionally they may encounter problems. This is most common with heifers having their first calf, and with small-boned cows bred to large bulls.

HAY

This topic is dealt with in more detail later in this chapter, but know that you will need to provide a source of hay for your cattle. In most areas, most of us are able to allow the animals to graze during the summer months. In winter, however, hay must be provided. Here is a basic question: What is hay? It's simply grass that has been cut and cured for later use as food for animals.

Hay is stored loose, in small square bales or in large round bales. Hay prices vary widely across the country. Around here, it is usually sold by the bale. In the West, hay is normally sold by the ton. Small square bales weighing about 50 to 75 pounds will normally run from $1 to $1.50 for mixed-grass hay. Alfalfa can run up to three to five dollars per bale. Large bales come in many different sizes according to the make and size of baler turning them out. The farmer can usually let you know the equivalent in square bales and base the price accordingly. As for loose hay, I can tell you that it is simply a lot of work! I don't know of anyone putting up loose hay other than the neighboring Amish farmers. Even

A young bull feeds on a big bale of hay.

many of them are switching to ground-driven square balers pulled by their teams of husky horses.

Some time ago, I heard this question: Is hay the same as straw? No. Hay is an irreplaceable food source for our grazing animals, especially in winter. Straw is a by-product of the grain-harvesting process. It is the dead stem and leaves of a grain stalk that are left behind after the seeds have been removed from the seed head by the harvesting equipment.

Putting up loose hay is real work. If you have a very small place, it might be practical, but if you plan to feed more than a single cow or a few goats, then consider making or buying baled hay.

A few large hay bales in my field. They will be moved with a tractor and three-point hitch bale spike.

Straw has no real nutritive value, though it is valuable as a bedding material. Wheat straw is the most common type, but any of the cereal grains such as oats, barley, or rye can yield good straw after harvesting.

A mature cow will need roughly one-third to one-half of a bale of hay per day in winter or on a site where pasture is not available. As I mentioned, we feed hay only in winter, along with a bit of mixed-grain feed.

FENCING

Good fences are necessary to keep cattle in. A cow or steer grazing indiscriminately through the neighborhood may or may not incur the wrath of the neighbors—but why take the chance? Chances are it wouldn't make you or the cattle too popular.

The subject of fencing is dealt with in depth in chapter 7. In the meantime, however, here are some thoughts specific to cattle fencing.

If you're using standard fencing, I recommend sturdy woven wire on stout posts. Woven wire comes in different heights, but the 39-inch will do fine. When putting up woven fencing, allow a couple of inches extra at the bottom and top. After it is erected, stretch and add a strand of barbed wire on the bottom and the top along the entire length. Cattle will really stretch to get to tasty plants outside their fenced area. These strands of barbed wire will convince them not to stretch under or over the top of the woven wire and will save you much in the way of maintenance and repair.

Some sections of our fence are barbed wire only. I prefer to use four strands of barbed wire, but three will suffice in a pinch. If you can, use four. It just makes a tighter fence.

Electric fence will work in most cases. It also offers the option of being easily movable to fresh pastures. Once the cattle are trained to recognize its ability to cause discomfort, you should have no problem. The so-called training is nothing more simply allowing them to bump or brush the fence while grazing. We used a single strand of electrified barbed wire on one pasture and kept in four large steers without a single problem or escape.

PASTURE

On good pasture, a couple of acres will maintain one animal. Throughout the country, the average is about one head to each 1 to 5 acres. Naturally, in drier climes, more acreage per head is needed. Plant varieties for pasture vary from region to region. Local farmers and ranchers, as well as your local agricultural extension service, can recommend the types best suited for your area. It is best if you can rotate the animals out of one pasture into another from time to time. This practice lets the pasture rejuvenate its plant growth and allows any parasites to die off.

It is a good practice to have your soil tested every year or so to determine what you need in the way of amendments. Your local extension service or fertilizer dealer can help you get the soil tests done properly. Testing will pay off in providing information on the proper balance of lime, nitrogen, phosphorus, potassium, and trace elements needed for your soil, and will result in better nutrition for your animals.

SHELTER

A beef cow that is used to the cold and in winter coat has a critical temperature of about 0 degrees. Below this temperature, extra energy is required to keep the animal warm. Cattle need a draft-free yet not airtight shelter. I used to think that this was a contradiction. However, realize that a good shed with three sides closed in and the open side facing out of the prevailing wind makes a good shelter. Do not make the shelter airtight. Cattle give off a lot of moisture, and if it cannot escape, all kinds of health problems in your animals will result.

Shelter for your animals doesn't have to be anything fancy, but it does need to be sturdy. These big animals stomping around can knock a lot of things loose. Cattle are not exactly graceful.

This brings up another point: If you are raising cows and calves together, you will soon see the need for an area in the shed or barn that permits access by the calves, but excludes the cows. This area—often called a creep pen—is where the growing calves can feed without having to compete with the larger cows. Again, it doesn't need to be anything fancy, but it does have to be sturdy. Usually, placing some stanchions about 16 to 18 inches apart will allow the small calves into their specified area, where they can pick at the calf starter feed and hay. Our own stanchions were made to be adjustable so that as the calves grew, we could open up the space to still allow them to pass through.

MARKETING YOUR BEEF

If you are raising cattle for market, you will generally have two options. First, you may want to sell feeder calves—animals of up to about 500 pounds. It usually takes about seven months to get the calves up to this size. Feeder calves usually bring a good price per pound.

If you wish to raise steers, it will take about 16 to 20 months or so for you to get the animal to a market-ready 1,000 to 1,200 pounds. Most of the time, we sell all our calves when they get up to about 450 pounds or so, except for the one or two we keep to raise for our own meat. These we keep until they reach 1,000 to 1,100 pounds.

Our Holsteins were kept for two full growing seasons. Five of the steers were trucked to the Louisville livestock market, where they brought a pretty fair price. The other two were kept for later sale to friends. We were paid at the market price on the day they were taken to slaughter. We could have easily advertised and gotten a higher price, but we were selling to friends, so the market price suited us.

Right now, we have beef-breed cattle running on our place—some Angus-Hereford crosses. They pretty well take care of themselves during the summer months and require just the normal feeding and watering in winter. The Angus bloodlines mean smaller calves and easier births. Crossing the two types of cattle gives a good, vigorous animal with a solid, desirable shape and meaty carcass.

Another real possibility for the small farmer or homesteader is to sell to a select market. By raising your beef organically—that is, with clean natural feeds and no additives or hormones—you will end up with a premium product that can command a high price if marketed properly. If, for example, you live near a medium to large urban center, people will be happy to pay more for your lean, farm-raised beef. A small, inexpensive advertisement in the local newspaper or at a nearby health food store or co-op will usually result in all the customers you want and more. This will require diligence to assure that your stock receives the natural, additive-free feed that produces the higher-priced beef.

Maybe you want to market locally. Even farmers and other country folks do not raise much of their own food these days. Advertise in the local paper and you will be surprised at the folks who are interested in buying good beef. If you have your own beef processed at a local meat processor, then you can offer to haul your customer's animal at the same time as an added sales pull. You will be able to get at least the going market price, and usually a bit more. You will be able to ask around among local meat processors, farmers, and others who have a good idea what you can get for beef. If you can guarantee that your beef is "additive-free" or "organically raised," then you can get a better price yet. Just the fact that your beef is raised on a small homestead and not in a "beef factory" feedlot means a lot in the way of producing clean, low- or non-medicated, additive-free beef. Our own beef is fed only grass and hay, with a smattering of grain during the winter months. We never confine a beef animal prior to slaughter for the purpose of "pouring the grain into it." In my experience, this does produce heavier cattle sooner, although I'm not sure the profit outweighs the cost of the extra grain. It also produces beef with a lot more fat on and throughout the meat. This "marbling," while desirable for gourmet cuts, is not really healthful. Our grass-fattened beef does us nicely, thank you.

So if you are interested in picking up a calf or two to raise for your own use and possibly to sell to family or friends, then raising bottle-calves may be the thing. Perhaps you would rather buy a mature bred cow or a cow and calf. Consider your alternatives and your resources to help decide on the operation that is best suited for you. Whether you raise just one animal for your own consumption or half a dozen to sell, you will be amply rewarded for your efforts.

CATTLE RESOURCES

For more information, look for these books. Some of them may be out of print, but patient and diligent searching have helped me add them to my shelf.

THE FAMILY COW, by Dirk van Loon, Garden Way Publishing.

RAISING A CALF FOR BEEF, by Phyllis Hobson, Garden Way Publishing.

A VETERINARY GUIDE FOR ANIMAL OWNERS, by D. C. Spaulding, DVM, Rodale Press.

THE STOCKMAN'S HANDBOOK, by M. E. Ensminger, Interstate Publishers.

THE COW ECONOMY, by Merril and Joann Grohman, Coburn Farm Press.

Starting Your Home Chicken Flock

One of the first types of livestock that many homesteaders try raising is the chicken. There is certainly no other species of animal more suited or more beneficial to the homestead. Meat, eggs, fertilizer, waste disposal, and pest control are among the stellar qualities of the home flock.

Several years ago, when we started out in the poultry business, so to speak, we began by looking over a couple of the catalogs available from reputable hatcheries. Selecting the types of chickens you are going to

Chickens are a valuable addition to the home livestock herd. These birds produce eggs and meat for the table.

order is not as easy as it sounds. But out of all the feathered makes and models available, we settled on a dozen each of Silver-Laced Wyandottes, Rhode Island Reds, and Buff Orpingtons. We knew that we wanted birds of the heavy breeds, for we were planning to butcher about two-thirds of them, then keep the rest as a small laying flock for brown eggs. These old homestead breeds of chickens lay those brown eggs. I am not saying that brown eggs are any different than white eggs, other than the color of the package. But I do know that you can sell home-raised brown eggs for a higher price than white eggs. I also like the old-fashioned, heavy breeds of chickens.

We ordered straight-run birds, which means that the birds are not sexed, but boxed and shipped just as they come from the incubators. Since we would be butchering most of them anyway, we felt that there should be plenty of layers to pick from for the laying flock.

You have a few choices in acquiring your birds. In spring, many feed mills or farmer's co-ops offer low-priced chicks when you buy 50 or 100 pounds of chick starter feed. The selection is generally somewhat limited with these offers, but they can be a good way to get your starter flock.

The sale barn or auction house is another source for a starter flock. However, be aware that many folks come to these sales to get rid of their old hens and burned-out roosters. Many chicken "collectors" also frequent these sales and often run the price up on the more colorful and unusual types of birds. The more common varieties of homestead-type chickens should go at a more reasonable price, though.

You may also be able to work out a deal with neighbors or friends to provide some starter birds for your flock, either as mature birds—usually older broody hens and randy roosters—or as newly hatched chicks.

The source I recommend is the mail-order poultry house. Probably every one of us has seen the advertisements for the large hatcheries in our favorite homesteading magazines. These mail-order hatcheries can provide a catalog with a much larger selection than you might find otherwise. And as surprising as it may seem, the mail never runs slowly with an order of day-old chicks. Almost without exception, mail-order chicks arrive thriving and peeping away. With chick orders, you will be notified of the shipment date by the hatchery. Then expect to receive a first-thing-in-the-morning call from the folks at the post office when the

I brooded our last chicks right in the chicken house. I added cardboard panels, which I stapled to the wall studs, to prevent the chicks from huddling and piling up in the corners.

birds arrive. You will probably be able to hear the chicks just as soon as you enter the building.

The large hatcheries offer the added benefit of providing not only lively chicks but also the ability to vaccinate them, clip their beaks, and generally fine service. It's their business.

Assuming you are starting with newly hatched chicks, let's look at getting them off to a good start.

Before your order of chicks arrives, be sure you have all the equipment for brooding them in place and working. When the post office calls for you to come and pick up your box of chicks, there will be little time to hustle around getting things ready.

Have a circular brooding area set up. This can be made from pieces of cardboard, metal, or almost any other material as long as it provides a draft-free environment and is tall enough (about 18 inches) to prevent the lively youngsters from hopping out over the sides. (Think about a few weeks down the road, when the little buggers really begin hopping and flopping about.) It is important to use a circular area to prevent the chicks from piling up in a corner and suffocating their siblings. We used a large plastic wading pool about 5 or 6 feet in diameter for our initial brooder area. I have also cut large cardboard cartons apart and stapled them to the interior studs of the chicken house. The corners were widely rounded to eliminate "chick pileups." We suspended a 250-watt red heat lamp about 18 inches above the bedding. It worked well until the birds were old enough to turn into the chicken house. The important thing is to introduce your chicks to an environment that is about 90 to 95 degrees. The heat bulb should be raised about 1 inch per week until the birds are old enough to do without it altogether—five or six weeks. A cheap thermometer will help you monitor the temperature in the brooding area. When we used a larger area, we set up two bulbs at slightly different heights. The chicks could utilize the one they preferred.

Two waterers that screwed onto quart fruit jars provided fresh water for the new chicks. Fresh feed was placed in a small feeder trough about 2 feet long. It has a loose top bar that prevented any chick from roosting atop it and soiling the feed.

We fretted and searched and pored over books and articles to come up with a suitable bedding material for our delicate new charges. We finally took the advice of an old Amish farmer at the feed mill and used ordinary clean straw. It worked very well. Beneath the straw we placed a layer of newspapers, and every couple of days the bedding was changed to help keep the chicks thriving and healthy. Other recommended materials include ground corncobs, wood shavings, rice hulls, or any commercial litter. Do not use sawdust for litter: The chicks will eat it.

Immediately upon receiving your shipment of chicks, take each one, dip its beak into the waterer, and allow it to drink if it wants. They will most likely be quite thirsty after their journey. This procedure serves not only to give them needed hydration, but also to acquaint them with their source of water.

We experienced a bit of a problem with cannibalism among our batch of chicks. It seems to have occurred with one of the initially weaker birds as the victim. Eventually, even after applications of pine tar to the victim, we ended losing two chicks to cannibalism. We used regular toenail clippers to nip off a tiny bit of the top beak tip of the survivors and applied a touch or two with a styptic pencil to stem the flow of blood. I do not know if the styptic pencil (alum) was somehow a cause, but we ended up losing a total of four more chicks after the "operation."

Once the young birds had begun getting their primary wing feathers, we were able to move them to the new chicken house. The timing was predicated less on any particular point in the bird's development than on the stage of construction of the chicken house! There the young birds had more room to scratch and run, and they adjusted quickly. Fresh feed and water were supplied and the same heat bulb was suspended from the rafters.

Upon completing the fenced chicken run, the small sliding door was raised and the chickens were allowed to come and go at will. They soon had removed every piece of greenery from the area and welcomed all grass clippings and kitchen scraps. The first night or two, some of them failed to grasp the concept of going back inside before dark, and I checked them to find them huddled in a corner of the pen. I gently tossed them back into the chicken house; after a couple of days, all of them would gravitate back inside as darkness neared.

One feature that I added to our chicken house, and heartily recommend to anyone constructing a similar building, is a cleanout door. Ours is designed a bit differently due to our site and circumstances, but works well. In one corner of the building, I built in a small door (about 2 feet by 2 feet) hinged at the top. Turn-buttons keep it closed from the outside. The door, being on the end of the building that's highest off the ground, allows us to move the wheelbarrow directly beneath the opening and shovel the old bedding and manure right into the 'barrow. With the chicken house directly adjacent to our garden, it is easy to get the material right onto the ground where it will do the most good.

When I built the roosts, I reverted to some old-time advice. Long ago, I'd been told that sassafras poles used as roosts keep mites away. Apparently the wood contains oils that help repel the little critters. If so, fine. If not, they still make great roost poles, for they grow abundantly in thickets and are thereby straight and tall as they stretch and compete for sunlight. The larger ones (2 inches or so at the butt) make the best roost poles. Incidentally, the smaller ones (1 to 1½ inches) make terrific beanpoles.

Another thing I had given thought to was how I would make nest boxes. The answer came when I read somewhere that ordinary 5-gallon plastic buckets could be used for the nests. I cut a couple of support boards to cradle three of the containers in one corner of the chicken house. After tracing the shape needed, I cut three crescents from scrap 1 x 4 stock and nailed them into the opening of the bucket to provide a short barrier to keep straw—and eggs—inside the nest where they belong. A friend I visited later had merely cut the original plastic bucket lid into the same shape and did the same job. Neat. The finished nests were anchored with a couple of nails to the supports. I also added a roost pole in front of the boxes, not so much for the birds to rest on as to provide a surface that they could come and go from.

We like to keep our flock confined to the run as much as possible, although on very hot days we let them run loose and find shade and scratch where they will. At first, we were concerned about the birds raiding the garden, but some improvised fencing took care of the problem before it occurred. Another alternative is to let the chickens out just an hour or so before dark. They will have plenty of time to roam about and scratch and feed, then will mosey back to the chicken house on their own as darkness approaches. It has worked very well for us.

Our intention from the beginning of the chicken-raising project was to get about three dozen birds, raise them to butchering size, butcher about two dozen, and keep the rest of the flock as egg producers for the family. This has worked out very well.

BUTCHERING

Butchering chickens is not difficult, although it is a bit messy. There are a couple of ways to begin.

If you've ever heard the phrase *running around like a chicken with its head cut off*, then you know what to expect when you begin the first method. Grasp the bird firmly by both legs and lay it across the wood block. Make a swift and sure swing with your sharp hatchet and cleanly remove the bird's head. Toss the bird aside and it will commence its little postmortem promenade, flopping around for a minute or so. Watching the headless birds flop, jump, and dance about is amusing in a macabre sort of way. In the meantime, you can grab another bird and repeat the procedure. This method allows the birds to bleed out while they flop around, so don't get too close!

A second way to kill the bird also sounds a bit brutal, but is just as humane. With a sharp, slim-bladed knife, insert the point into the bird's mouth and push it quickly upward and into the cranium. This should kill the bird; it also supposedly sends a signal through its nervous system that loosens its feathers a bit, making for easier plucking. I have tried this method and it does seem to work. Once the bird is dead, cut the head off, hang it by the legs, and allow it to bleed out a bit.

Once you get your birds killed, it is time to begin the remainder of the chore. While most of us probably think of plucking the feathers from the bird, I recommend skinning it. It makes the butchering chore much easier and cleaner.

If you do want to pluck the chicken, first dunk it in a pot of very hot, but not boiling, water. This helps loosen the feathers. As you pluck and the bird cools, dunk the bird again as necessary. After removing all the feathers you can by hand, you will find that a lot of small pinfeathers and fuzz still stick to the bird. These can be done away with by using a quick pass with a flame to singe them from the carcass. Either a lit, tightly rolled-up newspaper or a propane torch will work. Having tried all of these methods, I must admit that I opt for the skinning method.

Once the chicken is killed and the feathers removed, it is a relatively simple matter to remove the entrails. Cut from low on the abdomen upward to the breast. Reach in and remove the entrails, saving the liver and gizzard if you wish. The small greenish bile sac will likely be attached to the liver. Carefully remove it and discard it. The gizzard may be saved for cooking, but be sure to cut it open and clean it out as you prepare it for cooking. Cut and trim around the anus, removing all the gut. Cut off the feet at the drumstick joint, and you should have a bird that is ready to rinse and cook or freeze. When freezing chickens, we just rinse them well in cold water to clean and cool them, then put them in a large zip-top bag. Squeeze out all the air you can and freeze. Of course, you may also cut up the bird into frying pieces prior to freezing if you wish.

FRESH EGGS

Our primary motivation in getting a chicken flock started was to begin getting home-grown eggs. Once you have tried your own fresh, golden-yolked eggs, you will shudder at the thought of buying the anemic, cage-produced eggs at the store. All the good things (to a hen) like insects, kitchen scraps, grass clippings, grubs, worms, weeds, and so on that homestead hens get to eat certainly do make a difference in the eggs they produce, both in appearance and in nutritional value.

We try to gather our eggs at about the same time every day. It just gets to be sort of a habit, for the hens, and us, I suppose. In the photographs accompanying this section, you can see the nest boxes that we put in place for the hens to use. I recommend erecting a nest box for every three or four hens that you have. Even then, you may find that most of them will pick out just a few of the nests and use them almost exclusively. You should get an egg a day from your best hens. If the eggs are soiled, we simply wipe them off before placing them in a carton. Depending upon where you live, you can easily get from one to three dollars a dozen for rich, home-raised brown eggs.

POULTRY HINTS AND TIPS

Locate your chicken house as close as practical to your house and barn. If you locate it just an extra 25 feet away than need be, then you will end up putting in about 25 extra miles of walking over a year's time. That equals about eight hours of extra effort.

Pay attention to the shape of the eggs you get. Old-timers say you can predict the sex of the chickens that will hatch from them. Reportedly, the longer eggs produce rooster chicks, and the more rounded ones, hens.

If you do not keep a rooster, you will not get any fertile eggs and, hence, no chicks. If you plan to raise chicks from your flock, you will need to keep a rooster.

Consider putting a capful or two of apple cider vinegar in your chickens' water. It will provide the minerals they need.

Back in 1944, E. B. White offered the following advice for keeping chickens:

☞ Be tidy.

☞ Be brave.

☞ Walk, don't run.

☞ Never carry any strange object.

☞ Keep Rocks if you are a nervous man.

☞ Keep Reds if you are a quiet one.

☞ Do all your thinking and planning backward.

☞ Always count your chickens before they are hatched.

☞ Tie your shoelaces in a double knot.

POULTRY RESOURCES

Information and plans for chicken equipment can be found at:

NORTH DAKOTA STATE UNIVERSITY:
http://www.ag.ndsu.nodak.edu/ abeng/plans/BEEF_PLAN.htm.

UNIVERSITY OF TENNESSEE, AGRICULTURAL EXTENSION SERVICE:
http:// bioengr.ag.utk.edu/Extension/ExtPubs/PlanList97.htm.

PURDUE UNIVERSITY AGRICULTURAL PLAN SERVICE:
http://pasture.ecn.purdue.edu/~fbps/.

Raising Rabbits

One of the most efficient and nutritious animals that can be raised on the small place is the rabbit. They are particularly worth considering if you live on a small tract of land where the raising of other types of livestock is not practical.

Interestingly, Americans eat about 25 to 30 million pounds of domestically produced rabbit meat per year. All of that meat is produced in small backyard rabbitries, and in the many large commercial rabbitries. The animal is well adapted to both types of production.

For our purposes, we will concentrate upon the smaller-scale operation. Once you get into raising these interesting animals, you will probably find that you can develop a good homestead market for surplus rabbit meat, if you have any! Our family loves rabbit, and it can be cooked into a wide variety of tasty dishes.

A good starting point for the home rabbitry is a couple of does and a buck. From there, it will be easy to increase production if it fits into your plans. Two does will provide plenty of young fryers yet not be too

My home rabbitry. Notice the piles of rabbit manure under the cages. It makes great fertilizer or an addition to the compost pile.

much of a burden to care for. There are several good breeds of domestic meat rabbits. The two does we kept were New Zealand Whites. They have the characteristic white coats and pink eyes. The buck was a Californian. These animals grow to be about 9 or 10 pounds.

If I were starting over with rabbits, I believe that I would opt for all-wire cages in which to house them. My original cage was based on the popular drawings found in many books and government publications. It is framed with wood and featured two cages under one roof. A hay manger in the middle of the small structure separated the cages.

The main reason that I would make new cages from wire only is my experience that combination wood-and-wire cages provide too many places for urine and droppings, as well as spilled water and feed, to accumulate. In time, the buildup can create a health hazard unless it is cleaned out regularly. All-wire cages prevent the problem by eliminating areas where the buildup can occur. I believe that they are simply more sanitary. Rabbit supply catalogs and some good hardware stores carry the pliers and metal crimping sleeves that can help you turn hardware cloth and welded wire into neat and sanitary cages.

A heavy ceramic dish makes an ideal water dish for rabbits, which are notorious for overturning water dishes. Even ceramic dishes or any open containers are easily contaminated, however. But this is not usually a problem for the small rabbit raiser who can provide fresh water as needed.

Another possibility is the use of the simple tube-and-ball or "dewdrop" waterers. These neat little devices can be bought with a heavy plastic bottle or can be attached to a plastic soda pop bottle—although I have found that the thin, soft plastic of a soda bottle will collapse and not permit water to be dispensed. Whatever type of container you use, be sure to use a bottle large enough to hold a day's worth of water, or check the water often.

Feeders come in a wide variety. One of the best feeders is nearly impossible to find anymore. This was simply one of the old short coffee cans that were about 4 inches tall. The cans were easily attached to a small piece of board or wired directly to the cage wire to prevent overturning. They were just the right height for bunny feeders.

Feeders available on the market usually include a feed hopper in their design, into which may be placed several days' worth of feed. They are attached to the cage by cutting a hole in the cage wire. This places the feed trough inside the cage, while the feed hopper remains conveniently outside for filling. I prefer to feed daily, so as not to allow the feed to draw moisture. Some of these feeders come with a wire mesh bottom to allow the feed dust to fall through. This is an important point. Although we did not experience the problem, it seems that rabbits are pretty easily affected by inhaling this or other dust.

Once you get your animals and introduce them to their quarters, you will need to arrange for them to begin production of offspring. True to their reputation, bunnies are generally eager to cooperate in this respect.

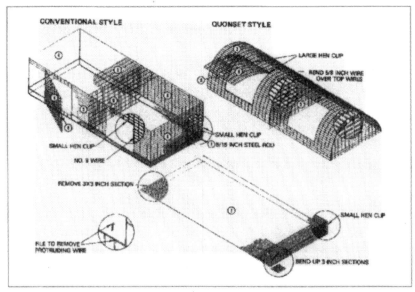

Rabbit cages are often made solely from wire. These types of cages allow for cleaner and healthier animals.

The does come into heat about every two weeks or so, but due to their makeup, they may actually be bred at any time with positive results. However, when the doe is interested, she will do a good deal of thumping with her hind feet, and rub her chin on the water or feed dish.

When getting your rabbits together, you need to remember to put the doe into the cage of the buck, not the other way around. Doe rabbits are very territorial; putting the buck into the doe's cage would jeopardize the health and safety of the buck, for she will give him a sound trouncing—if not seriously injuring him. A buck should have no problem servicing a couple of does; in fact, a maximum ratio of bucks to does is about 1:10 for good breeding results.

Place the doe in the buck's cage, and the buck should do the rest. Within minutes, he should complete his work, after which time the doe should be returned to her cage. It is normal for the buck to perhaps fall to the cage floor immediately after copulation. Don't be alarmed! I have found that if the doe is left with the buck for a few minutes, returned to her cage, then put back with the buck in half an hour or so, breeding is nearly certain.

After you feel certain that the doe has been bred, it is a matter of waiting the 30 days or so for the young to be born. In the meantime, you should place a nest box within the doe's cage. Prior to the doe giving birth, or "kindling", she will begin making a nest. You might want to provide some straw that she can add to the nest, which will be made up largely of hair that she pulls from her chest. The nest box should offer some seclusion and privacy.

The little hairless rabbits will grow quickly. You should see the young bunnies emerge from the nest box to feed when they are about 20 days old. It will get pretty crowded in the cage as the little ones grow. By about eight weeks—and none too soon for the doe—the young rabbits will be big enough to butcher as fryers.

If you plan to keep some for breeding stock, rabbits become sexually mature in five or six months. After that time, they may be bred successfully.

Here are some more rabbit-raising tips:

SITING THE RABBITRY. Rabbits do best where they do not get too much sunlight; this is why old garages or pole building work well as rabbitries. For the small rabbit raiser, the shady side of a building will work nicely. Shade and ventilation are especially important in summer. Conversely, during winter, awnings that unroll or drop down over the sides of the cage will help prevent drafts and retain heat.

LIFTING RABBITS. Lift rabbits properly—never by the ears. While at the local sale barn, I have seen grown men grab rabbits by the ears and go toting them off. To properly pick up an adult rabbit, pick it up by the scruff of its neck and put your other hand under its rump for support. The rabbit will appear to be sitting on your support hand yet is firmly held by the scruff of its neck.

For small rabbits, grasp the loin area gently and firmly. Your thumb will be on one side, your fingers on the other. The web of your hand will be across the back. The heel of the hand will be naturally pointed toward the tail of the rabbit.

KILLING RABBITS is not difficult. Although it might seem unpleasant the first time around, you will quickly get accustomed to it and should be able to accomplish the chore quickly and humanely. There are a couple of ways to do this.

Perhaps the simplest method is to grasp the rabbit by the rear legs and suspend the animal so that it can be delivered a sharp blow at the base of the skull with a stout stick or similar club. I had a short piece (16 to 18 inches) of ½-inch pipe handy that I used. After the rabbit flops around a bit, the head must be removed promptly so that the animal bleeds out properly. The easiest and quickest way to remove the head is merely to grasp it firmly in one hand, the shoulders of the rabbit in the other, and twist. It doesn't take a lot of effort to completely twist the head off the carcass. If the idea of doing this does not appeal to you, then sever the skin, meat, and fiber of the neck with a sharp knife. Then grasp the head and carcass as described above and twist enough to break the spine and remove the head.

BUTCHERING. Rabbits are not difficult to skin, although I have never mastered the art of getting the hide off in one nice piece. This hide is relatively thin and tears rather easily; I have never been left with any usable rabbit hides. Unless you wish to tan and use the hides yourself, however, this is not a big deal. Generally, rabbit hides are not very marketable unless you have a great number of them.

Once you have the critter skinned, then carefully open up the abdominal cavity with a sharp knife, cutting from the breastbone to the tail. As with any other meat animal, be careful not to puncture the entrails when you cut through the abdominal muscle layers. Once the entrails are exposed, reach up into the chest cavity and firmly grasp the organs found there. Pull them downward and keep going until you have the guts removed from the body. Some folks retain the liver and kidneys for later use, leaving them in the carcass. Cut or break apart the area at the anus and remove all of the vent gut.

Immediately rinse out the carcass, then put it in cold water for just a few minutes or place the meat in a refrigerator. This firms up the meat and makes cutting the carcass into frying-pan-sized pieces much easier.

When cutting up a fryer rabbit, you should end up with six or seven pieces. Remove each rear leg at the ball joint. Similarly, at the shoulders, cut into the meat at the base of the foreleg and remove each. Next, I usually cut the trunk into two pieces, cutting it in two just below the bottom rib. If you have not done so, split the rib cage down the breastbone. This opens the piece up a bit and helps it cook more thoroughly. Once you get the hang of all this, it will go quickly and smoothly. Don't be discouraged by those first attempts that might look like you tried to gnaw the carcass into pieces. Remember, the main purpose is to make the rabbit carcass fit in a skillet. If you do this, then you are successful. Freeze rabbit as you would other meat or small game. It is excellent in a wide variety of dishes.

RABBIT RESOURCES

Information and plans for rabbit equipment can be found at:

NORTH DAKOTA STATE UNIVERSITY:
http://www.ag.ndsu.nodak.edu/abeng/plans/BEEF_PLAN.htm.

UNIVERSITY OF TENNESSEE, AGRICULTURAL EXTENSION SERVICE:
http://bioengr.ag.utk.edu/Extension/ExtPubs/PlanList97.htm.

PURDUE UNIVERSITY AGRICULTURAL PLAN SERVICE:
http://pasture.ecn.purdue.edu/~fbps/.

Filling the Haymow

If you raise livestock for food or for pleasure, there comes the time each year when pastures die off and winter blows in. Most homesteaders and small farmers throughout our country live in areas where climate and weather make the feeding of hay a necessity at some time during the year. Very few of us live where homestead animals can forage on green pastures year-round. The livestock-raising backwoods dweller is simply going to be required to grow, purchase, or barter for hay as feed.

Few homestead jobs offer the opportunity for more plain honest work than putting up hay—sweat, muscle, and simple hard work. You see the results of your labor as the stack of bales grows.

The feeling of satisfaction you get when looking at your full haymow is comparable to admiring those full shelves in the cellar, lined with canned fruit, vegetables, and other home-produced and -preserved foods.

HAY TYPES

First off, for the novice, let's discuss the term *hay*. Some newcomers get confused between the terms *hay* and *straw*. *Hay* is simply plants—usually grasses and/or legumes—that are cut, allowed to cure in the sun, then gathered and stored as feed.

Straw is the dead stems of grain-producing grasses such as wheat, rye, or oats. These stems are usually baled after the grain is harvested from the fields. Straw has no food value but is valuable as bedding for livestock. Remember that hay and straw are not interchangeable.

With all of the wide ranges of climates in our country, and considering the different dietary requirements of homestead animals, it should be easy to see that the types of hay that will be available to you can vary widely.

Whenever possible, try to grow a legume or legume-grass mixture for hay. In comparison with grasses, legumes have three prominent advantages. First, they are higher in protein, vitamins, and minerals. Second, a higher yield can be realized from legumes. Third, the nitrogen-fixing bacteria present on legume roots take free atmospheric nitrogen out of the air, enriching the soil and the plant.

A mixture of legumes and grasses is often grown and recommended because of increased palatability, ease of curing, and better erosion control. Check with hay growers in your area and find out what is most widely grown.

When is your hay ready to cut? As a rule of thumb, cut clover crops when they reach the full-bloom stage. Red and alsike clover should be cut just before the full-bloom stage, however. Lespedeza makes fine hay and should be cut when it is in full bloom. Alfalfa should be cut when the crown of the plant begins to develop new shoots. This will be rather early in the plant development, usually at less than 25 percent bloom.

Sweet clover makes very good hay if it's not allowed to get overmature and stemmy. It should be cut just when the blooming begins or it will be quite tough.

Soybeans and cowpeas can also make good hay. If used for a hay crop, these legumes should be cut once the pods are at least halfway developed and up until they mature.

If you are cutting a small grain crop for hay, cut when the grain heads are in the milk stage to the soft dough stage for the best hay.

Hay that is left too long before cutting results in much leaf loss, or shattering. Along with the leaf loss goes much of the nutrition.

Put up the best hay you can. It is better to pay a bit more for what you know is good hay than to pay a cheap price for hay you have doubts about. Your livestock will be good examples of a modern acronym *GIGO*, or "Garbage In, Garbage Out." Just as we are what we eat, so are our livestock.

Generally speaking, early hay is better than late. If the hay crop is put up a bit early, it may result in a slightly lower yield, although this may not even be noticeable. However, the resulting hay will be of such higher quality that any decrease in yield should be offset by its nutritional value and digestibility. The shattering of leaves and seed heads of overmature plants will turn a good hay crop into junk food for your livestock.

WHAT MAKES GOOD HAY?

Whether you are buying hay or putting up your own, it is important to know just what makes good hay. Several factors influence the quality of a hay crop, and most are easily recognized.

☞ First, good hay is made from plants that have been cut at an early stage of maturity. This assures the maximum nutritional value as well as digestibility and palatability. Hay made during this stage should be fine-stemmed and pliable, not coarse, stiff, and woody.

☞ A good hay crop is leafy. This assures you of a high protein content.

☞ Good hay will have a nice green color to it. This indicates proper curing, good palatability, and high vitamin content.

☞ Good hay is free from a lot of foreign material like weeds and stubble. It is also uncontaminated by mold or lots of dust.

☞ Finally, good hay has a pleasant, fragrant aroma.

You have a few options when it comes to getting in your hay crop. Some small holders may want to put up some loose hay. You can also put up square bales, tightly packed and weighing about 40 to 80 pounds each.

Or you might opt to feed the large round bales, which are somewhat labor saving but take a tractor to move.

LOOSE HAY

Today nearly all of us are familiar with the manageable square bales of hay. Before square bales, though, hay was put up loose in the haymows of barns found on every farm. If you shun modern technology and are feeling especially "work brickle," you might want to try putting up loose hay. That is, you move the hay by the forkful onto your truck or wagon, transport it to the barn, and then fork it into the haymow. Obviously, this is going to entail a lot of manual labor and time.

It is still possible to find an old dump rake in working order. Not all of them have become lawn decorations! These first-generation hay rakes were a definite improvement over hand methods of gathering up hay. Many of these old horse-drawn rakes have had the tongue cut off and been adapted to pull behind a tractor. Basically, you operate a rake by drawing it through the field of cured hay. As the rake tines fill, a dump lever is activated to raise the tines and dump the hay into the windrow. As the field is repeatedly crossed, the hay is dumped at the same point along the field and the result is—or should be—long windrows of cured hay ready for baling or forking or loading. You should know, however, that these old rakes were designed long before mobile balers were invented: They're more suitable for the old horse-drawn hay loaders for which they were intended.

Getting the hay to the barn is another matter. Small batches can be forked onto a truck or wagon and hauled into the barn. Most of us simply do not have access to the loading and unloading equipment needed to use loose hay on a scale to support many head of livestock. Hay loaders—large machines used in the field to load tall piles of hay onto a wagon—are pretty much resigned to the pages of books. Hay forks and the metal tracks mounted high in the loft were used for moving the hay into the barn loft, where it was dumped. Again, these implements are generally seen only in antiques stores or in books.

Just so you know, even the technology-shunning Amish use square balers. They adapt them to run as ground-driven units, or by power take-off (PTO) from a horse-drawn power head.

Incidentally, as hay balers became more common, the packed, tightly bound bales were put up into the lofts of the same grand old barns that formerly held loose hay. Years of holding and supporting the tremendous weight of hundreds and thousands of bales of hay caused many of these barns to sag and degenerate prematurely.

I have put up loose hay before, and for me it's far too time consuming and wasteful to be an effective way of storing sufficient amounts of hay for my purposes. I'll just say that it was an interesting experiment. For practical purposes, let's stick with baled hay here.

SQUARE BALES

Once you decide that you are going start baling your own hay, you will need three basic pieces of machinery: a mower or hay conditioner, a rake, and a baler.

As a rule or thumb, if you plan to get your hay in a week or even two before your neighbors, then you will probably end up with some of the best hay. Good hay is young hay. Not immature, but young, leafy, and just tough enough to withstand the rigors of mowing, raking, and baling. If you hire any part of the haying done, such as the actual baling, the neighbors with the baler will most likely be able to get to your hay crop if they don't have their own on the ground.

For many homesteaders, it may not be possible or even desirable to own a hay baler. Perhaps you have just a small patch of hay and cannot justify purchasing, maintaining, and operating a hay baler. Some of you may not have any hay ground at all.

For those with fields producing a hay crop, you may decide to enlist the help of a custom baler. In my own case, I have cut and raked my hay fields and hired a neighbor to come and bale the cured hay into square bales. At the price most farmers charge for such work, it is difficult to justify purchasing a machine of my own.

The downside of hiring your baling done is that you are at the mercy of other folks, who'll come and do the baling when they want to do it or can get to it. Suppose you and your farmer neighbor both have hay lying in the windrow, ready to bale, and it looks like rain: You can guess whose hay is going to get baled first. Or you may be somewhere down the waiting list of customers for the baler. Finally, in some areas, it may actually be difficult to find someone to come and bale your hay crop.

Some homesteaders may decide that the time is right for them to look for a good used square hay baler. With most large-scale farms converting to large round bales, you'd think that balers producing the smaller, easy-to-handle bales would be flooding the market. I have found, however, that such is not the case. Many of the farmers with whom I've talked with want to hang on to their old square balers to bale the small odd patch of hay, as a backup baler, or maybe "just in case."

There are some good square balers out there, however, and if you look around you can pick one up at a decent price.

What's *a decent price?* This can vary widely, and it depends on a lot of factors. Your general area, the age of the machine, the condition of the machine, and even the person you are buying it from can and should all influence the price of your prospective baler. But you should expect to pay from $500 up to a couple of thousand dollars for a used baler.

Learn a little about a baler before you go and buy one. When buying, try to see your prospective purchase in action. I am no expert on maintaining a hay baler, but I do know that if you have one that ties one side loose and the other side tight; if you have one that turns out bales 6 feet long; if you have one that fails to knot the strings properly at all, then you have some headaches on the way. Most of these malfunctions can be taken care of with some simple adjustments, but others may require the replacement of parts such as "needles" or "knotters."

Remember, too, that you will need more than just the baler alone. Assuming that you have a tractor, and assuming that it has a live PTO with which to run the baler, you will still need a mower or cutter and a rake, in addition to the baler.

The old illustrations of the farmer cutting a swath with the sickle-bar mower are best left in our daydreams. With a decent crop of hay, an old mower will be popping pitman rods and rivets all day long as you try to cut the heavy crop. Today hay conditioners and disk mowers can efficiently lay a hay crop down in quick order. With the new disk mowers becoming popular, you may consider trying to pick up a good used cutter/conditioner.

Hay rakes are also a matter of concern. As I mentioned, I experimented with loose hay once. When I did, I used an old dump rake. More recently, I used an old five-wheel hay rake until a friend let me use his five-bar rake. There was no comparison between the two. Again, age and mechanical improvements can make a difference. Good used bar rakes are available for a few hundred to a couple of thousand dollars.

GO BIG

You may want to consider the relative convenience of using large round bales of hay in your feeding operation. Notice I said *relative* convenience. When feeding square bales, you must cut the twines and fork the hay into the manger or feed rack. When feeding round bales, you must first have a tractor with a bale spike either on the rear three-point hitch, or on a front-end loader. You must fire up the tractor and motor out to the hay bales, spear one, and wheel over to the hay ring—a special large metal hay feeder. Then you tip up the hay ring, remove the twines or netting from the bale, and drop it. Pull up and hop off again and drop the hay ring down over the new bale. This is done outside the barn in the feedlot or pasture, often in driving snow or rain.

Feeding large bales outside does offer a measure of convenience in that you need to feed only every few days. Square bales must usually be fed every day. Large bales are often stored right outside, although I like to put a tarp over them when I can. Large bales are less labor-intensive to bring in than square bales. In fact, a common lament from old farmers is that they can hardly find any teenage boys who want to put up hay anymore. That is why, they say, they decided to use large round bales.

BUYING AND BARTERING

For many folks, buying baled hay is the most practical choice for getting in the winter supply. During normal hay years, there are usually a number of ads in the local newspaper offering hay for sale. The local feed mill usually has similar ads posted on the bulletin board. Stop in at the local coffee shop and inquire about hay for sale.

There is not often a wide range of asking prices for baled hay. It seems that most farmers know what the others are getting for their hay crops and price their own accordingly. The price is more often affected by the amount of rainfall during the given year. A wet spring usually means a good hay crop and lower prices. A dry spring and poorer hay crop will mean higher prices per bale—simple supply-and-demand economics.

Buy the best hay you can afford. Follow the guidelines given on page 141 to help judge whether the hay crop is worth the price asked. You will be better off paying more for good hay on which your animals will thrive than buying old, overmature hay that will barely maintain the animals.

If you have a hay field but are short on equipment, you can sometimes make a deal to have neighboring farmers do your hay on shares. That is, they come in and cut, rake, and bale your hay for a share of it— half is not unheard of. This type of arrangement works well if you have a surplus of hay and an accommodating neighbor.

KEEP THIS IN MIND

If you are going to produce your own hay crop and want to produce the best and most hay possible for your acres, then there are three points to keep in mind.

☞ Be sure to choose plant varieties adapted to your area and climate. As with other crops, different types of hay plants will do better in different parts of the country. Check around and see what does best in your own area. See what your neighbors plant and what they shy away from. There is usually a good reason for each. A good thick stand of hay plants adapted for your area will produce higher yields of more nutritious hay, and will have finer stems and fewer weeds as well.

☞ Grow your hay crop on fertile soil. Go to the trouble of getting a soil test to determine just what elements your soil needs, then fertilize and seed your fields properly. You will have a much finer hay crop as a result. Remember *GIGO*—Garbage In, Garbage Out.

☞ Cut your hay at an early stage of maturity. This will assure you of having the most nutrients and the highest degree of digestibility and palatability for your hay. This factor probably ranks at the top as an influence on the makeup of your hay. Early cutting assures you of a high leaf-to-stem ratio. Early cutting also affects protein and fiber content—the older the plant, the lower its protein and higher its crude fiber. It is better to cut the hay a week or two early than a week or two late. You will end up with a slightly lower yield, but much higher-quality hay.

As I mentioned early on, putting up hay is good, honest work. It is hard work, but enjoyable. My boys like to put up hay, and even my wife and daughter enjoy helping. The scent of fresh-mown hay on a summer evening is one of those characteristic country experiences that become etched in your memory. And regardless of the method you choose, the knowledge that you have laid by stores for your livestock is a good feeling indeed. Conjure up a picture in your mind as you read these lyrics to Indiana's state song:

> *Oh, the moonlight's fair tonight along the Wabash.*
> *From the fields there comes the breath of new-mown hay.*
> *Through the sycamores the candle lights are gleaming,*
> *On the banks of the Wabash, far away.*

Keeping Bees

I believe that nearly every small farmer, gardener, or homesteader should have a colony or two of bees. Aside from the tremendous potential for producing usable and salable quantities of healthful sweetener, the bees will also do double duty as pollinators of crops, garden vegetables, orchard fruits, and flowers on your place. While wild bees can and do manage to do the job in most cases, a couple of thriving hives will ensure good pollination of your flowering plants. Too, there is no small amount of satisfaction in observing the winged workers gathering nectar from the various flowers and blossoms on your 'stead, knowing that the resulting honey is another crop coming off your own place.

The type—and color—of honey that will be produced by your colonies will be dependent, of course, upon the types of flowers they have to work on. In areas where large expanses of single plant types exist, predictable and consistent honey types are produced. Honey types identified with particular regions of the country are not uncommon. Good examples of this are the delicate orange blossom honey produced in the vast orange groves of Florida and the clear, golden clover honey produced in parts of the Midwest and High Plains. For the homesteader and home food producer, however, the plant types that the bees work is not nearly so important. In my area, we consistently get a relatively dark honey that is properly called mixed-wildflower honey. It is a duke's mixture of just about every flowering plant on the countryside. This type of honey is equal to, if not superior to the clearer honeys produced on the vast fields of clover or other single type of bloom. In fact, many consider mixed-wildflower honey to contain quantities of vitamins and minerals not found in any other types. I have honey customers who seek out this type of honey rather than buy the clearer versions. Whatever the comparative nutritional content, I am happy to remove the surplus honey from my colonies and use it through the year.

I have been fortunate in my beekeeping education. One of my uncles was an excellent beekeeper, and his hives produced many tons of quality wildflower honey. His results were not by accident, for he also spent many hours studying and observing the little critters that actually produced the sweet stuff. I used to visit him often and have seen his homemade observation hive—a single deep frame enclosed in a wood-and-glass container. The side windows were kept covered with pieces of cardboard unless actually observing the inhabitants, to provide the bees with the dark environment they like. The interesting thing about this observation hive is that it was located in the laundry room of the house, with the entrance in a specially made block at the window. The bees kept busy buzzing in and out through the little opening. Carefully removing one of the cardboard covers would reveal the queen bee being tended by her court. In would come the workers, wiggling and jiggling their figure-8 dance to tell the others of the source of the rich nectar they bore. I enjoyed watching the busy little one-frame hive, although I now wish I'd paid closer attention.

I have, tucked away, my uncle's notebooks from his years in Nevada, journals of bee activity, the swarms, production, and general condition of the individual hives.

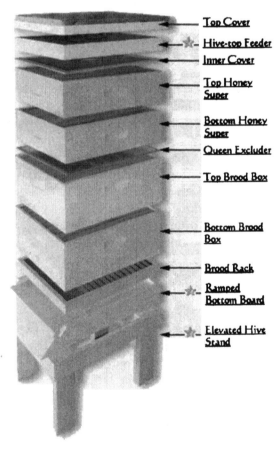

Top Cover
Hive-top Feeder
Inner Cover
Top Honey Super
Bottom Honey Super
Queen Excluder
Top Brood Box
Bottom Brood Box
Brood Rack
Ramped Bottom Board
Elevated Hive Stand

Here is an exploded view of a bee hive. Since this shows all parts that might be included, they would not necessarily all be found on any one hive.

In the accompanying illustration, you can see the basic makeup of the hardware in a typical beehive.

As you can see, there are several components to a beehive. First, an elevated stand makes a good base. It allows the hive to rest above surrounding weeds or grass and simply makes working the hive more comfortable. Next, the bottom board is placed on the hive stand. This allows a uniform space all along the front of the hive for the bees to enter and exit from. The hive bodies are placed on the bottom board. The bottom boxes of the hive are called the brood boxes or brood chambers. These are the boxes where the queen lays the eggs and the young bees are raised. Atop the brood boxes are placed the honey supers. Here, the workers will deposit most of the nectar and store the honey. They are the hive parts that you will extract your honey crop from later on. Between the brood boxes and the honey supers is placed a special screen called an excluder, which allows worker bees to pass through to reach

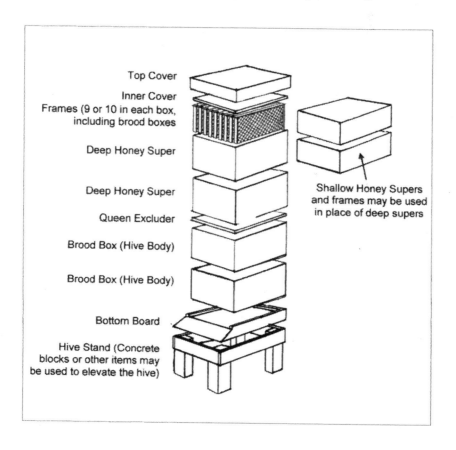

Top Cover

Inner Cover

Frames (9 or 10 in each box, including brood boxes

Deep Honey Super

Deep Honey Super

Queen Excluder

Brood Box (Hive Body)

Brood Box (Hive Body)

Bottom Board

Hive Stand (Concrete blocks or other items may be used to elevate the hive)

Shallow Honey Supers and frames may be used in place of deep supers the honey supers, yet prevents the slightly larger queen bee from entering. This keeps the queen from laying eggs in the honey supers and results in nice clean frames of honey.

Above the honey supers is an inner cover. This thin board is placed beneath the top cover and keeps it from being "glued" down by the bees.

While most texts illustrate the use of shallow honey supers atop the deep hive bodies, I have used the same size of deep supers or hive bodies throughout. While I suspect that this stems from my early instruction in beekeeping, using deep supers does have its benefits—most notably, I have to purchase only one size of wax foundation, and I can make or purchase the boxes all the same size as well. The main drawback to using deep supers is that they can weigh up to 100 pounds when full! However, overall there is less handling than when using shallow supers, and the bees work the deep supers well.

Another trick that I was taught is to use only 9 frames in the standard 10-frame Langstroth super. If you evenly space the frames in the super, the bees will naturally draw the comb out farther. This will put the cappings up higher above the edge of the frame and help make the uncapping chore much easier. You can easily make or purchase a spacer to help to ensure getting the correct spacing on the frames in the super—although spacing them by hand in just a few colonies is not a difficult chore.

Speaking of frames, this is a good place to describe just how the frames and combs are set up. Each of the light wooden frames comes shipped unassembled. With the provided instructions and hardware, you can put together plenty of frames in a relatively short time. After assembling the frame itself, you attach the wax foundation following the instructions that come with the equipment. The foundation is merely a wax sheet placed in the frame; it has a pattern of six-sided honeycomb cells pressed into it.

Once the foundation is set into the frame and secured, the frame is placed in the honey super; the bees naturally use the honeycomb shapes as a guide to build their comb upon. They will "draw out" the comb and then fill each cell with nectar. The nectar will be constantly fanned by workers in the hive. Once sufficient moisture is evaporated, the bees seal or "cap" each cell, and the honey is ready and stored.

OBTAINING YOUR BEES

For most of us, capturing a swarm of wild bees is not practical. I have helped capture swarms of bees that had taken up residence inside the walls of old houses or swarmed and attached themselves to someone's shrubs or trees in the yard. I've also helped capture a colony that a logger had disturbed when he dropped a tree that turned out to be hollow. Once you gain experience with bees, you will discover that there are opportunities to obtain bees in your area that will save you the expense of ordering package bees.

But package bees are the most common and most practical way for beekeepers, especially beginners, to get their honey operation going. Package bees are usually ordered in late winter or early spring from one of the several suppliers in the country. They will come to you via regular mail or by shipper. Believe me, the folks at the post office are pretty prompt to call you if you get a package of live and buzzing bees shipped to you.

Package bees are shipped in screen-sided boxes. They are usually sold in 3-pound quantities—and that amounts to a lot of honeybees. Inside the box is a smaller container that holds the queen bee and a few attendants. That small container is closed via a small sugar plug covered with a cork. The larger container with the rest of the bees should have a can of sugar water for them to feed on during the trip to you.

You should have your hive set up and ready before your bees arrive. Once you get them, remove four or so frames from the hive body. Remove the queen cage, then remove the cork that covers the candy plug in her cage. Suspend the cage between the two center frames of the hive. Gently but firmly shake the bees out of the shipping box into the space where you removed the frames. Make sure to shake several of the bees onto the area where the queen is located. Put the cover in place and don't bother the hive for a week. In short order, some of the bees will chew the candy plug from the queen cage. She should emerge and begin to lay eggs within a week, after the workers have drawn out some of the foundation into comb. After a week or two, check your hive to be sure that it is active and thriving. You are on your way to your first honey crop!

WORKING YOUR BEES

Although your bee colonies can pretty well be left alone to do their work, they will need to be checked periodically. When working around your bees, it is a good idea to wear light-colored clothing. They seem to get less excited when you do so. Using your veil, smoker, and hive tool, work calmly and steadily around your hives and you should have no problems.

When first working your hive, use the smoker as you begin. A smoker is a basic piece of bee equipment and consists of a combustion chamber, a bellows, and a funnel. The combustion chamber provides the place to burn the material with which the smoke is created. Try to get old, but clean, burlap for this purpose. Burlap ignites easily yet smolders well, which is what you want for the operation. Some folks use corncobs as fuel, but I cannot personally vouch for their effectiveness. Whatever fuel you use, be sure it is clean, preferably of a natural fiber or material, and does not give off any noxious fumes, harmful to you or your bees. The bellows on a smoker serve to help keep the fuel lit, and to provide the puffs of the smoke needed to work the hive. The funnel simply concentrates the smoke and directs it where it's needed.

Working a healthy colony of bees. Once you are comfortable with bees, you may find it easier to work without coveralls or gloves. Gentle bees help!

First, give a few good puffs of smoke directly into the hive entrance. Then remove the top cover and inner cover, and apply several good puffs of smoke into the super. The whole idea is to make the bees think that their hive is about to go up in smoke. Instinctively, the bees will load up on honey and prepare to evacuate the hive if necessary. Bees that are so loaded are not nearly as likely to

The helmet and veil are two of the most important parts of the beekeeper's equipment. Courtesy BeeCare.

sting as they'd be if you just took off the top cover and pulled out frames. Such behavior has evolved through millions of years and millions of generations of bees. When smoking the hive, take care not to puff the smoker so much or so hard as to create very hot smoke or actual flames. That will certainly kill any bees it comes close to, or will singe their wings at least. The idea is to create the cool smoke needed to calm the bees down and preoccupy them with the thought of the impending danger of fire.

With the top and inner cover removed, use your hive tool to lift a few frames out to examine them. Is the comb fully drawn out? Are the combs being filled with honey? Are the combs capped off and ready to extract honey from? Do the bees appear lively and healthy? After checking your colony, merely replace the inner and top covers. The bees will fan and clear the hive of any remaining smoke, and life in the colony will soon be back to normal.

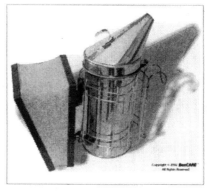

The smoker uses a simple bellows and smoldering fuel to produce smoke. The smoke is directed into the hive to calm the bees. Courtesy BeeCare.

REAPING THE HARVEST—TAKING OFF HONEY

When you have checked your hives and find supers full of capped honeycomb, it is time to remove your honey crop. When taking off honey, you must first remove the bees from the honey super.

In my experience, the best method is a commercial product called Bee-Go. This is a chemical solution called butyric anhydride. It is applied to an easily made "fume board" and put atop the hive in the place of the top cover and inner cover. The bees simply do not like the odors given off by the chemical and head farther down into the hive. Normally, nearly every bee has hightailed out of the honey super within a couple of minutes. With the use of shallow supers, you can probably clear a couple of supers at a time. Since I normally use deep honey supers, I can remove one cleared super and replace the fume board atop the next to get it cleared out as well.

Another chemical bee mover is one that I have not tried personally, but I've read that it's good stuff. Called Fischer's Bee-Quick, this product is a blend of natural oils and herbal extracts with a sweet, almost almond smell. This product should hold promise for the home beekeeper. Like Bee-Go, it is used in combination with a fume board to clear the honey supers.

You can easily make your own fume board at home. One method is simply to start as if you are making a regular telescoping cover for the hive. However, instead of plywood for the top itself, take a piece of cellulose-type insulation board (such as Celotex brand) and cut a piece the same size as a standard top cover. Assemble all the pieces to resemble a standard top cover. The difference is that the insulation board is quite absorbent and provides a good surface to apply the chemical solution to. Since the fume board is used only when taking off honey, it does not need to be waterproofed, and it can easily be stored in a large plastic bag or the like when not in use.

Another way to make a fume board is to simply use an old or extra hive cover. Staple a layer or two of ordinary burlap to the underside. It will act as the absorbent pad to which you will apply the chemical.

Apply the Bee-Go or Bee-Quick to the underside of the fume board as directed on the container. Place it atop the hive and wait for a few minutes for the bees to move down. If you have several supers to remove, take off the first cleared super and replace the fume board to continue to move the bees downward.

EXTRACTING HONEY

It is very difficult to extract honey without a mechanical extractor. If you are not using specially designed frames from which you will take sections of comb honey (honey marketed with the honeycomb intact), then you simply must find access to a centrifugal-type extractor. These are available in many sizes, including ones suitable for the small place. They can be made, but I have had better luck using a manufactured model.

Now that you have your full supers waiting, you will need to remove the wax caps on the combs. This can be done by using long heated knives. Some folks use two or three long blades, such as bread knives. Keep the blades immersed in a pot of very hot water and use the hot knives to slice the capping from the frame. As one knife cools, put it into the hot water and use another heated one. Slice off the cappings and let them drop into a pot or kettle—a lot of honey will drain from the cappings, and the wax is a valuable by-product.

You can also use an electrically heated knife to remove the cappings from the honey-laden frames. Such knives are available from any good bee supply house and simply use an electrical element to heat the blade. Use one in the same way as a regular knife—with a smooth back-and-forth motion to slice the cappings from the comb.

Place the decapped frames into the extractor with the top bar facing outward. This is important to extract all the honey. Honeycomb is actually built by the bees with the individual cell sloping very slightly downward toward the foundation. Therefore, by placing the top bar of the frame outward, you will be able to sling virtually all the honey out of the comb.

Some small home-sized extractors have the frames facing flat-side outward. Once some of the honey is spun out of one side, the frames are rotated and honey is taken from the other side. Then they are reversed once more and the extraction is completed. The reason for all this is to prevent the weight of the honey on the inside of the frame from causing the foundation to pull loose as the extractor is spun and the honey is taken from the outside comb.

As your honey is extracted from the comb, replace the empty frames in the super. Allow the honey to accumulate in the bottom of the extractor, and then drain it off. You should plan to run it through a few layers of cheesecloth to remove any bits of wax, pollen, or bees. Then simply decant it into the containers of your choice. I have used purchased honey jars with printed labels, and I have used quart and pint canning jars with hand-printed labels. You will have no trouble selling all the honey you want, regardless of the type of jar it comes in.

After extracting the honey from your supers, they will need to be cleaned up for winter storage. I usually allow the bees work on this chore. I set out the extracted supers, and the bees finish cleaning up any honey that might remain in the frames. After allowing a day or two for the frames to be cleaned up, examine each super for damage, rot, or other need of repair. The frames, too, are looked at to see if any are in need of replacement. Any remaining deposits of spur comb and propolis are removed. Next, I bag each super, frames and all, in a large plastic bag—the 50-gallon lawn-sized bags work well. I then place each super in the deep freeze for about a week—long enough to kill any wax moths, eggs, or larvae. Finally, the supers are put away, still bagged, to be used again next year.

Once you have extracted your surplus honey and made certain that your bees have enough left to tide them over the winter, it is time to ready them for the cold months ahead.

In most parts of the country, such preparation is simple. Mice can do a great deal of damage to a brood chamber, so a hive closure is a requirement when the rodents begin seeking winter quarters. A hive closure, which restricts the hive opening size, is easily made from a scrap of pine board. Make the closure board as long as the hive is wide. Cut a notch out of the bottom edge of the board about $7/16$ inch by 4 inches. The resulting opening is just tall enough for a honeybee to pass under. The device is lightly nailed to the main entrance of the hive and prevents mice from entering and setting up residence in the hive. It still allows for some ventilation during the cold months and for the honeybees to pass through and make "cleaning flights" on any day warm enough for them to get out.

There are two very serious threats to bees and the beekeeping industry at this time. In some areas, entire colonies of bees have been wiped out.

The problem is mites. Two species of mites have been wreaking havoc in many areas of the country as they decimate honeybee colonies and entire apiaries.

The tracheal mite is just what it sounds like, a minute critter that attaches itself to the inside of the bee's trachea, where it blocks respiration and absorbs body fluids until the host dies. It is not uncommon for affected honeybee to host several of the tiny parasites.

The Veroa mite is an external parasite but essentially does the same thing. These pests attach themselves to the host bee like ticks on a dog and work to absorb the honeybee's life fluids. The mites literally suck the host dry.

Fortunately, some very simple remedies or weapons for combating these pests are available. Crisco patties can be very effective in combating the Veroa mites. The patties are made by dissolving 2 parts sugar into 3 parts Crisco. Mix well and pour out onto aluminum foil, plastic wrap, or waxed paper. The thin patty can then be placed on top of the frames, under the hive cover. Apparently, the bees are attracted to the sugar and feed on it, at the same time coating themselves with a light oily film from the shortening. The film is believed to repel the mites. Beekeepers around the country are reportedly finding success using this method.

Another method that discourages the tracheal mites is also very simple. Just raise the cover on your hive and place two or three menthol cough drops atop the frames. Menthol crystals are also an accepted treatment for the mites, but somewhat tricky to administer effectively. The cough drop method is simple, effective, and does not harm any of the honey produced in any way.

There are other commercially available treatments available that you may wish to explore. Apistan strips are easily applied and will help with your mite problems. Continual research is being done to come up with other remedies to this serious problem.

A Beekeeping Calendar

Here is a helpful guide to attending to your bees throughout the year. A more complete calendar for your particular can be located by visiting your local agricultural extension office.

JANUARY

☞ Check the hive entrance. Be sure it is not blocked by snow, dead bees, or other matter.

☞ Check your supplies and order or make things that you will need for the coming season.

☞ Review your records and see where you can make changes and improvements.

FEBRUARY

☞ Watch for your bees making "cleaning flights" from the hive. You should begin to see them making their first flights on nice days.

☞ Begin to assemble your honey supers for the coming honey flow.

☞ Lift the hives to check for presence of remaining honey stores and bees.

☞ Order package bees if needed.

MARCH

☞ Inspect the colonies. Medicate if needed.

APRIL

☞ Check the colonies. Observe for crowding and swarming. Provide plenty of space in the hive.

☞ Install package bees.

☞ Cease medications.

MAY

☞ Check the colonies for drawn comb. Add supers if needed.

JUNE

☞ Check the colonies. Remove and process your spring honey flow if needed.

JULY

☞ Check the colonies to be sure they have plenty of super space for honey storage.

☞ Contact your honey markets if needed.

☞ Bore a ⁹/16-inch hole in or beneath the grip of the first super above the queen excluder to provide a ventilation hole and an upper entrance for workers.

AUGUST
☞ Check the colonies for full supers. Begin to remove the honey supers. Process the honey and allow for fall nectar flow.

SEPTEMBER
☞ Inspect for stores of honey. Be sure the bees have plenty stored away.
☞ Apply Apistan strips, menthol, or your chosen treatment for mites.

OCTOBER
☞ Install a hive opening reducer.
☞ Market your honey and products.

NOVEMBER
☞ Continue marketing.
☞ Clean up equipment, repair, and replace.

DECEMBER
☞ Sit by the stove, and have a cup of tea . . . with honey in it, of course!

Beekeeping Resources

The following books are loaded with beekeeping information:

FIRST LESSONS IN BEEKEEPING, by C. P. Dadant, *American Bee Journal,* Hamilton, Illinois. First published in 1917, this classic book on beekeeping is an excellent resource for the beginner. It covers all aspects of the pursuit of beekeeping, in a format and volume suitable for the novice. Highly recommended.

BEEKEEPING IN THE MIDWEST, by Elbert R. Jaycox, University of Illinois, 1976. This is another superb handbook on the beekeeper's craft. While it pertains especially to the Midwest, it covers the physiology of bees, equipment, and many other topics of universal interest. In particular, it has some excellent pages and illustrations on making your own bee equipment. This is one of my personal favorite books on the subject of beekeeping. It is available from the University of Illinois at Urbana-Champaign, College of Agriculture, Cooperative Extension Service, Circular 1125.

HOW TO KEEP BEES AND SELL HONEY, by Walter T. Kelley, Walter T. Kelley Co., Clarkson, KY 42726, 1983. This book by Mr. Kelley appears to be a compilation of information possibly from the old *Modern Beekeeping Magazine*, of which Mr. Kelley served as editor. It contains a wealth of valuable hints on beekeeping, as well as much basic information. It is packed with photos.

THE HIVE AND THE HONEYBEE, edited by Dadant and Sons, Dadant and Sons, Hamilton, Illinois, 1946–1986. Here is the trusted, authoritative volume on beekeeping. It goes in depth on a multitude of topics of interest and concern to the serious beekeeper. This textbook-quality volume is profusely illustrated with photos, charts, tables, and drawings, and is thoroughly indexed. I'd recommend this book, especially once you get going in beekeeping.

FOLK MEDICINE, Dr. D. C. Jarvis, Fawcett Crest Books, 1958. I mention this book here because it contains some very good information on the value of honey in maintaining good health. Note that the information contained in *Folk Medicine* regarding the feeding of honey to infants has in recent years been proven to be unsafe.

ABC AND XYZ OF BEE CULTURE, A. I. Root, A. I. Root Co., Medina, Ohio, 1978. This volume is an alphabetically arranged encyclopedia on beekeeping. Within its 700-plus pages are hundreds of topics of value and interest to the beekeeper. Hundreds of illustrations, as well as a glossary and index, are included. This is a highly recommended text, particularly once you get the basics down.

For beekeeping supplies and information, check out the following sources:

WALTER T. KELLY CO., 3107 Elizabethtown Road, Clarkson, KY 42726, www.kelleybees.com.

DADANT & SONS, INC., 1 South Second Street, Hamilton, IL 62341-1399, www.dadant.com.

THE A. I. ROOT CO., P.O. Box 706, Medina, OH 44258-0706, www.airoot.com.

BRUSHY MOUNTAIN BEE FARM, 610 Bethany Church Road, Moravian Falls, NC 28654, 1-800-BEESWAX, www.beeequipment.com.

BEECARE, P.O. Box 1070, Leander, TX 78646-1070, www.beecare.com.

DRAPER'S SUPER BEE APIARIES, INC., 1-800-233-4273, www.draper-bee.com, for package bees and supplies.

5

FOOD: STOCKING THE LARDER

Food Preservation

Food Dehydration

Storing and Using Wheat

Winemaking at Home

Food Preservation

For the homesteader, home preservation of food is as natural an activity as laying in the winter wood supply, putting up hay for the livestock, or planting and tending the garden. It is following the principles of putting by stores in times of plenty for use during lean times. For many of our fellow country folks, however, home food preservation is a dying or dead art. Even many farm folks—the very people who feed our cities—don't produce or preserve their own food. Most have become, like their city counterparts, used to living a hand-to-mouth existence. Many people would no more think about putting up quantities of their food than they would refining their own gasoline. It is unfortunate that home canning, freezing, and drying of home-produced food is so relatively rare. But, come to think of it, folks like us are relatively rare, too.

It has only become true relatively recently in our history that Americans have ceased to store food and supplies for hard times. Historically, and up until the present generation, this was done to provide for the seasonal lean times. Today it is done for the same reason. It can be a matter of principle. Although perhaps not wealthy in a material sense, a good homestead is a potential storehouse of food, equipment, and know-how for use during hard times, seasonal or otherwise.

To become truly self-reliant, some system of food preservation must be put in place on the 'stead. Much camaraderie and fellowship can be had in gathering to harvest, prepare, and preserve home produce. As with most homestead chores, youngsters not only can be given an opportunity to help out, but soon become valuable aides in gathering and processing home-produced food. They quickly become proud of the good work they do and in knowing that something is expected of them. They take pride in their contribution to the family group. These times spent together are good for the children—and for the family as a whole. Yet another possibility is that two or more families can share produce, labor, and equipment and turn out great quantities of home-canned or -frozen food. Too, the gathering can make for a very pleasant social event, with everyone visiting while sharing in the work. In group canning bees, everyone has a job—from the young child to the grandparents.

BULK FOOD BUYING

In addition to food produced right on the homestead, you will in all likelihood be required to purchase a certain number of supplies from commercial outlets. Although you might prefer it to be otherwise, there are still some things that cannot be produced on the farm. And as long as you have to shop, you might as well get the best buys possible on the items you choose, right? For us, bulk buying presents many marked advantages for stocking our shelves and freezers. First and most obvious, of course, is the money you will save. Big money. When buying in case lots, unpackaged bulk, and so on, you can save 50 percent or more. Also, consider buying goods in institutional-sized containers. Now, 5 pounds of dry yeast or 5 gallons of dishwashing liquid may sound like a lot, but when you figure up the savings, you will indeed be impressed at your good buy. It is true that the initial outlay of cash can be considerably more when purchasing in these large quantities, but it doesn't have to be prohibitive. First, save just a bit, and when you do make a shopping trip, pick up a case or two of a particular sale item you are shopping for. The next trip, do the same on another item, and so on. Soon the stock will add up, and your larder will be bulging with provisions and supplies.

Another way to offset the cost of one of these major shopping trips is to squirrel away funds over a long period of time just for the purpose of stocking the shelves. We make a couple of really big shopping trips each year to replenish supplies of some household goods, staple foods such as dried beans and pasta, plus other often-used items. We generally use one of our "cookie jar accounts" to finance these excursions, and normally bring home some unexpected bargains as well as the sought-after items.

Now, storage of all of these goods takes a good deal of space. In the homestead dwelling, there is

Any odd space can be turned into a storeroom. Here are some shelves stocked with canned goods and other items. Buying case lots can save you big money over the long run. In addition, it cuts down tremendously on the trips to town.

usually found—or should be, anyway—a sizable pantry and/or cellar in which to store home-produced food. Expanding on the same idea—say, by lining the wall with more shelves and bins—you can create plenty of storage space for bulk purchases and a regular "store" in your home. In fact, when our oldest son was about five years old, I made a special sign for him declaring our supply room his GENERAL STORE. He liked being asked to run downstairs to "the store" to get a can of this or a jar of that.

Most of us know the feeling of security that comes from having those cellar and pantry shelves full of canned, dried, and otherwise preserved home produce. The feeling is compounded when the shelves also contain supplies of those products that we need and use often, but are not able to produce on the farm. It is a good feeling, knowing that if the roads get shut down by a severe snowstorm or similar inconvenience, we have enough provisions to get by. Too, economic disasters are not impossible, nor unheard of. The same feeling of self-reliance and security exists in knowing that if the grocers, markets, and banks shut down, we homesteaders will be getting by nicely.

HOME CANNING

Of course, home canning of foods and produce is a natural activity for those of us on the small place. A good pressure canner and a hot-water bath canner should be in every homesteader's kitchen. We use the pressure canner for just about everything we can, for safety's sake. This device is basically an airtight kettle that uses pressurized steam to achieve the high temperatures necessary to kill

Home-canned produce on the shelves. It is a good feeling to have stores laid by.

all botulism-causing bacteria. Pressure canning is the only method recommended safe by the USDA for canning low-acid foods. The high temperatures made possible inside the pressure canner ensure the destruction of bacteria inside the jars. A word of warning here: You will need to learn how to operate your particular pressure canner by reading the owner's manual that comes with it. If you have purchased a used pressure canner, and you do not have an owner's manual, you can obtain one by contacting the company that manufactured it. Pressure canners do require you to pay attention while using them, but they are relatively simple to operate and perfectly safe when used according to guidelines given with them. Every home canner should have one.

The old-fashioned hot-water bath canner has fallen out of favor for most home canning, particularly with the advent of the home pressure canner. The hot-water bath is simply a large covered kettle with wire racks to hold the canning jars. For many foods, the temperatures simply do not get high enough to kill all of the bacteria present. However, for most whole tomatoes, tomato juice, and other high-acid foods, the hot-water bath works well. Be sure to consult your local county extension service for the latest, up-to-date information on home canning.

FOOD PRESERVATION RESOURCES

The texts listed below contain a wealth of information on home canning:

PUTTING FOOD BY, by Janet C. Greene et al., Plume Books.

STOCKING UP III, edited by Carol Hupping, Rodale Press.

MAKING THE BEST OF BASICS, by James Talmadge Stevens, Gold Leaf Press.

If you are interested in setting up a long-term food storage plan, there are some good computer programs available to help you determine just how much you might need to store. Try these Internet links to get you started:

http://www.geocities.com/Athens/Forum/5499/fs.html.
http://www.millennium-ark.net/News_Files/LTAH_Food_Store5.html.

A lot of good food storage information is also available from these sites:

http://www.waltonfeed.com.
http://www.happyhovel.com.

All these sources can help get you on your way to filling and organizing your pantry shelves.

Food Dehydration

The drying of food as a means of preservation has been around for a long, long time. For countless generations, populations in suitably dry climates all around the globe have dried meat, fish, fruit, and vegetables in times of plenty as a way to provide for the leaner months of the year. My grandmother used to tell us of helping to spread apple slices on the top of a tin shed roof for drying when she was a child. An aunt once described stringing fresh young bean pods on a long, heavy thread and hanging them to dry, coming up with what they called leather-britches beans. A friend has told us about placing trays of sliced fruits and vegetables on cheesecloth-covered trays in an old car that he had. The trays were placed on wood strips lying across the dashboard, the seat backs, and the rear deck. The car's windows were rolled down just a bit to allow some of the moist, heated air to escape. This made a pretty effective, if somewhat bulky, food dryer! Obviously, all of these were simple and imperfect food-drying systems, but do show ways in which food can be dried at home.

Essentially, dehydration of food removes the moisture that provides the environment conducive to the growth of bacteria. Removal of the moisture results in a product that can be stored for months or even years.

For the present-day homesteader, hunter, hiker, or camper, dehydration is still a valuable method of food preservation. Fortunately for those of us in the less arid climates, methods exist that enable us to dry suitable quantities of foods at home without having to spread the food out on our rooftops. In fact, a really good food dehydrator can be made right at home.

For the past several years, some round plastic food dehydrators have been available at retail outlets, by mail order, and from infomercials on TV. These units introduced many people to food drying. The ones I examined, however, were too lightly constructed to stand up to many years of regular and sustained use. They also lacked the capacity to do much in the way of drying a large quantity of food. While they provided the user with a good introduction to food drying, most of these food dryers, I expect, have wound up at yard sales or stuck away on a shelf.

Other commercially available dehydrators that I have seen used were large, high-quality units. These models are mounted on rollers and about the size of a portable dishwasher. They can dry a considerable quantity of food at a time, and were being put to heavy use by the family who owned the two of them. They are way too expensive for me, though.

When I decided to begin food drying, I did so after visiting with the folks using the floor-model

This interior view of the dehydrator shows trays of jerky being added. Some construction details are visible as well.

dehydrators described above. These friends showed me containers of dried diced carrots, onion slices, apples, and other fruits and vegetables. What impressed me the most about this method of preservation was the amount of space saved by drying the foods. For example, a 5-gallon bucket full of fresh carrots could be sliced, steamed, dried, and made to take up the space of a shoe box. Half of a 5-gallon bucket of apples, when sliced and dried, fits nicely in a gallon-sized freezer bag.

Since building our own dehydrator, we have dried jerky, apples, strawberries, carrots, onions, green beans, bananas, fruit leathers, and several other fruits and vegetables. Some of these were experiments, but we use the dryer each year to put up several bushels of sliced apples. These treats make a healthful and tasty alternative to junk snack food for the whole family, much better to munch on than potato chips.

Below are instructions for building a food dryer similar to ours. As with all the homestead projects that I describe, the main point to remember is to use your imagination, intuition, and abilities when building your own. Use what you have or what you can obtain easily and cheaply. Make your food dryer to suit your own circumstances. It might be nearly identical to the one described or a vastly improved version.

I began by purchasing light polycarbonate trays, then designed and built the dryer cabinet around them. After considering various materials for constructing the trays from scratch, and after studying the effects of these materials on some foods, I decided the trays were what I needed. The acids in some foods may react unfavorably with certain metals such as aluminum screen. Wood, as used in dowel-rod-type trays, may absorb food tastes and odors. Fiberglass screen can leave minute fiberglass splinters sticking to the dried food. Galvanized screen is out, because its zinc-based coating reacts with foods. One material that I have not tried but that may warrant experimentation is nylon screening. If stretched tightly on light wooden frames, this material might be durable enough to withstand repeated use. I do not know of any health problems posed by the use of the material on dryer trays. The trays we used were simply better than any alternative I could come up with at the time. I have not regretted starting with them.

Whatever the size or material of your trays, design the cabinet size around them, allowing for sufficient room below for the heat element and room to easily fit the trays within. I am providing the measurements below to serve as a guideline for your own construction process, because the type and size of trays that you come up with may vary from the ones I devised. Our dryer measures 48 inches tall by 14¾ inches wide by 16 inches deep. This allows the trays to be easily slid in and out, allows for framing of the cabinet, and places everything at a comfortable working height. The trays themselves measure 13¾ inches square. A slightly different-sized tray is available from Excalibur Dehydrators; see the contact information at the end of this section.

In the accompanying photographs, you can see some of the construction details of our dryer. I made base of heavy 1-inch particleboard because that is what I had. One-quarter-inch plywood made up the sides and top of the cabinet. I ripped 1 x 2s for the framing in the cabinet and for the cleats that support the drying trays.

A fan is mounted near the bottom in the back of the dryer. Ordinary screen wire covers the 6 x 6 opening. Holes cut near the top of each side are covered on the inside with strips of screen and allow moisture and air to escape while keeping insects out.

If you do not have one, a wide variety of suitable fan and motor assemblies is available from W. W. Grainger Distribution Group, 1901 Plantside Drive, Louisville, KY 40299. Request one of the firm's catalogs—but note that this is an electrical supply wholesaler. You may have to have a retailer order this unit for you. Order fan-motor assembly #7C7-27. The cost was less than $20. Just remember to use a relatively small fan (about 4 inches in diameter) and move the air rather slowly through the dryer. You want the fan to ventilate the box and move the heated air throughout. You do not want to cool the food on the trays.

The heat source is a ceramic heat coil screwed into a regular porcelain lamp base. The lamp fixture is secured to the base and wired either directly to a three-prong plug or through a thermostat. The coil was purchased from a local hardware store and is rated at 600 watts. At the time I built mine, the cost was less than five dollars, but that was a few years ago. The porcelain lamp base cost approximately a dollar. At the time I am writing this, the ceramic heat coils are becoming more difficult to obtain. Thanks to our ever-watchful

This ceramic heat coil uses a standard lamp base. They are available in 500 to 1,000 watts.

federal government, excessive regulations have caused many manufacturers to cease making the pieces. I have included one source at the end of this section.

Although it isn't absolutely necessary, I next added a thermostat assembly that I had scrounged up. This addition helped maintain an even temperature, as well as cutting down on tending and tray rotation. The thermostat easily handles the appropriate 100- to 150-degree temperature range. If you purchase a thermostat, specify a fairly narrow temperature spread for the on-off cycle.

Old unmatched hinges for the door and hooks and eyes for the closures were scrounged from the workshop.

DRIED APPLES

Since dried apples are so popular at our house, I will get you started by giving you the directions for drying them as an example of how simple it is to dry foods. First, the fruit must be cut into approximately ¼-inch slices. I use one of the countertop clamp-on slicers that core, slice, and peel the apples in one operation. It takes maybe three to five seconds to process one apple with one of these peelers. I have looked over several models, tried a few, and prefer the one I purchased from Back To Basics Products (see the end of the section for address). With this peeler, one simple knife cut is all you need to produce a handful of neatly prepared apple rings. By the way, you can save the peelings and cores and make a nice batch of apple jelly from them later.

As I peel the fruit, I place the rings in a bowl containing a solution made from a half cup or so of lemon juice and about 2 to 4 cups water. This acid bath prevents the apples from turning brown as they dry. I have also heard of some folks dipping the apple rings in plain 7-UP or Sprite for the same purpose. This also adds just a bit of sugar to the apple rings.

After dipping the apples, I place them in a plastic colander to drain and then arrange them on the dryer trays. Leave just a tiny space between the pieces of fruit. You do not want them to overlap—this could result in incomplete drying and later spoilage where the pieces overlapped. Let them dry to a chewy, leathery consistency and they are ready to store. This should take several hours. It is also helpful to rotate the trays every couple of hours, moving the trays with the less dry slices down toward the heat source. We have found that the 10 trays full of freshly dried apples fill up a 1-gallon zip-top plastic bag. After bagging, they are stored in the freezer. We do this only to add some shelf life to the finished product; freezing is not necessary.

The finished dried apples make great snacks for work, camping, hiking, or TV munching. They make a really good apple pie as well; just add a little extra liquid to your regular recipe.

Vegetables are similarly easy to dry, usually requiring a simple steaming prior to going into the dryer. Steaming, or blanching, of the vegetables before they are placed on the trays accomplishes two things. First, it seems to soften the food a bit, possibly allowing quicker and more thorough drying. Second, and most important, it kills enzymes that cause deterioration in the nutritional value, keeping qualities, and even the color of the dried food.

One secret to successfully drying fruits and vegetables is to use only the best of your garden. Cut out any bad spots or bruises. Some texts advise throwing out bruised or blemished fruit and vegetables entirely. While I haven't found this to be necessary, I do cut out any and all bruises and bad spots. Just use care and put only the best that you can into the dryer.

MAKING GOOD HOMEMADE JERKY

Jerky was once a common and vital trail food for many. It was light—jerky weighs about one-quarter the amount of fresh meat. It kept well—properly dried and stored, jerky can easily last through a year. It could be eaten without the need for preparing a fire or using utensils, which would slow down the traveler. Many a frontier traveler merely shaved or gnawed off a chunk of jerky and chewed while walking or riding.

Traditionally, jerky is merely strips of thinly sliced meat that have been dried. This method of meat preservation was adopted from the Indians and involved hanging the meat to air-dry on wooden racks. Sometimes, where insects or humidity were a problem, a low smoky fire was built under the drying meat. The smoke, from burning just about any hardwood, imparted flavor and perhaps helped in the preservation process as well. The low fire was important because too much heat would cook the meat instead of allowing it to dry.

Today hikers find jerky lightweight, satisfying, and easy to carry. Hunters often carry some for a quick snack or lunch. I sometimes take a few pieces along when I'm out cutting wood. Whatever the reason, jerky is still a versatile, tasty, and nutritious food. It is a good way to preserve deer or beef or other good, lean meat. In fact, here at our place, we have been digging down into the bottom of the freezer, cleaning it out to prepare for having another beef butchered. So I am using up some roasts and other cuts by converting them to jerky.

A CUT-AND-DRIED METHOD

I've made jerky in the traditional way by cutting and drying thin strips of lean meat. For making jerky, beef or deer is ideal. After trimming the fat, sinew, and membranes from the meat, marinate it overnight. Use one of the marinated recipes provided here, or experiment with your own. Each strip of meat is pierced near one end with a toothpick. The strips are then hung from a wire oven rack that I suspended above a woodstove.

I recommend using frozen meat to make jerky. Many parasites exist in both domestic and wild animals that can be transmitted to humans. Freezing of the meat helps kill these critters. As a rule of thumb, meat that is less than inch thick should be frozen for about 30 days; thicker pieces, for 60 days or more.

Jerky should be made from good lean meat only. Trim off as much fat as possible. Fat will not allow the jerky to dry as thoroughly as it should. Fatty jerky will not keep as well either—the fat may turn rancid.

Slice the trimmed meat into long strips about ¼ inch thick. If you work with the meat before it is completely thawed, it will be much easier to slice. Slice the strips with the grain or along the length of the muscle fibers to make chewy jerky. Cut across the grain, or across the muscles, to end up with more tender jerky. I personally prefer the cross-grain slices.

MARINADES AND SEASONINGS

For most of us, the thought of eating jerky that has been merely sliced up and dried doesn't sound too appealing. Granted, unseasoned and dried beef or deer strips do taste a bit bland. In fact, the first time or two I made jerky, I underseasoned the meat and it lacked the flavor I was hoping for. On the other hand, I added far too much black pepper to some antelope jerky once. It would make your eyes water! To save you some of the same trouble, below are some good ways to prepare the meat before drying.

Easy Jerky Marinade

1 c. pickling salt
1 gallon water

Mix the brine well and allow the strips to soak for about 24 hours. Pat them dry and place in the dryer.

Many folks prefer their jerky slightly spiced or peppered. This is pretty much a matter of taste (particularly when using hot peppers!), but here is some good spicy marinades for jerky.

Jerky Marinade (for 1 pound of meat)

½ c. soy sauce
1 Tbsp. Worcestershire sauce
½ tsp. black pepper
¼ tsp. ground hot pepper
¼ tsp. garlic
½ tsp. onion powder
1 tsp. hickory-smoke-flavored salt

Cajun-Spiced Jerky (for 1 pound of meat)

¼ c. soy sauce
½ tsp. black pepper
¼ tsp. garlic
1 tsp. salt
2 tsp. Cajun spice

THE SQUIRT-GUN METHOD

Not all jerky is made from the sliced strips of meat. A rather new twist on jerky making involves using a device that looks like a cross between a cake decorator and a caulking gun. This jerky gun squirts out a neat, uniform strip of meat for drying. The method works well but does require running the meat through a grinder to allow it to be pushed through the gun. There are a couple of ways to do this. If you have an old crank sausage grinder, it will do a fine job. I opted for modern technology and used the electric food processor. It did a great job. Either appliance should turn out meat minced finely enough for squirting through the gun. Using this method, the resulting strips of jerky are a little more manageable to eat, having been made from tiny bits of ground meat rather than a single strip of meat fibers.

There are a few manufacturers of these "jerky-guns." The one we have and use is made by American Harvest and was purchased at the local Wal-Mart.

To season the meat, I used a home blend as described above on one batch of jerky, and used the seasonings provided with the gun in another. Both were good, and I believe it's just a matter of preference.

When using the meat marinades above with a jerky gun, cut back on the amount of liquid listed. You will be mixing the spices and other ingredients right in with the ground meat, so the drier it is, the better and faster it will dry. In fact, the packets that come with the kit include dry ingredients only.

DRYING THE JERKY

As I mentioned, I have made a lot of good jerky by hanging strips of meat from an old oven rack suspended above the woodstove. This general method does a first-rate job and is preferred by many people. Naturally, if you do not have a food dryer or do not live in a climate with sufficiently low humidity, this will be a really good method to try.

When drying your jerky, first dry it for an hour at about 160 to 180 degrees. It is important, though, not to get the meat too hot. After that first hour, adjust the heat source itself or the distance of the meat from the heat source, so that it runs from about 140 to 160 degrees. Remember, you do not want to cook it. Keep an eye on it to test it for readiness.

The key is to heat the meat slowly enough to dry it without over-cooking. If you heat too fast, the outside gets crusty while the inside is not dry enough. But you do need to heat the meat quickly enough to get it out of the danger zone (40 to 140 degrees) as quickly as possible.

You can test your jerky to see when it has become dry enough by just breaking a piece of it. Take a piece from the dryer or rack and allow it to cool. Then just break the piece in two. It should not break cleanly— that is, snap in two. Rather, it should bend and then sort of splinter and break, much as a green stick might. Give it another few hours after that. Remember, though, that overdrying is preferred to underdrying. With the latter, any retained moisture could allow bacterial growth and spoilage.

When the jerky is sufficiently dried, remove it from the heat source. If there are beads of oil present, pat the strips dry with a paper towel. I then store the jerky in large plastic zipbags and put them in the freezer. This is not essential, but it does add storage life to the finished product. At least be sure to keep the jerky in a sealed container. Dried jerky takes up moisture readily. Even if you dry jerky enough to prevent growth of microorganisms, over time the meat could reabsorb enough moisture to allow the little critters to grow again.

Making jerky is a practical method for preserving meat on just about every place. Once you try making your own jerky, those small, overpriced jerky strips found in the convenience store will seem much less appealing. In addition, it can stretch the use of your dehydrator beyond the gardening season.

DRIED FLOWERS, ANYONE?

My wife has also used our food dryer to dry sprays of flowers such as baby's breath, statice, and globe amaranth for use in dried bouquets, wreaths, and swags. It worked quite well for this, too, as she prepared those items for sale. Herbs can also be dried with little or no preparation. Simply use the best ones you can pick, spread them evenly on the dryer trays, and turn the heat to a moderate setting, about 140 to 150. You should end up with some beautiful and fragrant dried plants for sale or use.

DEHYDRATING RESOURCES

For more information on drying specific foods, I recommend consulting a good book on the subject, such as *Making the Best of Basics: Family Preparedness Handbook*, by James Talmage Stevens (Gold Leaf Press). This has a terrific section devoted to food drying. One of the early editions of this book provided the inspiration for our own dehydrator.

Stocking Up III is another fine food-preservation manual. It is edited by Carol Hupping of Rodale Press. It covers this and almost all other aspects of food preservation.

For some of the items listed in this article, contact:

W. W. GRAINGER, INC. You can visit its Web site at www.grainger.com to browse the on-line catalog. Use the site's search function to locate a Grainger outlets near you. You can also write to W. W. Grainger, Inc., 100 Grainger Parkway, Lake Forest, IL 60045-5201.

AKINSUN HEAT CO., INC., is a source of ceramic heat coils. Contact 1531 Burgundy Parkway, Streamwood, IL 60107, 1-630-289-9393, www.akinsun.com. Two models are available: #CS 1003-01 (500 watts) and #CS 1003-02 (660 watts).

EXCALIBUR FOOD DRYERS, 6083 Power Inn Road, Sacramento, CA 95824, 916-381-4254. These folks have a Web site under construction at www.excaliburdehydrator.com. They make high-quality food dehydrators. They also have trays available periodically. Call them for availability and prices.

BACK TO BASICS PRODUCTS, 11660 South State Street, Draper, UT 84020, 1-801-571-7349, www.backtobasicsproducts.com. This firm offers the top-notch apple peeler mentioned in this article and other similar food-preparation devices.

NESCO AMERICAN HARVEST. For information on the American Harvest Jerky Works Kit, contact: P.O. Box 159, Chaska, MN 55318-0159, 1-800-288-4545, www.nesco.com.

Storing and Using Wheat

One of the staple foods used by almost every homesteader is wheat. Whether grown or bought, purchased as flour, or ground at home, wheat provides, literally, our bread of life. Whole wheat can be made into hundreds of tasty and nutritious breads and foods and is deserving of its prominent place in our diet.

With most of today's store-bought flours bleached, enriched, softened, and saturated with preservatives, grinding your own flour can make not only good economic sense, but good health sense as well. Home wheat storage is practical, because flour that is stored at room temperature for over a month loses practically all of its food value. With your own supply of stored wheat, however, you can easily and quickly produce a week's worth of fresh whole-wheat flour. For those of us interested in self-sufficient, self-reliant living, wheat offers much by way of helping us sever unnecessary ties to the "supermarket economy," as well as providing more nutritious food for our families and ourselves. Let's take a look at some good ways to obtain, store, and use this golden grain.

HOW MUCH TO STORE?

Now, that's a good question. A lot depends upon how many are in your family and how much you can or will use wheat. I am going to give you a variety of ways to use the grain, but just exactly how much you will use a stored supply of wheat is for you to decide. Here are the guidelines for a one-year supply given by the Federal Emergency Management Agency (FEMA):

ONE-YEAR SUPPLY—FEMA RECOMMENDATIONS

Adult Males, Pregnant or Nursing Mothers,
Active Teenagers 14–18..275 lbs. wheat
Women, Youths 7–13, Seniors ....175 lbs. wheat
Small Children age 6 and under...60 lbs. wheat

As you can see, the amount of wheat needed for storage can add up pretty quickly. By the time you figure an average couple with three children, you can expect to set about anywhere from 600 to 1,100 pounds of wheat. That translates to somewhere between 12 and 25 buckets. An important factor to remember when laying in your supply is simply this: Use it! A year's supply of wheat will not do any good just growing old on the shelf. If your family is not used to the processing and using of fresh raw wheat, then phase it in over a period of time. Make a special event out of grinding, sifting, and baking with it. (This is a good time to tell your youngsters the story of the Little Red Hen.)

For those who wish to obtain their wheat in bulk, unprocessed form, I offer the following suggestions: First, locate a good source of the grain. If you can grow your own, so much the better. You will then have total control over your wheat from seed to finished loaf. Growing, harvesting, processing, and using wheat on the home scale may be impractical for many, due to acreage, time, or desire. However, if you live in an area where wheat farming is common, you can usually work out a deal to purchase a few bushels from one of the local farmers. If you are a stickler for using organically grown grain, you will probably have a more difficult time locating a source, but keep looking. They're out there, and becoming more common. Another source to consider is the local feed mill or agricultural co-op. There you can probably get the grain already dried, although you may wish to clean it a bit before storage. Commercial suppliers of bulk grains and foods for home use are around, providing another source of wheat. Check a few of these out and compare their products, prices, and shipping costs. Some are listed at the end of this section.

Possibly more important than how the grain is raised is the type of wheat you have and how it is stored. For the home baker's use, a dark hard winter or spring wheat is probably best. These types tend to store best. To prepare the wheat for storage, you must first be sure that it is clean enough for human use. To do this, I have used old-fashioned wind power to clean the wheat from the chaff, also known as winnowing. Toss shovelfuls of wheat into the air on a windy day, or in front of a large fan. The chaff is simply blown away, and the whole grains will drop onto your tarp, plastic sheet, or whatever. You may have to do this a few times to obtain grain clean enough to suit you. The method works well, and I don't know of a better one to clean your grain.

Next, you must make sure that the grain is dry enough to be stored. For home storage, wheat should contain no more than 10 percent moisture. This low moisture content will help inhibit insect infestation, as well as preventing molding and spoilage. As I mentioned above, you may be able to get wheat that has already been dried from your local feed mill or co-op. But unless you are drying an extremely large quantity or live in an especially humid area, you should be able to easily dry more than enough to suit your needs. To dry the grain, you may use a food dryer, although the time involved in drying such small quantities at a time might make this method prohibitive. I have spread out large quantities of cleaned wheat on a sheet of black plastic on the deck located on the south side of my house. After a hot afternoon, the direct heat and air combined with the reflected heat from the house lowered the moisture sufficiently to allow me to complete the storage process. I checked the moisture percentage on an ordinary moisture meter that most grain farmers have. If you purchased wheat locally, the farmer might test your dried wheat for you. The local grain elevator will have a moisture meter and can probably test it for you as well. Finally, if you are really serious about regularly laying in a home wheat supply, you might purchase your own tester. Expect to pay at least $150 for one, though. Check your farm supply store for availability, brands, and prices. A source for obtaining more information is listed at the end of this section.

If the sun-drying process takes more than one day, merely cover the grain with another plastic sheet come evening, and resume drying in the morning. Note that wheat draws moisture, so watch to keep your grain from being exposed to very high humidity.

Now that we have the wheat cleaned and dried, we are ready to place it in storage. I recommend using 5-gallon plastic buckets for this purpose. They will hold usable quantities of wheat, and are light enough to handle easily. Their round design allows air to circulate between them, and they usually have a gasket lining the lid that provides an airtight seal. Finally, you can usually get all of them you need for little or nothing from local restaurants, delis, bakeries, or other businesses that purchase bulk food supplies. I do not put the wheat directly into the buckets; I prefer to put it into a plastic bag first. To do this, I bought some nondeodorized 13-gallon kitchen-sized garbage bags. Line each bucket with one of the bags, folding the excess down over the top of the bucket for the time being. Pour in enough of the cleaned and dried wheat to come within a couple of inches of the top. At this point, I took an ordinary cotton ball and added a dozen or so drops of carbon disulfide, which I obtained from a local drugstore. (As with any chemical compound, exercise caution in the handling, use, and storage of carbon disulfide.) I then placed the dampened cotton ball into an ordinary baby food jar and secured the lid, through which I'd punched several small nail holes. I placed the jar, bottom-end up, into the wheat itself so just its bottom was exposed. Inverting the jar in the grain allows the fumes to spread throughout. I then gathered up the excess plastic bag and, removing as much of the air as possible, twisted it shut and attached a wire tie. The lid was placed atop the bucket and tapped firmly into place. This fumigation treatment should take care of any residual creepy-crawlies that might lurk in the grain and destroy any eggs that may have been deposited. Wheat that has been treated in this manner and kept in a cool dry place should remain good for years. Before using the fumigated wheat, I remove the jar and allow the grain to air out for about 24 hours.

I have also participated in group canning sessions where dried wheat was used to fill a number 10 can to within ¼ inch or so of the top. Next, I put an oxygen absorber packet on top of the wheat. A lid was put in place, and the can was placed on the electrically powered canner. The machine rolled a perfect crimp as it sealed the lid onto the can. The cans store nicely on shelves in the basement and are of a convenient quantity to work with.

Obviously, the home miller will need a method of grinding the wheat into flour. There are dozens of different grain mills available, from hand-cranked steel burr mills to electric-powered stone mills; you can spend just about any amount you want on a wheat grinder. I have used an old Corona hand-powered mill with steel burrs for several years with great results. The only change I have

I usually grind the wheat twice to get the fine flour needed for baking.

considered is to possibly add a small pulley and set up the mill to use with bicycle power or a motor. As with many purchases, you will need to evaluate the amount of use that you expect the grinder to see against the cost of the machine. Decide whether you can use the steel burr grinder or want to get stone-ground flour. Do you want an electric model or will a hand-powered one do the job?

Wheat is a surprisingly versatile grain. Of course, far and away its most popular and most suitable use is for making browned and fragrant loaves of fine bread. However, this cereal can be used in other ways.

One of my favorite uses of wheat comes as a by-product of the grinding of a batch of fresh wheat flour. After I grind up a quantity of wheat into flour, it is sifted and put aside to use in breads and cakes. I take the coarse "leavings" and either let them soak overnight in water, or start it directly in the morning. Take about 2 cups of the coarse cereal and add about 6 cups of water. Set it on the stove to simmer for about 40 minutes. Once it has thickened nicely, spoon it into bowls, add a dollop of butter, and some honey, and sit down to a real stick-with-you breakfast! This makes one of the best hot cereals I've ever tasted.

Another good use for wheat is to use the whole kernel or berry to make bulgur. This wholesome and versatile food is made by steaming or soaking the whole-wheat berry. The result can then be used in a wide variety of dishes, from soups to crunchy snacks, from main dishes to side dishes.

To make your own batch of bulgur, you will first need to take a large pot such as a cold packer and place a rack in the bottom. Add water almost to the level of the rack. Put a cup of wheat, a cup of water, and a dash of salt into a smaller pot and place it on the rack. Next, cover the large pot and place it on high heat for about 15 minutes. Reduce the heat and steam until the wheat absorbs all the water in the smaller pot. Once the wheat kernels have fluffed up nicely, you can remove and use them or store them for up to two weeks in the refrigerator.

Bulgur may be used as a hot breakfast cereal by adding milk and sweetener. You can also make a very tasty snack by lightly seasoning a couple of cups of bulgur, spreading it out on a cookie sheet,

A ball of dough being kneaded before being shaped into a loaf.

and toasting it in a moderate oven until it is lightly browned and crunchy. Bulgur can be added with good results to any dish that calls for rice or barley. Many soups and salads are enhanced by adding this ingredient. Use your imagination in utilizing this healthful food.

Of course, the most widely accepted use for wheat is for the making of bread. This basic food can be easily prepared at home and is satisfying not only in its preparation but in its nutritional value as well. Your own rich brown loaves of bread will bear no resemblance to the pasty slices that come from the supermarket.

Here are a few recipes for whole-wheat bread that you should enjoy.

Whole-Wheat Bread 1 (2 loaves)

1 Tbsp. dry yeast
2½ c. warm water
¼ c. plus 2 Tbsp. honey
3 Tbsp. oil
6 c. whole-wheat flour

First, dissolve the yeast in the warm water. Add to ¼ c. of the honey in a large mixing bowl. Then add the oil. Add the flour to the liquid mixture. Knead the dough until it is smooth, then cover and let it rise until it is doubled in bulk. Punch down the dough and form into two loaves. Place the loaves into two greased 9 x 5 loaf pans and allow to rise again until doubled in bulk. Bake the loaves in a preheated 350-degree oven for about 30 minutes.

This is a good basic recipe to which can be added other ingredients to provide flavor and texture. Consider adding a few raisins or some cinnamon, sunflower seeds, bulgur, or chopped dates to give the bread a different and tasty twist.

Whole-Wheat Bread 2 (1 loaf)

1 pkg. yeast
3 Tbsp. dark brown sugar
¾ c. warm water
2¾ c. whole-wheat flour
3 Tbsp. nonfat dry milk powder
3 Tbsp. vegetable oil
1 tsp. salt
1 large egg or 2 large egg whites

Stir the yeast and sugar into the water and let it stand until foamy, about 5 minutes. Into a large mixing bowl, put the rest of the ingredients and mix well. Make a depression in the center, pour in the yeast mixture, and work it into the rest. Put the dough out onto a floured board and knead until smooth and elastic (about 10 minutes). Transfer the dough to a large plastic bag, squeeze the air out, and seal the top of the bag. Place the dough into a bowl to rise in a warm location. Allow it to rise until doubled in size, about 1 hour. Punch the dough down and shape it into a smooth ball. Place the smooth side up on an oiled baking sheet and cover it loosely with oiled plastic. Let it rise in a warm spot until doubled in size, about 45 to 50 minutes. Preheat your oven to 375 degrees. About 15 minutes before baking, put the rack in the center of the oven. Lightly dust the top of the loaf with flour. Place the loaf in the oven and bake until the bread is well browned and sounds hollow when rapped on the bottom. This should take about 30 to 35 minutes. Remove the loaf from the oven and pan. Place it on a cooling rack.

Whole-Wheat Bread 3 (6 loaves)

8 c. milk
3 pkgs. yeast
¾ c. water
1 c. plus 1 Tbsp. sugar
12 c. whole-wheat flour
¾ c. shortening
½ c. molasses
2 Tbsp. salt

Scald the milk. Dissolve the yeast in ⅔ cup of the water while the milk is cooling. Dissolve 1 cup of the sugar in the hot milk. Stir all the ingredients in a large bowl, turn out onto a floured board, and knead for about 5 minutes, adding flour a little at a time, if necessary. Knead the dough for about 5 minutes. Let the dough rise until doubled in bulk (about 1½ to 2 hours). Knead the dough down and shape it into six loaves. Put in greased loaf pans. Let it rise again in the pans until doubled. Bake in a preheated 375-degree oven for about 40 minutes. Turn the loaves onto a wire rack and allow them to cool.

There are many more recipes and uses for wheat. Your own experimentation will yield great results in cooking with this great cereal grain.

WHEAT RESOURCES

If you would like to learn more about wheat storage and use, I recommend looking for the book *Making the Best of Basics—Family Preparedness Handbook*, by James Talmage Stevens, published by Gold Leaf Press. This excellent book deals with a wide variety of topics for self-reliant living.

If you cannot find a source for buying wheat locally, you might want to check out these mail-order suppliers:

WALTON FEED has been around for more than 50 years and has a great selection of grains and other dried foods. Contact 135 North 10th Street, P.O. Box 307, Montpelier, ID 83254, 1-800-847-0465, www.waltonfeed.com.

EMERGENCY ESSENTIALS has been providing emergency supplies since 1987. Contact 352 South Commerce Loop, Suite B, Orem, UT 84058, 1-800-999-1863, www.beprepared.com.

To purchase moisture meters:

FARMEX INCORPORATED, 10325 State Route 43, Streetsboro, OH 44241, 1-800-821-9542, www.farmexinc.com. Farmex MT3 units are available at Rural King and other farm supply outlets.

Winemaking at Home

The art of winemaking is an ancient and time-honored one. My guess is that some early man let his grapes or juice set a little too long, and a strange, yet not unpleasant taste accompanied the ingesting of the fermented foodstuff. After gorging himself on the mysterious concoction, he probably ended up collapsing on the floor of the cave and began seeing pink mastodons walking across the ceiling. Perhaps he decided that he could repeat the experience by deliberately allowing the grapes to ferment. The rest is history.

From the days of early human allowing natural fermentation of fruit and juice to occur in crude vessels, to the high-tech, computer-controlled, stainless-steel wineries of today, the basic process of winemaking has remained unchanged. Very simply put, wine is made when yeast converts fruit sugar to alcohol. Winemaking involves influencing and controlling the fermentation process to obtain wine of a desired flavor with the desired degree of sweetness and alcohol content.

The home winemaker can create a multitude of tasty and well-made wines. As with the other foods produced on your home place, you'll know exactly what ingredients are in the finished product. You don't need to use potentially harmful chemicals or clarifying agents, yet you can still end up with superb wines, suitable for serving to even the most finicky friends. Of course, not every wine will please every taste, but that, again, is one of the pleasures of making your own wine. You can experiment with ingredients, sugar content, yeast types, and fermentation methods. By recording the information, you can repeat your successes and discard the failures. In fact, even bad wine can be permitted to complete the fermentation by exposing it to air, resulting in some good and very usable vinegar. Good wine recipes are also something to pass on to offspring, much as a grandfather passes down a treasured shotgun.

Essentially, home winemaking is just another part of being as self-sufficient as possible. By possessing the knowledge and ability to make your own fine wines at home, you can save a good deal of money, depending upon your level of wine consumption. Good homemade wine is just another product and result of a successful self-sufficient and self-reliant homestead. It is a good use of fruit produced on the home place. In many cases, even home-produced honey can be used to sweeten your wines.

Of course, the government has exercised control over even the making of homemade wine. Current regulations from the U.S. Bureau of Alcohol, Tobacco, and Firearms permit the head of a household to make up to 100 gallons of wine or beer for each adult in the household, with a 200-gallon limit. Such production is limited to beverages produced for consumption in the home. I'd suggest that you locate the ATF office serving your area in a directory listing federal government agencies, and contact them for further information. Note, too, that the regulations apply to the making of wine and beer only, and not whiskeys, brandies, or other *distilled* spirits. The making of such beverages is a big governmental "no-no," frowned upon by the ATF and punishable by fines and jail time.

The actual process of making wine is not overly complicated, but it does require a bit of time in the kitchen and enough space to allow the fermenting juice to do its thing. Simple setups such as the one illustrated are very serviceable and dependable. In fact, I use one or more of the jug-and-tube arrangements nearly every time I make wine. For larger batches, 5- or 6-gallon glass jugs are available from winemaking supply or some industrial outlets. The caps of these large jugs can be fitted with a commercially available air lock or can easily, and at no cost, be rigged up to work just like the milk jug and tube as illustrated. For the more ambitious winemaker who anticipates many evenings of wine guzzling around the winter woodstove, I recommend purchasing a used whiskey barrel or two to be used as the fermenting vessel. But remember that it takes a pretty good wine appetite to down 50 gallons of homemade wine. Additionally, especially for the beginner, a 1- or 2-gallon mistake is easier to get rid of than a 50-gallon one. So follow the general directions given here and enjoy some mighty tasty wine that you'll be delighted to serve to your friends. Once you get the hang of it, don't be afraid to experiment with ingredients or to adjust the sugar content to better suit your taste. You will make a few mistakes, but even many of those will be quite drinkable! After a while, though, you will end up with a favorite wine of your own making and will likely have a hard time answering requests for samples of bottles of the delightful drink.

The accompanying illustration shows how easily a home fermentation setup can be made for little or no cost at all.

As you can see, an ordinary plastic milk jug is recycled to become the fermentation vessel. The cap of the jug is punched to accommodate a length of plastic tubing, which in turn runs into a jar of water. This arrangement forms the air lock and provides an escape for the gases forming within the fermentation jug, yet allows no air into the vessel to spoil the wine. The tubing that I used was just the size to allow me to use a

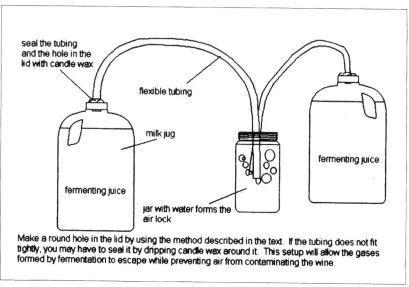

seal the tubing and the hole in the lid with candle wax

flexible tubing

milk jug

fermenting juice

jar with water forms the air lock

fermenting juice

Make a round hole in the lid by using the method described in the text. If the tubing does not fit tightly, you may have to seal it by dripping candle wax around it. This setup will allow the gases formed by fermentation to escape while preventing air from contaminating the wine.

A typical home winemaking setup.

fired .357 magnum pistol case to neatly punch the hole in the plastic jug lid. The tubing fit tightly into the hole, but I sealed it with a bit of melted candle wax just to make sure there were no leaks. You can easily make several of these jugs and tubes and run them all into the same vessel of water.

You may also purchase air locks in a variety of styles for use on different fermenting containers. In the photographs, you can see some that are fitted to caps that screw onto plastic jugs. A larger threaded air lock is one I made to fit a 6-gallon glass carboy. More common are air locks that use friction-fitted stoppers inserted into the jug or bottle. Whichever style or method you decide to use, the main thing to remember is to be sure that it is airtight.

Air locks for making homemade wine. The first two fit onto ordinary plastic milk jugs. The third has been adapted to fit the cap on a 6-gallon glass carboy.

It is important to use clean and sanitary equipment when making wine. Be sure to wash all your equipment thoroughly to prevent contamination by wild yeast, mold, or bacteria. I generally use just plenty of hot soap and water to clean my containers and equipment.

Be sure to have a place where you fermenting wine can sit undisturbed. Further, the temperature of the fermenting wine has a great effect on how the finished product will turn out. It is important to place your wine in an area where fermentation temperatures can remain between 70 and 75 degrees without a lot of variation. If the temperature is too cool, then fermentation may stop before all the alcohol is made. If the wine-to-be is allowed to get too warm, then the finished product could have an off taste.

If you are not particularly averse to adding chemical ingredients to your wine, then you may want to consider the use of Campden tablets when starting your wine. Campden tablets are dissolved into the raw juice prior to fermentation. One crushed tablet per gallon of water or juice is stirred in well. The tablets release sulfur dioxide in the juice and kill the wild molds and bacteria that occur naturally in the fruits and can cause off tastes in the finished wine. You may also crush several of them and add them to the water used to clean your equipment. Campden tablets are available from all the main suppliers of winemaking ingredients and are quite inexpensive insurance for good finished wine.

The recipes below are the same ones that we use here at home to make many very good wines. Try them yourself, and adjust the ingredients, if necessary, to make the wine acceptable to your taste. The first recipe includes the essential method to be used with other recipes. On subsequent recipes, additional instructions are included as necessary.

Just about any type of grapes can be used for this recipe. The resulting wine will please just about anyone.

Grape Wine

4 lbs. grapes
1 gallon boiling water
3½ lbs. sugar
1 pkg. dry yeast

Pick the grapes from the stalks and crush them by hand. Pour the boiling water over them and leave to soak for 48 hours. Strain and put the juice through a jelly bag or similar material to remove as much of the fine pulp as possible. Put the juice in a large pan and heat slightly. Add the sugar to the warm juice (the sugar will dissolve better in the heated juice than if it were cold). When the sugar is dissolved, sprinkle the yeast on top and stir in. Put the soon-to-be wine into the fermenting vessel, attach the air lock, and ferment for 14 days or until bubbles are no longer emitted from the plastic tube. After fermenting is complete, siphon the new wine into a clean container, being careful not to shake the container and disturb the sediment in the bottom. Place the container in a cool place to permit further settling of solids. If any sign of fermentation is present, reattach the air lock; it won't hurt a thing. Otherwise, just cap the container. After a few months, again siphon off the wine. This time it should be much clearer. It should now be ready for bottling and/or drinking. If this wine is stored in gallon plastic jugs or corked glass bottles, it will continue to age and improve in quality.

Note: Remember, siphoning the new wine prevents the sediment (also called the lees) from being disturbed. Be careful when siphoning not to let the wine go back through the tube and stir up the lees.

The process of siphoning off the wine to allow the sediment to settle out is called racking. Usually one racking is all that is necessary to produce a good clear wine; however, the wine may be racked two or three times if required.

Black Raspberry Wine (my personal favorite)

4½ lbs. raspberries
1 gallon boiling water
3½ lbs. sugar
1 pkg. yeast

Crush the raspberries, pour the boiling water over them, and leave to soak for 48 hours. Strain the juice and pulp through a jelly bag. Heat the strained juice to near boiling and simmer for 2 minutes. Pour the hot liquid over the sugar and stir until all the sugar is dissolved. Allow the brew to cool, then sprinkle the yeast on top and stir in. Funnel into the fermenting vessel and attach an air lock. Ferment for 14 days or until fermentation ceases. Bottle as with Grape Wine. Enjoyed on a cold winter evening, this wine is pure ambrosia!

Cherry Wine

6 lbs. cherries
1 gallon boiling water
4 lbs. sugar
1 pkg. yeast

Crush the cherries and pour the boiling water over them. Leave to soak for 48 hours. Strain through a piece of muslin and then through a jelly bag. Heat the juice to near boiling and simmer for a couple of minutes. Pour the hot juice over the sugar and stir until all the sugar is dissolved. As soon as the sweetened juice is cool, sprinkle the yeast on top and stir in. Put into the fermenting vessel, attach an air lock, and ferment for 14 days. Bottle as with Grape Wine.

Blackberry Wine

5 lbs. blackberries
1 gallon boiling water
4 lbs. sugar
1 pkg. yeast

Crush the berries and pour the boiling water over them. While the pulp is still hot, strain through a piece of muslin and then put through a jelly bag. Heat the strained juice to near boiling and simmer for a couple of minutes. Pour the hot juice over the sugar and stir until all the sugar is dissolved. As soon as the brew is cooled, add the yeast and stir in. Put into the fermenting vessel and attach an air lock. Let the wine work for 2 weeks or until fermentation ceases. Bottle as with Grape Wine.

Honey-Berry Wine

1 c. honey
1 c. crushed strawberries
4 lbs. sugar
1 gallon water
1 pkg. yeast

Put the honey and fruit into a large vessel. Boil half the sugar in a quart of the water for a couple of minutes. Cool and add to the honey and fruit. Put in a gallon of boiled and cooled water. Add the yeast. Boil the remaining sugar in a quart of water. Cool and add. Put the brew into the fermenting vessel and work until all fermentation stops. Siphon, rack, and bottle. This is a good one!

This is not a real whiskey—that is, a distilled liquor. The wheat added to the wine gives it a whiskeylike appearance and taste. It is another very good wine.

Up-North Whiskey

1 gallon water
4 lbs. sugar
2 lbs. wheat
2 lbs. raisins
4 large oranges
1 pkg. yeast

Heat the water to boiling and pour over the sugar. Stir until dissolved and add the wheat and chopped-up raisins. Cut up the oranges and add the "fresh-squoze" juice into the rest of the brew. Allow it all to cool, then add the yeast and stir in. Pour into the fermenting vessel and allow to work until all fermentation stops, usually in 2 to 3 weeks. Bottle as with the Grape Wine.

Strawberry Wine

1 gallon water
4 lbs. strawberries
2½ lbs. sugar
1 pkg. yeast

Boil the water and pour it over the crushed fruit. Let stand for a few hours, stirring occasionally. Strain well through a jelly bag. Heat the mixture to near boiling and simmer for 2 minutes. Pour over the sugar and stir until all is dissolved. Allow the whole mess to cool, sprinkle the yeast on top, and stir in. Put it to working in the fermenting vessel, and once all fermentation has ceased, rack and bottle.

This is an easily prepared wine using frozen grape juice concentrate. Tasty! Note: Try using frozen concentrate of white grape juice. It makes a delightful white wine.

Welch Wine

7–12-oz. cans frozen grape juice concentrate
7–8 lbs. sugar
1 pkg. yeast
5 gallons warm water

Mix the juice concentrate into the warm water. Make sure that all the juice dissolves. Add the sugar to the mixture, stirring until all is dissolved. As soon as everything is cooled to approximately room temperature or slightly above, add the yeast and stir in. Pour into your fermentation vessels and attach air locks. Let the wine work until all signs of fermentation stop. Siphon off and bottle.

Wild Grape Wine (using wild fox grapes)

8 lbs. wild grapes
2 gallons boiling water
5 lbs. sugar
1 pkg. yeast

Strip the grapes from the stalks and crush them in a large crock or pan. Pour the boiling water over the fruit and let soak for 48 hours. Strain

the juice through muslin, and then through a jelly bag. Heat the juice
to near boiling and add the sugar, stirring until all is dissolved. Once the
mixture is cooled, add the yeast and stir in. Funnel into the fermenting
vessel and attach the air lock. Let it work for 14 days or until fermentation ceases. Siphon off and bottle.

Country Peach Wine

5 lbs. fresh ripe peaches
1 gallon water
4 lbs. sugar
1 pkg. yeast

Cut up the peaches and remove the stones. Heat the water to boiling
and pour over the fruit. Let stand for a few hours. As soon as the mixture cools well, crush the fruit well by hand. Let the mixture stand for
48 hours. Crush the fruit well again, then strain through fine muslin.
Heat the juice to boiling and simmer for 10 to 12 minutes. Next, pour
the hot juice over the sugar and stir until well blended. Allow the whole
solution to cool, then add the yeast by sprinkling it into the juice and
stirring it in. Put the liquid into the fermenting vessels and allow it to
work for about 14 days or until it stops. Siphon off and bottle. This one
is a real taste of summer on a cold winter day!

Apple Wine

6 lbs. good-quality apples
1 gallon water
4 lbs. sugar
1 lb. raisins
1 pkg. yeast

Using clean apples, grate them and discard the cores. Put the grated fruit
into the water and soak for 48 hours. Stir occasionally, then crush with
your hands and strain through fine muslin. Put the juice through a jelly
bag if you have one. Heat the juice just to boiling and simmer for 5 minutes. Pour the hot liquid over the sugar and stir until all the sugar is dissolved. Add the cut-up raisins. When the mixture has cooled, sprinkle
in the yeast and stir until blended. Attach an air lock and ferment for
14 days or until fermentation ceases, then siphon, strain, and bottle.

Wild Plum Wine 1

2½ lbs. wild plums
2½ lbs. sugar
½ tsp. yeast nutrient
½ tsp. pectic enzyme powder
1 Campden tablet
1½ tsp. acid blend
1 pkg. wine yeast
1 gallon water

Use only sound, fully ripe fruit. Remove the pits and crush the fruit. Put all the ingredients except the yeast and water into the primary fermentor—a large crock or bucket will do. Add the yeast as directed. Normally, if using tablets, 1 tablet per gallon of sugar is called for. Heat the water and add to the crock. Stir to dissolve the sugar. Cover with a plastic sheet. When the must has cooled to room temperature, add the yeast. Stir the must daily for 5 to 6 days. Strain out all the fruit pulp, press it, and put the juice in with the must. Siphon into gallon jugs or similar containers and attach the fermentation locks. In about 3 weeks, fermentation should cease. Rack the new wine. In about 3 months, rack it again. Once the wine is clear, bottle it. This wine is best when aged for about a year.

This is an even simpler recipe that will turn out about a gallon of very tasty lighter-bodied wild plum wine. Make as directed above.

Wild Plum Wine 2

5 lbs. wild plums
3 lbs. sugar
1 pkg. wine yeast
yeast nutrient tablets
1 gallon water

For a heavier-bodied wine, try this recipe. It will also yield about a gallon of wine.

Wild Plum Wine 3

8 lbs. plums
4 lbs. sugar
1 pkg. yeast
yeast nutrient tablets
7 pints water

This is for a large-scale batch!

Raisin Jack

22 lbs. raisins
5 lbs. prunes (pitted)
1 case sweet oranges
8–10 lbs. cornmeal
140 lbs. sugar
12 pkgs. dry yeast

Grind the raisins, prunes, and oranges together. Put the cornmeal in a cloth bag and put into a half barrel or large crock. Dissolve 40 pounds of sugar in 5 gallons of hot water, and dissolve the yeast in warm water. Add this to the fruits. Stir and press the cornmeal bag twice daily for about 7 to 8 days. Press out all the juice and put into a 50-gallon wooden whiskey barrel. Dissolve another 100 pounds of sugar in hot water, put into the barrel, and fill to the top. Put a hose or tube through a stopper and fix securely into the bunghole of the barrel. Lead the tube into a jar of water to make the air lock. Top off the barrel with water each day for 1 week.

BOTTLING YOUR WINE

Bottling your homemade wine does not need to be anything fancy. In fact, I often leave it in plastic milk jugs after having racked it once or twice. Just make sure that there is no air getting to the wine or it will turn to vinegar. Of course, that can still be used in cooking, but even if you cook a lot, I doubt that you will have much need for a gallon or two of wine vinegar.

Many folks save wine bottles and have their friends do the same. You can bottle your wine in bottles with threaded tops and caps. I have bottled lots of it in this type of container.

Our own homemade wine.

You may also use what is called "cork finish" bottles, which are wine bottles that are manufactured to take a straight-sided bottle cork. These bottles may be saved, obtained from friends, and even often gotten free from a restaurant where you have a contact. Corks and the corker are available from wine supply shops and are simple to use.

The corker I have used resembles a giant duck call—a large wooden cylinder. With this device, a cork is place into a slot in the cylinder and the device is placed firmly atop a filled bottle. A wooden plunger is then tapped with a mallet or small hammer until the cork is shoved down a tapered cylinder and into the bottleneck. Once the plunger is fully depressed, lift off the corker and you will see the cork seated flush with the bottle top. Then all you have to do is devise and apply a label of some sort—as simple or as elaborate as you wish.

Winemaking at home can be a very enjoyable and rewarding pursuit. As with most other facets of self-reliant living, try to use what you have or can make or scrounge. Experiment with your own types of fruit and proportions of ingredients. I'm sure that you will come up with some very drinkable wines, made at home, from the best ingredients available.

WINEMAKING RESOURCES

Some sources for winemaking supplies include:

BUTLER WINERY, 1022 North College Avenue, Bloomington, IN 47401, www.butlerwinery.com.

E. C. KRAUS, 733 South Northern Boulevard, P.O. Box 7850, Independence, MO 64054, www.eckraus.com.

THE WINEMAKING HOMEPAGE, http://winemaking.jackkeller.net/shops. asp. This Web site lists winemaking suppliers all over the country. You might find one in your local area.

6

WOOD & WOODLOT MANAGEMENT

The Homestead Woodlot

Chain Saws

Heating with Wood

Firewood

The Homestead Woodlot

I am not a professional forester, nor do I play one on TV. I have, however, dealt with them in my profession and have used their services on
my own property. I have also heard many horror stories from landowners who chose not to go to the expense of hiring a consultant forester to
assist them in conducting a timber sale—and have then had some ter-
rible experiences in dealing with timber harvesters.

Your woodland can be a valuable crop producer, fuel supply,
wildlife habitat, and general recreation area for your family. A well-man-
aged forest or woodland will yield many benefits, including:

☞ The environmental effect of having many oxygen-producing trees.

☞ Increased numbers and species of wildlife.

☞ Marketable timber.

☞ Firewood.

☞ Recreation—camping, hiking, and more.

☞ Privacy—your woodlot secludes or screens you from the neighbors.

☞ Aesthetics—the mere pleasures of have a forest area to wander in.

THE CONSULTANT FORESTER

You don't need a vast forest to warrant the use of a forester. In fact, any
woodlot with marketable timber can benefit from the services of a qualified forester.

I ran into one landowner who related to me that some fellows had
stopped by and offered to buy some timber on his property since they
were cutting on the neighbor's place anyway. After some talk, the buyers offered the landowner what seemed to be a large amount of money
for his "marketable timber over 14 inches in diameter." It seemed like a
pretty good offer, so he signed on the dotted line.

This landowner is an older fellow and hasn't been on a hike through
his woods in 10 years or more. He had no idea how many or what kind
of trees he had just sold the timber buyers. He also didn't realize that
most timber buyers, when buying on a diameter cut, are measuring "at
the stump." Now, go out and look at some of the trees on your place. A
tree with a 14-inch stump is going to taper rather sharply before it gets

to an even, straight stem. In fact, in these parts, a 14-inch stump can be supporting a 10-inch stem. But loggers can get a marketable "tie cut" out of that—that is, a stem just large enough to be squared off to make a railroad cross-tie.

In essence, a sale like the one above is seriously harming the overall health and productivity of the woodland, removing individual trees way before they have a chance to reach their prime, and costing landowners thousands or tens of thousands of dollars.

This account is not intended to be a wholesale indictment of all timber buyers and loggers, but it is intended to serve as a warning to woodland owners—market your timber as you would any valuable product or merchandise. Timber buyers are out to make money. If they can maximize their profits simply because you don't know what or how much you're selling, then the buyers are in a position to make a big profit.

Outright timber theft often occurs under the guise of a legal timber sale. In fact, it occurs more often than we like to admit. Often the loggers "unintentionally" cross landowner boundaries and harvest some of the neighbor's trees.

By using a consultant forester, you have the benefit of training and experience going for you. The forester can inventory and mark select trees to sell, and can tailor the sale to your wishes or management decisions. A forester will mark trees based on a measurement called DBH or "diameter at breast height." *DBH* is a common forestry term and is used since stump diameter can be very misleading as to the actual tree trunk diameter and resulting number of board feet of lumber contained in a tree. For this reason, foresters use the universal DBH measurement when inventorying and marking a timber sale.

Consultant foresters will benefit you in several ways.

☞ They can tell you exactly what you have to sell. This is very important. Many, perhaps most, landowners have little idea just what types of trees they have in their woods, let alone the sizes, grades, or marketability of those trees. Foresters can inventory or "cruise" your woodlot and give you an accurate figure of what marketable timber is there, how much (usually in board-feet), and advice on the best species to market.

☞ They can assist to any degree in setting up and conducting the sale of your timber. They can do the inventory, mark the timber, post for closed bids, and contact good prospective bidders. They can field inquiries from those prospective buyers and assist at bid openings.

☞ Very importantly, consultant foresters can advise on *when* to market your timber. This is crucial in maximizing the return on your timberland.

☞ They can advise and even assist in developing your woodland to realize its maximum potential. Some of this can come in the form of TSI or "timber stand improvement." TSI involves removing certain vegetation or trees for the purpose of improving the overall health of the woodland. It includes cutting grapevines that can literally strangle large timber trees. Here in the East, wild grapevines can make the climb to the crown of a tall white oak tree in the matter of a few years. From there, the vine spreads throughout the crown, competing for leaf space, choking the tree itself, and lowering the quality of the tree. Other TSI includes marking and/or removing "wolf trees"—those stems that are severely crooked or deformed and will have little or no marketability in the future. Sometimes, too, trees simply need thinning to allow more sunlight and nutrients to reach the remaining stems.

Consultant foresters are advisers. They recommend sound forest management practices for landowners. However, it is important to remember that they do so to your specifications. For example, if one of your concerns is having plenty of wildlife den trees on your property, then make this known to the foresters. They'll make sure your forest management plan includes leaving some of the big old hollow beech trees for raccoon dens and woodpecker nest sites. They work for you, and you have the last word in the management of your woods.

Consulting foresters usually work on a percentage basis. However, they will earn you far more than their cost to you—not only in dollars, but also in a healthier and more diverse woodland.

For more information on consultant foresters or getting in touch with one in your area, suggest contacting your state forestry office or local county extension office. Either place should be able to put you in touch with certified and qualified consultant foresters. Ask for references and do some checking with former clients.

Chain Saws

Let's face it. One of the most needed tools around the home place is the chain saw.

You don't have to be a clear-cutter to need a good dependable chain saw. Their uses around the homestead are many.

☞ Cut "wolf trees" for good timber management and firewood.

☞ Cut trees for lumber and timber.

☞ Clear brush.

☞ Saw out beams and boards (with the proper attachments).

☞ Even rough carpentry in remote sites.

Be sure to follow the manufacturer's recommendations on the fuel-to-oil mixing ratio. These folks know how their engines are designed and what they need to run properly. This can be a bit of a headache when using different makes of machines with different mix ratios, but it will pay off in the long run.

When mixing your fuel, splurge and buy a high-quality mixing oil such as Sta-mix, Stihl, Homelite, or another name brand. The few cents more you will pay for it are worth it.

It is easy to get a saw that is too small or too large for use on your place. Too small a saw will be suitable for some light limb lopping and similar uses, but will leave you wanting when it comes time to get in the winter's wood. On the other hand, too large a saw will simply be too large, heavy, and unwieldy to comfortably use and will likely leave you simply aching after a day's cutting. A good and sensible compromise is a midsized saw. Chain saw manufacturers recognize the need and the large market for this type of saw and make a wide variety of models to fill the niche. These midsized chain saws are powerful enough for nearly any use around the small farm or homestead. They are also light enough that they do not wear you out. With a 16- to 20-inch bar and chain, these saws weigh in at about 12 to 14 pounds.

A good midsized saw will most likely fit your normal homestead operations. For the occasional very large tree to be felled, you may opt to enlist a friend or neighbor, or even a professional. On many large trees I have taken down, however, I've been able to get the job done by just making slow, deliberate, and careful cuts . . . and being mindful of the wind direction!

ECHO has a good reputation for turning out solid, dependable chain

The Echo CS4400 is a dependable saw big enough to handle almost any chore on the place. Courtesy Echo, Inc.

saws that hold up well on the farm. My current saw is an Echo, and I have had nothing but good luck with it (knock on wood! . . . no pun intended). I did opt to have a 20-inch bar installed on it when I bought it.

HOMELITE chain saws, just like the parent company, have been around for a long time. Inventor Charles Ferguson created the first gas-powered generator and founded the Home Electric Lighting Company back in 1921. In 1994, Homelite became a part of Deere and Company (John Deere), of farm tractor renown.

As best I can tell, Homelite has maintained its same production quality and offers many saws suitable for farm and homestead. It markets through many of the mass retail outlets, making these saws quite available, but perhaps lacking when it comes time for service.

HUSQVARNA is a quality saw well known among loggers and commercial cutters. The firm's "air injection" system is unique to its saws and is liked by many who use one.

The Husqvarna 350 is plenty of saw for many users. Courtesy Husqvarna.

JONESRED is a company most of us hear little or nothing about. It does, however, have a solid reputation among loggers, tree trimmers, and other professionals.

POULAN is another brand that is widely available in the discount store line. Those who use these saws seem to really like them. However, as with the Homelite saws, service may be somewhat difficult to obtain when needed.

STIHL is one of the best-known names in chain saws. I have used, but never owned, a Stihl, but know them to be really good machines. The professionals I've talked with have told me that over the years, design and construction changes have made the saws somewhat less

The popular Stihl 029 Farm Boss is hard to beat. Courtesy Stihl-USA.

dependable than they used to be. Others swear by them, though. When using one of their saws recently, I was really pleased at just how well it cut. Overall, for the average small place, I don't think you could go wrong one of these saws.

SHARPENING THE CHAIN

Chain sharpening is something of an acquired art. However, it is not mystical. Chain sharpening is basic to saw operation and maintenance. Either hand files or special electric grinders may be used when sharpening your saw chain. Study and follow the directions given in the manual that came with your saw. The main thing to know here is to get the proper size file for your chain and to maintain the proper angle as you make each stroke. Take your time and you should be able to get the knack of it quickly.

Even though I sharpen my own chains, I still have them professionally sharpened every fourth or fifth time. This simply makes sense to correct my accumulated mistakes.

Important note: Be sure to file the drag links occasionally. These links help move the wood out of the saw cut and keep the cut going smoothly and efficiently. If the links are not occasionally filed, they will prevent the actual cutting links from making a good biting contact with the wood. They are filed using a small flat file. Half a dozen strokes or so with the file is usually sufficient to keep the drag links in good working order.

WHICH SIZE SAW IS BEST FOR YOU?

TYPE	GUIDE BAR LENGTH	WEIGHT (approximate)	USES
Mini or lightweight saws	8–12"	8½–10½ lbs.	Light and occasional use for limbing, cutting small logs, and felling very small trees.
Midweight saws	14–20"	12–14 lbs.	Frequent log cutting and felling of small trees.
Heavyweight saws	over 20"	13½–22 lbs.	Professional use—not generally recommended for consumers.

Chain saw kickback can result in death or serious injury. The force of the saw chain striking an object throws the saw violently back toward the operator, sometime with disastrous results.

Kickback can occur when the saw chain around the tip of the guide bar touches any object, such as a nearby log or branch. It can also happen when the wood being cut closes in and pinches the saw chain in the cut. To avoid kickback:

☞ Don't touch the tip of the bar to any object while the saw chain is running.

☞ Always hold the chain saw firmly with both hands.

☞ Use the proper grip. Grasp the forward handle with your left hand, palm down, wrapping your fingers around the handlebar, keeping the bar in the webbing between your index finger and thumb. Grasp the rear handle firmly with your right hand.

Maintain a firm grip and steady stance when using your saw.

☞ Boring cuts require burying the nose or tip area of the saw into the wood being cut. This can cause kickback, so exercise special care making this type of cut.

☞ Use a well-balanced stance.

☞ Avoid cutting limbs above mid-chest height.

Safety equipment, such as this helmet with hearing protectors and face shield, is necessary for safe saw operation. Don't skimp on safety gear. Courtesy Stihl-USA.

☞ Use a sawbuck or similar device to support and hold logs when possible.

Other safety tips:

☞ Always hold the chain saw firmly with two hands.

☞ Use the proper grip.

☞ Use the proper stance. Don't lean forward or sideways to cut.

☞ Let the chain saw do the work. Don't try to force it through the cut.

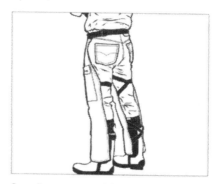

Saw chaps are a useful piece of safety gear. The rugged chaps protect the wearer against accidentally running the saw into the leg. Courtesy Stihl-USA.

☞ Be aware of the downward or outward path the saw will take after the wood is cut. Keep your legs out of this path.

☞ Watch for springback of limbs being cut or of a second branch being held by a limb being cut.

☞ Take your hand off the trigger between cuts.

☞ Avoid sawing from a ladder or from a stance in a tree.

☞ Use wedges to avoid pinching the bar when cutting larger pieces.

☞ Know where the saw is going at all times.

Heating with Wood

On the homestead, an important part of becoming more self-reliant and self-sufficient is production and operation of your own home heating source. Of course, more attention will probably be given to this subject if you live in Baudette, Minnesota, than in Brady, Texas, but most of us live somewhere in between. There is no doubt that the use of wood for heating and cooking can save you money. Getting in and burning wood for fuel can also give you a feeling of connecting with the past, particularly if you shun the modern contrivances such as hydraulic splitters (I'll keep my chain saw, thanks). The use of wood for fuel can even be a political statement. If you depend upon wood for fuel, you can have your own renewable source of fuel for heating and cooking. You depend less or not at all upon oil companies, gas companies, coal companies, or electric utilities. Burning wood can be an ecological statement, too. Wood is a form of solar energy. Through the God-given miracle of photosynthesis, carbon dioxide and water are transformed into organic material. When the tree dies, bacteria go immediately to work to convert it back to carbon dioxide and water, with the nutrients returning to the soil. When a tree is burned—for fuel or otherwise—the same ingredients are released: carbon dioxide, and water, as well as ashes. If the burning process is complete and efficient, the energy stored in the wood is released as heat and the original components are recycled back to the earth. There is no disruption of natural cycles, merely the speeding up of a natural process.

Wood heat is a logical alternative for the home. In the past, wood supplied up to 90 percent of America's energy needs. This dropped to less to 1 percent by 1970, due mainly to our growing dependence on cheap fossil fuels. After the 1973 oil embargo, the cost of those "clean modern fuels" shot through the roof, and people began to look again at wood for heating and cooking fuel. The woodstove business suddenly became a multimillion-dollar industry. However, in 1973 there were fewer than one dozen stove manufacturers in the whole country! Fortunately, after the surge of new stove designs and the near glut of dealers in the 1970s, a good number of excellent designs of woodburners have survived, and it is still easy to find a good stove suitable for many years of use in the home. Consider the type of stove you wish to put in your home. There are literally dozens of different kinds of woodstoves on the market today. Most, however, fit into one of the following categories: circulating stoves, radiant heaters, or combination stoves.

CIRCULATING STOVES. These stoves are usually some variation on an inner combustion chamber constructed of heavy sheet metal or cast iron and lined with firebrick. Surrounding it is a sheet-metal cabinet, spaced so that a natural flow of air is created to flow out of a louvered top surface. Basically, it's a stove in a box. The cabinet or outer shell stays considerably cooler than the stove itself, so these types of stoves are especially suitable where infants or small children may accidentally come into contact with the woodburner. Circulating stoves are highly efficient and should definitely be considered by the prospective buyer.

The Wonderwood stove from U.S. Stoveworks is a proven and dependable design. The cabinet surrounding the stove helps direct heat and protects against direct contact with the combustion box. We have heated our home for many years with a stove such as this. Another heats the garage and workshop. Courtesy U.S. Stoveworks.

RADIANT HEATERS. This category takes in a considerable number of stoves available today. They're usually made of sheet metal, cast iron, or heavy welded steel. The old pot-bellied stove falls into this group, as do many of the modern airtight stoves on the market. These stoves transfer heat directly by radiant energy and indirectly by convection currents set up by airflow over the stove surface. Many of the better-made models are nearly as efficient as the circulating stoves.

COMBINATION STOVES. This type of stove combines the looks and operation of a conventional radiant stove with the capacity for the operator to open the doors and view the fire as with a fireplace. Overall, the stoves work rather efficiently, depending on how much time is spent in the open-door "fireplace" mode.

Whichever stove type or design you choose, you will need to get acquainted with it once you get it in place. Each woodstove seems to have its own personality, requiring the owner to get to know the quirks and traits peculiar to that individual stove. For example, I have two stoves obtained from the same manufacturer. One I use in the house; the other, in my workshop and garage. The two are essentially littermates, identical in make and appearance. However, each requires its own particular settings of the dampers and burning controls. Each seems to burn just a bit differently. It will take a while to get to know the optimum settings and adjustments for your stove. There is really nothing mysterious about it, however. You will soon learn to recognize how to get the best results from your stove.

Any woodburner must be situated a safe distance away from any combustible material to prevent the radiant heat from causing a fire. If

Another type of system is the outdoor wood furnace. Benefits include keeping wood, bark, ashes, smoke, and insects outside.

your stove is U.L. (Underwriter's Laboratory) listed, be sure to follow the manufacturer's recommendations for setting it up in your home. Different types of stoves may require different amounts of free space around them as a "safe zone." When setting up a woodburner against an unprotected wall, I'd recommend a minimum of 36 inches clearance. One or even 2 feet of clearance will not do! Below is a table indicating some minimum clearances for different types of installations.

MINIMUM CLEARANCES

TYPE OF PROTECTION	STOVE SIDES	STOVE-PIPE
Unprotected	36"	18"
¼" fireproof millboard	36"	18"
¼" fireproof millboard spaced out 1"	18"	12"
28-ga. sheet metal on ¼" fireproof millboard	18"	12"
28-ga. sheet metal spaced out 1"	12"	9"
28-ga. sheet metal on ⅛" fireproof millboard spaced out 1"	12"	9"
22-ga. sheet metal on 1" mineral fiber bats reinforced with wire mesh	12"	12"

Safe distances for floor clearances are less than those for the sides and back of the stove. Furthermore, accumulating ashes in the woodstove add an insulating layer. Use the table below as a guide to floor distance for a woodstove. Be sure to extend the floor protection out beyond the stove itself to allow for protection from embers and sparks. A minimum of 18 inches in front and 6 inches for the back and sides is recommended.

FLOOR CLEARANCES

LEG LENGTH	PROTECTION NEEDED
18" or more	24-ga. layer of sheet metal
6–18"	24-ga. layer of sheet metal over ¼" layer of fireproof millboard

6" or less   Use 4" of hollow masonry laid to provide air
                              circulation through the masonry layer covered
                              by a sheet of 24-ga. sheet metal

Once you have decided which stove is best for you and have determined the best installation setup, it is time to turn your attention to the chimney. If your house already has a chimney, I certainly recommend having it inspected prior to installing your woodburner. Professional chimney cleaners have the equipment and expertise to tell you whether your chimney is in condition to safely use. They can tell you what repairs, if any, would be needed, and can often do those repairs.

If you are putting a woodstove in a house that has never had one before, it is a good idea to get some help from someone who really knows how to install a good chimney. Check, too, with your insurance company representative. With the increasing popularity of woodburning stoves over the past several years, insurance companies have really tightened their requirements on chimneys and flues. In fact, some rather prominent companies flatly will not insure your home if it has a woodburner in it. Most companies that do insure homes with woodstoves provide helpful literature on locating and setting up woodstoves in the home. Also, most companies certainly will not insure you if you are using a stove that is not U.L. listed.

There are a variety of chimney materials available, some good, and some not so good. I frequently see a stovepipe projecting out the side of a house or mobile home with little or nothing to insulate it from the surrounding wall. Often these stovepipes are merely run through a hole in a piece of sheet metal that has been put in an opening replacing a window. Small wonder the insurance companies get upset.

For a really good and safe chimney, enlist a friend or professional who knows and builds chimneys. They will be able to guide you in the selection and construction of your smokestack. A couple of rules of thumb to keep in mind in chimney construction: First, make certain that your chimney is at least 2 feet higher than the highest point of the roof within 10 feet. Second, if you are installing a chimney through a flat roof, be sure that it extends at least 3 feet above the point where it enters the roof. Both of these simple rules will help ensure that your flue will draw properly, prevent downdrafts, and minimize the danger of fires from sparks.

There are a variety of materials for constructing flues. One really good choice is the triple-wall stainless-steel pipes. These insulated sections of stainless steel will help keep down the danger of fire and resist the rusting that drastically shortens the life of regular stovepipe. They are relatively easy to retrofit into an existing home and can be safely installed in mobile homes. They are somewhat expensive initially, but their durability and adaptability to many installation situations make them a prudent choice in many cases.

What most of us think of as ordinary stovepipe can also be used in many installations. This old standby comes made from different gauges of metal and, as a result, varies in its durability and life span. The lighter-weight, blued metal is usually of about 14-gauge metal. The heavier 24-gauge pipe is much more durable. If choosing stovepipe for your chimney material, definitely opt for the heavy-gauge pipe. The security and peace of mind are well worth the added cost.

Masonry flues are a bit more appealing to the eye and can last for generations with proper care. They are often constructed of brick alone, brick with clay tile liners, masonry block and liners, or other configurations. I recommend the use of clay tile liners in the flue. They take the heat well and help create a good smooth surface on the inside of the chimney. Due to this smooth surface, they also seem to offer a bit less surface area for creosote to cling to. This brings up another topic altogether.

One special concern in heating with wood is the danger of chimney fires. These fires usually result from ignition of combustible materials deposited on the inner walls of the chimney during the burning process. These materials are usually called creosote. In Grandma's day, the old woodstove was often kept glowing, literally, to compensate for the wind whistling in around windows and doors. Insulation was unheard of, and even the stoves themselves left much to be desired in terms of burning efficiency. It was difficult not to burn a hot fire. As a result, deposits of combustible materials left on the chimney walls were lessened. Granny also often intentionally "burned out" the flue by burning newspapers or other scraps in the stove. In some cases, though, flue deposits still built up, flues still burned out, and sometimes the house went up with them.

Today's superinsulated and airtight homes, combined with the use of superefficient, airtight stoves, do away with the need for burning high, intense fires. This combination, while consuming less fuel, also greatly contributes to the danger of flue fires.

Low fires help cause the quick and serious buildup of creosote and other deposits in the chimney, which, if not removed, set the stage for a flue fire.

As the low fires simmer and smolder, the smoke rises slowly, cooling as it goes. As it cools, the creosote, soot, and tars left from the incomplete wood combustion in the stove are deposited on the walls of the flue. This layer can be black and sticky or quite dry and crumbly. It can run nearly the entire length of the flue. Once the inside of the chimney is nicely coated with creosote, the first hot fire can ignite the mess—and I do mean *ignite!*

For those of you who have not had the experience of witnessing your chimney catching fire, just try to imagine the noise created if a freight train were to pass through your house. The event is a real attention getter! There is also the real danger of the fire severely damaging the flue due to the intense heat that develops—as high as 3,000 degrees. Consider, too, that a flue fire can cause secondary ignition of your roof as it spews out flaming bits of creosote and ash. The internal framework of the house itself can also be ignited either from direct contact with flames from a now faulty flue, or in rare instances from spontaneous combustion caused by the intense heat.

Flue fires resulting from the buildup of creosote often occur during late fall or early spring. These periods are often subject to spells of relatively warm weather when the need for a hot fire is reduced. These periods often also coincide with heavy creosote layers in the flue itself. Either the flue wasn't checked and cleaned prior to the burning season, or the whole season's worth of deposits are sticking to the chimney walls early in spring, just waiting for the first hot fire to ignite them.

Another contributor to the buildup of creosote on chimney walls is the burning of green or unseasoned firewood. All wood is going to leave some deposits of unburned chemical compounds on the flue walls, but green or unseasoned wood increases the danger exponentially due to its moisture. The cooling effect of the moisture upon the ascending smoke, coupled possibly with the increased presence of certain chemical elements, causes the buildup to be more rapid. The best way to prevent such buildup is to not only clean the flue regularly, but also burn the highest-quality, best-seasoned wood that you can get.

Firewood

Newcomers to woodburning may be asking, "Now that I have the stove ready to go, just how do I go about finding a supply of wood for my woodburner?" Well, hopefully, your 'stead will have a nice-sized woodlot from which you can harvest low-quality, misshapen, damaged, or diseased trees for use as fuel. The benefits will be twofold: First, you will be providing space and nutrients for the higher-quality trees in your woods, and second, you will have a virtually endless supply of firewood for your own use.

If you must gather all or part of your wood from other sources, here are several suggestions for locating a supply for the cutting.

Contact the closest state or national forest office; low-cost firewood permits are usually available. You will likely be assigned an area from which to gather your wood. Often that will be in an area of a recent timber harvest where the remaining treetops lie in abundance.

Contact neighbors who may have had a recent timber harvest. Ask to cut up some of the remaining tops for fuel. If they also burn wood, you might try to work out a deal for cutting on shares, cutting some for them and some for you.

Check with the local sawmills. They quite often have virtual mountains of "edging strips"—pieces left after the log is cut into lumber. These strips, when cut into suitable lengths and allowed to season, make excellent cookstove fuel. My grandma used to use edging strips as her sole kitchen stove fuel. The mills often have some pretty good-sized pieces left, which can make good heating fuel as well. Around here, the sawmills also cut a lot of railroad ties. The short leftover pieces or "tie ends" make outstanding stove fuel once they are allowed to season. They run about 8 inches high by 10 inches wide. Since they are scraps, the usable pieces usually run anywhere from 8 to 24 inches in length. They are a popular source of fuel where they are sawn, so search early for your supplier if you choose to go this route.

Get in touch with the local timber harvesters. Find out where they are cutting timber locally and contact the landowners for permission to cut wood after the harvest operation is complete. Too, as the logs are yarded prior to loading onto trucks, they are often "butted." This means that large pieces of the log are cut off the butt end and left in the log yard. If you cut up many of these chunks, however, watch the piece you cut. After the logs are dragged in, they can have a lot of chain-dulling dirt embedded in the bark. It's not a bad idea to use an ax to chip away the bark where your saw will be cutting these pieces.

Contact tree removal companies in your area. They often cut and burn trees in the normal course of their work. In fact, much good wood is shoved into the chipper and spit out as so much mulch. Many of those same trees could be cut up into good stove wood. The folks at the company may be able to help you by contacting you when they have wood available.

The following tables illustrate the relative heating value of different species of wood. The first table is from the USDA Forest Service and lists the relative heat of 33 dry woods. In this table, hickory equals 100, and the density values presented are in comparison to water. Remember that denser woods burn longer; less dense woods ignite easier and burn faster.

HEAT VALUE OF VARIOUS TREE SPECIES

TREE SPECIES	DENSITY VALUE	HEAT VALUE
Osage orange	.78–.83	112
Dogwood	.70–.79	100–107
Hop hornbeam	.70–.75	100–101
Hickory	.70–.74	100
Oak	.60–.73	86–99
Black locust	.69–.70	95–98
Blue beech	.65–.71	93–96
Beech	.64–.66	89–91
Hard maple	.58–.65	83–88
Birch	.55–.64	79–86
Mulberry	.59–.63	84–85
Apple	.58–.62	83–84
Ash	.57–.61	81–82
Southern pine	.51–.60	73–81
Elm	.50–.59	71–80
Walnut	.52–.55	74
Soft maple	.47–.54	67–73
Tamarack	.49–.53	70–72
Cherry	.50–.52	70–71
Sycamore	.49–.52	70
Gum	.48–.52	69–70
Douglas fir	.45–.51	64–69
Sassafras	.44–.46	62–63
Chestnut	.42–.44	59–60
Spruce	.41–.44	59
Tulip/yellow poplar	.40–.42	57
Hemlock	.40–.42	57
Cottonwood	.38–.41	54–55
Balsam fir	.36–.40	51–54
Redwood	.33–.40	47–54
Aspen	.37–.39	53
Basswood	.37–.39	53
White pine	.35–.37	50

In the next table, from the U.S. Department of Energy, a wide variety of wood species are compared in the heat value per cord in BTUs. This table will assume that there are 80 cubic feet of solid wood per cord and 8,600 BTUs per pound of oven-dried wood. Now, all this sounds pretty scientific, but it does give us a good index for comparing the value of many species of wood.

HEAT VALUE PER CORD (in BTUs per cord)

HIGH (24–31)	MEDIUM (20–24)	LOW (16–20)
Live oak	Holly	Black spruce
Shagbark hickory	Pond pine	Hemlock
Black locust	Nut pine	Catalpa
Dogwood	Loblolly pine	Red sider
Slash pine	Tamarack	Tulip poplar
Hop hornbeam	Shortleaf pine	Red fir
Persimmon	Western larch	Sitka spruce
Shadbush	Juniper	Black willow
Apple	Paper birch	Large-toothed aspen
White oak	Red maple	Butternut
Honey locust	Cherry	Ponderosa pine
Black birch	American elm	Noble fir
Yew	Black gum	Redwood
Blue beech	Sycamore	Quaking aspen
Red oak	Gray birch	Sugar pine
Rock elm	Douglas fir	White pine
Sugar maple	Pitch pine	Balsam fir
American beech	Sassafras	Cottonwood
Yellow birch	Magnolia	Basswood
Longleaf pine	Red cedar	Western red cedar
White ash	Norway pine	Balsam poplar
Oregon ash	Bald cypress	White spruce
Black walnut	Chestnut	

As you can see, there is a big difference in the quality of wood for use in a woodburning stove. Obviously, this is important when culling and cutting trees on your place for firewood, but it can be even more important if you purchase or barter for your stove fodder.

Since the price paid for firewood can vary widely, be sure to learn to recognize the various species of wood by the bark. In doing so, you can avoid, for example, paying premium prices for aspen or elm firewood. If you end up paying high prices for low-quality wood, the cost-effectiveness of woodburning drops drastically and quickly.

Too, the importance of burning seasoned wood cannot be stressed enough. Green wood typically has a moisture content of at least 80 percent. At this moisture level, more than 15 percent of the heating value is lost. In addition, green or unseasoned firewood contributes tremendously to the buildup of creosote in the flue. This is due to the wetter, cooler smoke given off and the higher content of chemical and particulate matter.

Granted, your firewood will probably not be dried to the extent of the oven-dried wood used in setting the table values listed above. But by cutting your wood in winter, spring, or early summer, stacking it, protecting it from rain, and allowing it to air-dry, you should have sufficiently seasoned wood for use in almost any stove. It is a good idea to cut your firewood a full year ahead to allow for thorough seasoning. Many folks who burn wood will only cut their wood during the winter months, when the sap is down. They believe that this results in quicker and better seasoning and better-burning firewood overall. I can't think of any reason to disagree with them, if only because the weather during the winter is so much more pleasant for woodcutting.

If you are buying your firewood, determine when the wood you are purchasing was cut—*seasoned* is such a vague term.

Since we're talking about buying wood, you should be aware of different terms used when cutting, selling, or buying firewood. First of all, while most of us have heard of "a cord of wood," too few actually know what that term measures out to. A *cord*, or actually a *full cord* of wood measures 4 feet high by 4 feet wide by 8 feet long. This stack measures out to about 128 cubic feet when you count all the space between the various pieces of wood in the stack. A full cord provides about 80 cubic feet in volume of solid wood.

A *rick* of wood is half of a full cord, or a stack of wood measuring 2 feet by 4 feet by 8 feet. A *face cord* is a pretty deceiving term and may mean different things to different people. Generally, a face cord is a stack of wood measuring 4 feet by 8 feet of whatever length of wood is being supplied.

An even more general term is *pickup load*. Many advertisements in small-town newspapers, and so forth, offer wood for sale by the pickup load. Most often, the folks selling the wood do try to give you a full load for your money, but here, as with almost any transaction where money is involved, there are those who will try to beat you out of a few pieces of wood. Wood can be piled loosely in a pickup truck or it can be stacked tightly. Even just tossing it on (depending on whether you are buying the wood or selling it!), you can get more or less on the truck. The important thing is to know what and how much you are buying before you buy it. If you have doubts, unload and stack the wood before paying for it to get a real idea of what you are getting for your money.

The following ledger sheet provides a tongue-in-cheek account of one man's experience with getting started in burning wood. Your own expenses and experiences may or may not equal his!

EXPENSES FOR BURNING WOOD FOR ONE YEAR

Stove, pipe, installation, etc.	558.00
Chain saw	249.95
Gas and maintenance for chain saw	44.60
4-wheel-drive pickup, stripped	24,759.04
4-wheel-drive pickup, maintenance	538.00
Replace rear window in pickup (twice)	610.00
Fine for cutting unmarked tree in state forest	500.00
14 cases of beer	167.30
Littering fine	100.00
Tow charge from creek	50.00
Doctor's fee for removing splinter from eye	125.00
Safety glasses	29.90
Emergency room treatment (dropped log, broke toes)	278.80
Steel-toed safety shoes	49.50
New living room carpet	800.00
Paint walls and ceiling	120.00
Chimney brush and rod	75.00
Splitting maul and wedges	39.00
Gasoline-powered log splitter	1,295.00
15-acre wooded lot	9,000.00
Taxes on wooded lot	357.00
Replace coffee table (chopped & burned while in high spirits)	125.00
Divorce settlement	56,922.00
Total first year's costs	96,793.09
Less savings over "conventional" fuel—first year	−124.74
Net cost of first year's wood burning	**$96,668.35**

7

FENCES &WALLS

Fences

Electric Fences

Building a Stone Wall

Fences

Yes, the old adage is true: Good fences make good neighbors. Good fences provide a solid reference point from which boundary disputes are kept from erupting. They can keep livestock in . . . or out. They can provide an aesthetically pleasing border to a property. Generally, the condition of your fences reflects your attitude toward your homestead or property.

When building a fence, there are many different materials and styles to consider. However, there are some tried-and-true rules that should not be skipped or skimped on. Some of these have been taught to me; others I have learned the hard way.

You may think that a fence doesn't need to be all that sturdy to contain your particular livestock. However, a horse using the top wire to scratch its neck, or a cow snuffling under the bottom wire to reach the grass that is greener on the other side, can soon cause a lot of sagging and premature fence failure. In addition, you may be more concerned with keeping critters out than in. This is often the case when fencing sheep. The problem is not so much keeping them in as it is keeping predators such as dogs and coyotes out. It is a case of wanting and needing to build a good tight fence.

First of all, when buying fencing, it is easy to be tempted into buying the cheaper brands of wire. Let's face it, fencing is not cheap to put up, in terms of either money or labor. However, I have found that fencing is like a lot of other things: You can pay for it now or you can pay for it later.

When you shop around for barbed wire, you will quickly notice a difference in the price of various brands. Barbed wire is one item where the cheaper brands have done all right for us overall. They stay bright and shiny with good galvanizing. It seems to me that they do tend to become somewhat brittle over many years, but I've noticed this mainly when repairing or removing a strand. I've been told that the higher price of a fence wire reflects the amount of copper contained in it. Since copper is relatively soft and malleable, this possibly accounts for the relative brittleness of the cheaper wire compared to the better workability of the higher-priced wire.

Woven wire is sold by the gauge of the wire: The heavier the wire, the pricier the fencing. Remember that when you are sizing the wire, the greater the number, the smaller the wire's diameter. That is to say, 12-gauge wire is heavier than 14-gauge wire. Also, the type of wire called "field fence" will not have the same number of vertical wires as does regular woven wire. Field fence wire usually has the vertical wire or "stays" placed on 12-inch centers. Normal stock fence has 6 to 8 inches between the stays.

When it comes to buying and using woven wire, I have found that the cheaper brands just do not hold up. They are made of lighter-gauge wire that is not tough or durable enough, especially if you have children who periodically use the fence for a ladder to the other side. On the rolls I have used, the galvanized coating seems to have eroded away relatively quickly; the wire rusts easily.

In short, go for the better brands of woven wire. It will be worth it. Benefit here from my experience and lapses in judgment.

Woven wire is manufactured with tension-producing crimps spaced along the run. If you overstretch your fence wire as you are installing it, these crimps will be stretched beyond their limits, and you will end up with a sagging fence. Similarly, if you do not provide sufficient tension when stretching the run of wire, time, gravity, and the weight of the wire itself will cause the fence to sag. Use fence stretchers, not just a tractor or truck, to stretch wire. Fence stretchers or come-alongs provide gradual and adjustable tension on the run of wire. This is nearly impossible to do if just using a tractor or truck, when overstretching is the normal result.

FENCE POSTS

A fence can only be as good as the posts that hold it up off the ground. Fence posts are generally referred to by three different names: corner posts; brace or slave posts; and line posts. Let's take a look at the last of the three types.

Line posts are the ones that will run the length of your field or pasture. Right away, let me give you the benefit of my mistakes: Don't skimp on the number of posts you use. Early in my fencing days, I tried to make a set number of posts cover more length than I should have. Instead of the 10 to 12 feet that I should have allowed between posts, I placed them about 16 feet apart. It wasn't too long before the fence began to sag and I was going back and adding posts. So remember to place your line posts no more than 10 to 12 feet apart when stretching barbed wire or woven wire. The added work and cost of adding the few extra posts will pay off.

You may use wooden posts for which you will have to dig postholes, or you might decide to use steel T-posts, which can be driven into the ground with a sledge or post driver. Steel posts are quick and easy to use and come with wire clips that are used to attach the fence wire itself. A post driver is not much more than a piece of heavy steel pipe, closed on one end. It is placed down over the top of the post and repeatedly slammed down to drive the post into the ground. These work really well where few rocks are encountered. On my own rocky place, I have often had to shift the post one way or the other and redrive it after hitting a large rock. My own post driver is made from a piece of old truck drive-shaft. The end is heavy and solid and well able to withstand the repeated blows of driving the steel posts. In the illustration, both drivers are depicted with optional handles. They may be added by welding ½-inch-diameter smooth rod, bent to appear approximately as shown.

Wooden posts come in a wide variety of sizes and types. Depending upon where you live, some native woods make very good and long-lasting fence posts. In my area, some favorites are locust, cedar, mulberry, and Osage orange. Ask around in your own area. The locals should know which species make the best posts. If you are buying posts at a farm auction or auction house, be sure you know the species of wood the post are made from. You don't want to end up paying cedar prices for sassafras posts.

When using wooden posts, ordinary fence staples are used. These are available in different lengths depending upon the type of wood your posts are made of. Generally, if you are using softer posts, use a longer

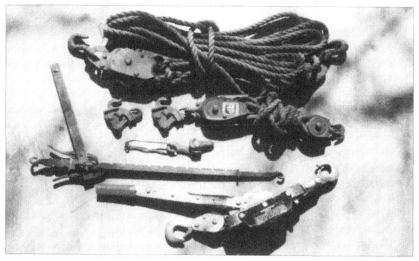

Tools needed to erect fence. Shown from top to bottom: stretchers for woven wire fence, stretchers for barbed wire, a ratcheting come-along, two clamps that attach to barbed wire, and (at bottom) a wooden, fence stretcher. To use this, it is unbolted; the woven wire is placed between the boards, then bolted back together. The device helps to keep the fence wire evenly stretched.

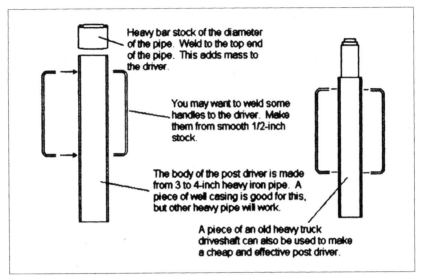

Heavy bar stock of the diameter of the pipe. Weld to the top end of the pipe. This adds mass to the driver.

You may want to weld some handles to the driver. Make them from smooth 1/2-inch stock.

The body of the post driver is made from 3 to 4-inch heavy iron pipe. A piece of well casing is good for this, but other heavy pipe will work.

A piece of an old heavy truck driveshaft can also be used to make a cheap and effective post driver.

Making a homemade post driver.

staple. Harder woods require a shorter staple to do the same job. Believe me when I say that trying to drive a 1½-inch-long staple into a locust post is not an easy task! That is what the inch staples are made for.

When driving fence staples, drive them at a slight angle to the vertical axis of the post. This keeps both points of the staple from sinking into the same vertical grain of the wood (and splitting it) and helps make a more secure fence.

FENCE CORNERS

Your fence corners can pretty much determine how well your fence is going to bear up. Proper construction of fence corners and terminal points, such as gate posts, is essential. There is a tremendous amount of tension on a given run of fence, and it takes some pretty stout posts and anchors to support it.

When constructing your corners, you will generally, want to use a larger and longer post for the corner. Today, treated corner posts of 6 to 8 inches in diameter are commonly available. These posts are usually about 7 to 8 feet in length and are set a bit deeper in the postholes, usually 2½ to 3 feet. I have used corner posts cut from long-lasting native woods such as locust, mulberry, and cedar. I have used posts cut from sections of used telephone and electric poles. I have used old railroad cross-ties. I have used store-bought corner posts made from pine or other conifers and treated with copper-arsenate solution, which is now more closely regulated. All of these have worked well where they were used. Naturally, I would like to always use the treated posts, but economics have not always allowed this. One trick I learned from my dad is to coat the exposed end of wooden posts—particularly corner posts—with a thick coating of roof tar. This will seal the end against moisture and help prolong the life of the post.

Once you have dug the hole for your post, whether with a tractor-driven auger or the old standby method of using clamshell-type post-hole diggers, it is important to properly set the post itself. Many texts advocate using gravel in the bottom of each hole to permit draining away from the post. Other writings suggest even using concrete around each post. While these may be good ideas for just a few posts, I have seen very few places where they're very practical.

In most cases, you can securely set the fence post by first placing it into the hole and lining it up with the others. Next, shovel a bit of dirt into the hole on each side of the post and tamp it in. I have a stout piece of 1¼-inch pipe that I use for a tamper. It is about 7 feet long and slightly bent at a point about 2½ to 3 feet from its lower end. This allows me to tamp the post and keep my knuckles from getting scraped on the post as I do so . . . another lesson learned. My dad had a piece of tough hickory that he used for a tamping rod. He cut the hickory pole the same length—about 7 feet—and perhaps 1½ inches in diameter. He put the piece of green wood between some stakes so that the same bend on the lower end was created. The piece was allowed to dry out in this position, and when it was taken from the form, it was permanently and perfectly shaped for tamping. He used it for many years.

You can do all right by eyeballing most of the posts to make sure they are plumb. When setting a gate post, you might want to use a level to be certain it is as close to vertical as you can get it. Keep adding a bit of dirt, then tamping, more dirt, more tamping, until you fill the hole. Any remaining dirt can be shoveled up around the base of the post and will help direct water away from it. It is important to add a little, tamp a little, add a little, tamp a little until the post is solidly tamped in. If you try to add all the dirt at once and then tamp it in, the post will not be at all solid.

A cross-piece will add stability to the corner. If you are using a wooden cross-piece, you can notch into the corner and brace posts and set the cross-piece into the notches. Tension supplied by the brace wire will hold the cross-piece in place. You might want to toenail the cross-piece into each post to be sure. That also helps keep the piece in place while you are constructing the corner. If you are using a pipe cross-piece, a nail in each post will give you a point from which to hang the pipe until you tighten the wires. Cross-pieces can be made from wood, pipe, old steel fence posts, or even old bed rails. In a couple of spots near the house, I had a few extra treated landscape timbers that I used.

Brace wire is not the same as fence wire. It is usually available at supply stores in large coils for a nominal price. Brace wire is usually sold as #9 gauge and is fairly pliable. In a pinch, I have even used barbed wire as brace wire, but I don't like to do this.

The critical part of constructing a post corner is the proper positioning of the brace wires. A properly constructed corner can be seen in the photograph on page 226. If you are using a brace wire as shown, it is essential that the brace wire runs from the base of the corner post up to the upper portion of the brace post. This is because the tension is *pulling* against the wire. The top of the brace post is anchored to the most stable point on the corner post—the base.

If you are using a post as a diagonal brace, place it so that it runs from the top of the corner post toward the bottom of the brace post. This way, the tension will push the most movable part of the corner post—the top—against the most stable part of the brace post—the base.

In the photograph on page 226, you can see a corner post to which a horizontal wooden brace and a horizontal wire brace were added. There is no strengthening of the corner by using diagonals. As you can see, the post has pulled inward, toward the direction of tension of the fence wire.

If you are at the end of a fence run and plan to hang a gate there, you want to construct the fence at that point as you would a corner. That is, use a heavy corner post, a stout brace post, and diagonal wire from the base of the corner toward the top of the brace post. Now, since there will be the added weight of a heavy gate hanging on the corner post, add another diagonal wire running from the base of the brace post to the top of the corner post (or gate post, in this case). In this way, the weight of the gate will be pulling the top of the corner post against the base of the brace post. This will make the gate less likely to sag (see the illustration).

When placing the brace wire, you will be using just over twice the length of the span between the diagonal corners. That is, start a fence staple near the base of the appropriate post. Run the wire up and around the other post and through another staple that you have placed at a point near where the top of the fence wire itself will be. Run the wire back down and through the same staple at the base of the first post.

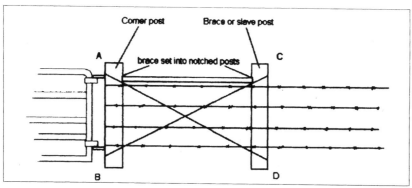

When running fence wire from the corner post, you must have a brace wire running from B to C. That way, the top of the brace post is pulling against the most stable point of the corner post (point B). Adding a gate will require a brace wire run from point A to point D. This will support the weight of the gate pulling the top of the gate or corner post against the most stable point of the brace post (point D).

There are a couple of ways to anchor the wire. Some folks run the wire back onto itself and make several wraps, then anchor it with a couple of staples. I have not found this to be necessary, however. I drive another staple slightly around the post from the first and run one end of the wire through it. Drive the staple in tightly, then bend the wire back on itself. Do the same on the other side. Then you can add one or two staples on the loose ends to hold them securely in place. This arrangement will hold well.

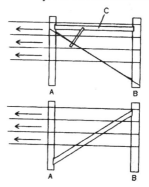

Tension needs to be applied to the brace wire to make sturdy the corner post and brace post. Use a piece of wood, pipe, rod, or similar hardy material. Cut a piece about 16 to 20 inches long. Place one end between the two strands of the brace wire that you have just secured. Simply begin twisting the wires, using the pipe or rod as a lever to tighten them. Once you

In this diagram, the tension of the fence wire is pulling the top of the brace post against the base of the corner post—the most stable and solid point. Notice that a horizontal brace is used. In this diagram, the tension of the fence wire is pulling the corner post into the diagonal wooden or pipe brace. It, in turn, is pushing against the base of the brace post—the most stable and solid point. Note that no horizontal brace is used here.

have them taut as a drumhead, let the end of the lever rest against the horizontal brace that you have placed between the posts. Tension should keep the rod in place. If the lever seems like it might slip off the brace post, simply drive a nail into the brace for it to rest against. Repeat the entire process, if necessary, on the other diagonals. You can see in the photographs how I have run the wires and how the levers rest against the horizontal brace.

A properly braced corner.

Improper construction of fence corners can cause drawing and sagging. This corner has the brace wire place horizontally about halfway up the post. It allowed the tension on the fence to pull both the corner post and brace post, resulting in a sagging fence.

Electric Fences

Electric fences are, in many cases, a homesteader's dream. These fences are adaptable, durable, portable, and easy to put up. I know of several farmers who have grazed large herds of cattle for the past 40 years using just electric fences. Nothing more than a single strand of barbed wire and a good fence charger stood between these cattle and bovine freedom. In fact, once accustomed to the unpleasant jolt of an electric fence, even the largest of bulls can be confined with an electric fence.

In erecting an electric fence, you will need posts, insulators for those posts, wire, and a good fence charger.

Some of the most economical posts available commercially are the ones made from ⅜-inch steel rods. They are relatively inexpensive and do a good-enough job of holding the fence wire up off the ground. Steel T-posts are popular and available in several lengths. For electric fences, the shorter ones do nicely. Of course, wooden posts work just fine. Whichever type of posts you use, be sure to purchase enough of the appropriate insulators to mount your fence to the posts. With the electrical current running through the wire, it must be insulated from the posts or the charge will run to ground, rendering the fence ineffective. Dozens of different insulators are available to meet just about every need. A stop at your fence supply store can fix you up with the ones you need. Most electric fencing jobs I have done required a combination of materials. A hefty wooden post for a corner here, some steel rods alternated with some T-posts, and perhaps a ceramic insulator tapped into an old corner tree there: Use what you have or can come up with. I have found that farm auctions are good places to buy fencing supplies cheaply—perhaps with the exception of wooden posts. At more than one auction, I have purchased

Many folks find that electric fence meets their needs. Here is some ribbon wire, made from long-lasting plastics with interwoven wires to carry the electrical current. It has the advantage of being highly visible, so it is much less likely to be accidentally knocked down by livestock or deer.

a bucketful of electric fence insulators for a couple of dollars, and also got the bucket! Gates—often referred to as "gaps"—can be created just about anywhere along the run of fence. Plastic spring-loaded handles are available where you buy the insulators and wire, or you can make one from a scrap of PVC pipe and a bit of heavy wire.

I have seen electric fence wire available in either aluminum or steel. I have opted to use the lighter-gauge steel wire. I have found it easy to work with and tougher than the softer, albeit more visible, aluminum wire. I have also erected a more permanent electric fence using alternating wooden posts and steel posts and stringing a single run of barbed wire along them using the appropriate insulators.

Solar fence chargers like this one are good for remote sites. The wire running from the white insulator is connected to the fence wire. The other wire runs to a ground rod driven into the earth near the post.

Available now are several varieties of electric fencing made from durable plastic woven ribbon with fine stainless-steel wire woven right into it. This material offers the added advantage of being highly visible. As such, it is very useful for fencing horse paddocks as well as keeping deer and other varmints out of the garden.

Fence chargers themselves are pretty much trouble-free. They are made to run off regular household electrical current, with heavy dry-cell batteries, or with small solar panels. With the solar fence chargers available, it is possible to have charged fences in areas where there is no normal electrical power and without the worry of replacing an aging dry-cell battery. The solar units are fairly priced, and can be much cheaper to buy than to add the cost of running electrical power to the cost of a regular fence charger.

Fences are a long-term investment on your property. They are not cheap to install, but they are relatively inexpensive to maintain if they are erected correctly the first time. Spend some time planning and putting up your fences, and you will save time and worry.

Building a Stone Wall

The natural beauty of a stone wall has been romanticized in poem and picture for hundreds of years. There is a soothing permanence that can be seen in a well-built stone wall. I have built a couple of simple stone walls over the years and thought I'd share what I have learned about the process of building and working with stone.

Our area is very rocky, and a few folks make pretty decent money just "harvesting" and selling fieldstone. They work up and down the streams and creeks in the area, hauling load after load of heavy stone out in old pickup trucks. The "crick rock," as it is often called, is sold by the ton to a local dealer, who then sells it all over the state and region. Most of it eventually ends up as a part of fireplace mantels in high-dollar homes, as veneer on exterior walls, lining walkways, and so on.

Recently, we had a planting bed that needed rebuilding. The bed had initially been made of old railroad cross-ties, but over the years the wooden pieces had finally begun to do some serious rotting. I decided to replace the wood with a fieldstone wall, made of stone from right around home.

Once I had gathered the stone at the construction site, I decided that I would have to cut or split a few of the pieces to make the puzzle fit together. Cutting stone versus splitting stone can perhaps best be compared to cutting wood versus splitting wood. When cutting, you are going across the grain; when splitting, you are going with it.

Cutting or splitting a stone will give you a piece that will fit better into a given spot. It will also—and not unimportantly—give you a stone that is much easier to handle! I'll admit, I haven't tried this on Rocky Mountain granite or Vermont marble, but the method works really well on good old southern Indiana sandstone. I

Yes, rock can be split! Using an old hatchet and hand sledge, rocks can be split to the general size and shape you need for a project. Give it a try.

used a common hand sledgehammer and an old hatchet that I had in the toolshed. I used the hatchet as a sort of wedge, struck by the hand sledge to create breaks in the stone where I wanted them (approximately!). Oh yes, always use some good eye protection when cutting or splitting stone.

Let's get started. Pick out a nice-sized rock and roll it to where you can work on it. First, look at the stone. Size it up. Walk around it, turn it over, and look at the way the structure "flows." Many stones have a sort of grain that runs along their length. I guess it is the result of the eons of compression of the material that eventually becomes the stone. Pick out a good line that goes along with the shape of stone you need. You may have to look over a few rocks to get the one needed for a particular spot. Don't worry; you will use the misfits later. I've found that nearly every stone ends up in a spot that seemed made just for it.

Once you have picked out the stone, be sure it is on a flat, solid surface. Cutting a stone is done in baby steps. That is to say, using the small sledge and the hatchet, start at one side of the rock and first lightly score a line along the cut you intend to make. Next, place the hatchet near one end of the line and begin solidly tapping it with the hammer. Go back and forth along the scored line, moving from end to end, all along the stone. Keep it up. Eventually, you will worry the stone to pieces! Keep tapping, all along the line. Soon, you will begin to see a hairline crack develop and feel the hatchet stick as it begins to wedge into the forming crack.

The way I figure, it works like this: The light, but solid taps of the hammer on the hatchet send structure-crumbling shock waves through the stone, beginning at the point of contact. By using the light taps of the hammer, you are in more control of the eventual fissure and break than if you really pound away on the stone. Try to resist the temptation to start whacking harder on the hammer. You will only end up with a jagged break going somewhere other than where you wanted it. Trust me on this! In fact, it's a good idea to have a few practice stones to mess up, but I believe you'll be surprised at how well this method works. Note, too, that the structure of the stones themselves may differ. Even in the same general area, different stone can look, feel, and work up differently.

These stones can be split just about as easily as they can be cut, perhaps even more easily. If you turn one of these rocks up on its side, you can usually see the flow or "grain" along the length of the rock. To split such a stone, just locate the point where you wish to begin and start tap, tap, tapping along the grain, just as you did when cutting the stone. Soon you will see the hairline crack begin to form; then the stone will cleave into two pieces, much like a split piece of firewood.

A picturesque and functional rock wall can be made by dry stacking stones. Notice how the joints are lapped.

I chose to put the wall together without using any mortar. This method is referred to as dry stacking.

Now, when it comes to dry stacking the wall, I have found a few simple things to watch for. First, lay a course of stone as level as you can. It will make the rest of the wall much easier to construct if the foundation is level. Make these stones as large and as uniform as you can. Next, stagger the joints of the stones as much as possible. As you can see in the photographs, I have staggered the stones to give almost a laid-brick look. This ties everything together better and will result in a sturdier and longer-lasting wall. Use rocks as large as you can handle. Since gravity and friction hold a dry-stacked wall together, larger stones will simply stay in place better than smaller ones. The smaller stones can be used to fill gaps or provide some leveling. Plan to lay your rock wall so that it slopes inward about 1 inch for each 12 inches of rise or height.

I hope you enjoy working with stone. Building with materials that came right off the home place can be especially satisfying. Building something that lasts is just as satisfying.

STONE RESOURCES

For more information on building with stone, consider reading the respective chapters found in:

BUILD IT BETTER YOURSELF, by Bill Hylton and the editors of *Organic Gardening Magazine*, Rodale Press.

BACK TO BASICS, edited and published by Reader's Digest Books.

8

BARNS, SHEDS, & OUTBUILDINGS

Pole Buildings

Other Structures

As you begin to plan your country place, it will quickly become apparent that you will need a place to store and house all of the tools, livestock, equipment, hay, feed, and material that you will be accumulating.

In fact, once you find your place in the country, you may consider putting up a building or two even before you build your house. This will allow you to keep your tools, machinery, equipment and even livestock right on site while you prepare to construct your home. Besides, you will learn, if you haven't already, that you can never have too much storage space.

As with any building project, be sure to construct your barn or shed where there is good drainage. This will keep the building drier inside and help to prolong its life. It will simply make less of a mess in and around the building, particularly if you have livestock moving in and out of it.

Another thing to consider when planning your farmstead building is the direction of the primary prevailing winds. There are a couple of reasons for this. First, by placing the back of a shed into the wind, rain and wind will not be blowing in on the livestock, machinery, or hay in the building. In addition, by placing the building downwind from your dwelling site, odors can be kept to a more satisfactory level.

When planning your buildings and layout, consider "economy of steps." Poorly laid-out farmyards can result in many miles of extra walking over the course of several years. Keep your steps as few as possible and your chores will seem less of a chore. What are you going to be using the building for? Will it be for machinery, for hay, for livestock, or a combination of these or other things?

Pole Buildings

In these next pages, I'll refer primarily to building with pressure-treated poles or posts as the main structural supports—what are normally called "pole buildings." This technique offers many advantages to the builder. First is simplicity. A pole building costs considerably less than its foundation-and-frame counterpart. Conventional construction requires the forming and pouring of concrete foundations and footers, framing with dimension lumber, and more. Pole construction, on the other hand, simply requires the builder to dig a hole with hand diggers or a mechanical digger, set the poles, and begin framing up the building. Secondly, since there is much less material used, the cost will be less.

A pole building under construction. You can see the main posts, the ribbing, and roof in place. This particular building also has a sliding door and track along the front.

In my area of southern Indiana, the neighboring Amish community has created whole industries on the pole building trade. From manufacture of roof trusses, to rolling out the 5-V channeled roofing, to sending crews over a five-state area to erect the buildings, these hardworking builders can attest to the cost-effectiveness and durability of pole construction.

The pole building principle can be applied to just about any size of building. Our 8-foot by 24-foot chicken house and toolshed were built using this method. So were my barn and implement shed. The possibilities are limited only by your imagination.

There are many materials suppliers for these versatile and practical buildings. If your building experience is limited, consider contacting a couple of these local materials stores as you begin your own project. There will likely be personnel on hand who can help you with everything from planning, to selecting materials, to putting up the building.

LAYING THINGS OUT

When it comes time to actually lay out the building with stakes and string, remember the "6-8-10 Rule" from chapter 2. A square building is a must, especially when working with precut sheets of wood or metal siding and roofing. The simple 6-8-10 Rule will help ensure that your building will be square. As a final check, once you have the corners marked, measure diagonally corner to corner. The distances should be precisely the same if your layout is square.

Once you have the corners marked and square, it's time to dig in.

Dig the holes. Ordinary clamshell posthole diggers are available at any good hardware or building supply store. These are implements of honest work. That is to say, you will know you've done something after spending an afternoon digging enough 3- to 5-foot-deep postholes to accommodate your building poles. Powered portable diggers are often available at tool rental centers. These are simply gasoline-powered augers and require two hardy people to run. Tractor-mounted hole diggers that run off the power takeoff are also available. If you get into rocky ground, a spud bar may need to be used to break up the stones into smaller pieces that you can remove by hand or with the diggers.

The hole for a shed or pole barn usually needs to be at least 8 inches in diameter; 12 inches is much better and not much more work. For a building of this type, I dig the holes at least 3 feet deep. In areas of deep frost penetration, such as our northern states, 5-foot holes are not unheard of. Once I have dug the hole to the proper depth, I often toss a flat rock into it for the butt of the pole to sit on.

When setting poles for buildings, you might pour in a couple of bags of dry Quickrete-type bagged concrete mix around each pole. Don't add water; just pour the dry powdery mix into the hole around the pole. It will absorb enough water in a few days that it will set up like, well, con-

This shed on my place houses the manure spreader and a few other implements. You can see how the metal siding is attached over a wooden lumber-and-pole frame.

crete. If there is still space to fill, just toss in some dirt and tamp it to fill the hole the rest of the way. Have some long scrap lumber and stakes handy so that you can plumb the poles and secure them in the position that they will need to be in as the project progresses. Plumb each pole in two directions, and secure the brace.

Barns, sheds, and outbuildings are good places to utilize recycled lumber and materials. The pole barn that I currently use has scarcely a purchased board in it. The poles themselves were made by ripping used railroad ties with a chain saw. These ties had been used on a bridge, so they were longer than usual and had not been in contact with the earth. They have stood well for nearly 25 years.

The rest of the material was gathered from salvage projects. The used corrugated roofing tin came from a friend's poultry barn that was being torn down. Much of the lumber came from old houses and other salvaged buldings. In projects like this, where finish carpentry is not necessary, used material can do the job very well and at a lower cost.

Don't be afraid to tailor the measurements to the lumber you have on hand. If a 10-foot-wide shed would be nice, but you have a stack of 9-foot lumber that you have salvaged, then adjust your plan to utilize the lumber you have. In the end, no one will know but you. Using lumber and other materials salvaged from old buildings that you have torn down can go a long way toward saving you money on your project.

Other Structures

A successful farmstead will necessarily have more than one outbuilding on the place. Whether a chicken house, an implement shed, a hog house, a pump house, or a small general-purpose barn with a horse or cattle stall, barns and outbuildings can be as specialized as you need them.

Illustrated here is a plan for a building projects that will likely fit into your homestead scheme. This illustration and many others can be found on some very good Internet sources for farm plans, namely:

MIDWEST PLAN SERVICE:
http://www.public.iastate.edu/~mwps_dis/mwps_web//frame_p.html.

NORTH DAKOTA STATE UNIVERSITY EXTENSION SERVICE:
http://www.ag.ndsu.nodak.edu/abeng/plans/index.htm.

CANADA PLAN SERVICE:
http://www.cps.gov.on.ca/english/frameindex.htm.

The first two sites have archived hundreds of old U.S. Department of Agriculture farm plans and make most of them available to download at no cost. They also can provide larger-format printed sheets for a very nominal fee. These sources are definitely worth checking out. The plans are not all-inclusive—that is, they are not complete working blueprint sets—but they give you a good idea of some of the construction details and an overview of the project. They are good for basing your own project upon. The third site listed, from Canada, offers a wide variety of farmstead plans in either metric or imperial measurements. All are good sources of information.

Barns were one of the most important structures on an early American farm. There were many superstitions that centered on barns. Farmers of long ago might paint a mural on the barn door showing the animals that would bed in the barn as a way to trick witches. Others might hang a worn horseshoe above the door for good luck—just be sure to hang it with the open end up to catch the good luck! Point the open end downward and you will be pouring out your luck. Hex signs were painted onto many old barns in order to bring good health and bountiful harvests. While building a barn, farmers often made a point of using a single piece of beech lumber in the frame to ward off lighting strikes.

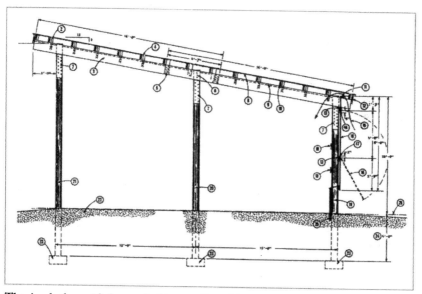

The simple three-sided open shed is versatile and fairly simple to build. It can be used to house livestock, store hay, or keep machinery in. Illustration from Canada Plan Service.

These traditions helped people explain things that were simply beyond explanation in their time.

OUTBUILDING RESOURCES

For all kinds of barn hardware:

JUST BARNS, INC. 1676 Route 78, Java Center, NY 14082, 1-585-457-3080 or 1-800-836-4271, fax 1-585-457-3160, http://www.just-barns.com.

In addition to the plans and sources listed, a couple of really good books that have information on this subject are:

BUILD IT BETTER YOURSELF, by Bill Hylton and the editors of *Organic Gardening Magazine*, Rodale Press.

PRACTICAL POLE BUILDING CONSTRUCTION, by Leigh Seddon, Williamson Publishing.

9

THE FARM POND

Site Selection

Watershed

Dam

Other Considerations

Any picture of a successful homestead that you conjure up will likely include a quiet, rippling farm pond. Indeed, these icons of country living deserve to be considered when planning your own place. Scenes of children fishing or swimming on a sunny day, or simply the summer sky reflected in your own pond, should help stir your interest in creating a farm pond for your place.

The benefits of having a farm pond are many. Ponds can be constructed for fishing, swimming, landscaping, irrigation, fire protection, livestock watering, wildlife habitat, water-quality management, or home water supply.

Ponds help prevent soil erosion and protect water quality by collecting and storing runoff water. A well-constructed and -located farm pond can add much value to your place, in both aesthetics and dollars.

The Agricultural Stabilization and Conservation Service (ASCS) and the Natural Resources Conservation Service (NRCS) will provide you with much assistance in planning your pond. They also administer cost-sharing programs that you may qualify for. Contact your county's soil and water conservation district office for more information and to contact your local agents.

Pond construction is not cheap. Excavators charge from about $65 to $125 per hour for projects of this type, depending upon the locale and the size of the machine doing the work. An average-sized pond can end up costing you $5,000 to $10,000, depending upon the types of spill-

A quiet farm pond offers many benefits for the owner. Here is a typical pond, complete with dock and small paddleboat.

ways and outlets you choose to add, soils encountered, and other factors. However, this cost can be offset if you qualify for and choose to participate in one of the cost-share programs.

Site Selection

Site selection is perhaps the most important single factor to consider when building your pond. Locating, sizing, and designing the shape of a pond have a lot to do with the terrain, soil type, a suitable water supply or watershed for the pond, and potential impact on downstream properties vulnerable to water damage if the dam fails. A pond should be designed to blend well with existing ecological features.

A good pond site contains:

☞ Level topography that provides for economical construction.

☞ Soil with sufficient clay to hold water.

☞ An adequate water supply.

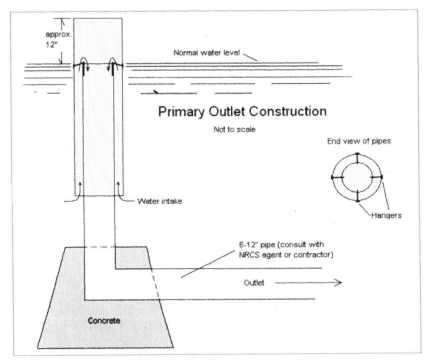

How to construct a primary water outlet for your pond.

The two main types of pond structures are excavated (dugout) ponds and embankment ponds (ponds constructed by damming a stream channel or a depression). Excavated ponds generally are found in relatively flat areas with a high groundwater table, while embankment ponds are common in terrain with more defined relief. Generally, excavated ponds are preferred and are less prone to washout by exceptionally heavy rainfalls.

To minimize maintenance during the life of the pond, it is best to locate the pond off-line rather than in-line with a stream. Be sure to ask your local NRCS agent about any necessary local permits that might be required to construct your pond. The requirements vary by state, county, and municipality, so check this out prior to beginning construction.

SOIL

The soil type of the area is important in determining the location for a pond. Sites with average to high clay content are ideal for ponds because they provide a tight base that reduces water loss, whereas those with sandy soil or shallow depth to bedrock do not. Because a pond is basically just a depression for holding water, the dam and bottom must be composed of soil that minimizes seepage. Clay soils do this, while sites containing gravel or sandy soils are unsuitable, often requiring costly earthmoving to obtain the fine clay soil needed. Areas with considerable limestone or shale are also unsuitable because of possible fractures, which create leaks. Swampy areas with mucky soils are poor sites because they are difficult to drain and costly to maintain.

The fine clay soils also are used to make up the core of the pond dam—the base upon which the rest of the dam is built. As described above, the clay soil helps seal the dam and prevent leaks and seepage.

Soil for pond dam construction should be excavated from the pond site itself, if possible. If that is not possible, borrow areas that are carefully selected may be used. Any borrow area that is not going to be underwater should be graded to drain freely and replanted to good grass cover. This will help control erosion and restore the symmetry and beauty of the landscape.

Watershed

The watershed required to supply a pond with 1 surface acre of water varies widely across the country. Suitable areas include just a few acres in the wetter areas of the country to 100 acres or more in the arid High

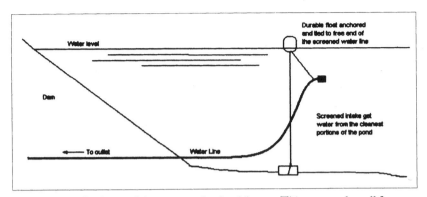

A water intake for the pond does not need to be elaborate. This type works well for most applications.

Plains and Southwest. Too small a watershed feeding your pond and it will simply fail to fill. Too large a drainage area for the pond site may make it unfeasible due to the potential for washout. Consult with your NCRS or ASCS agent to help determine your needs and the site suitability. Local excavators who are experienced in pond construction can also help you with site selection.

The upstream watershed uses are particularly important in selecting your pond site. Protected timber is perhaps the best watershed cover. Other suitable covers include grassland and pasture. These types of terrain provide an inflow of slowed and filtered water. Rowcrop fields are the least desirable watershed cover because of the large amount of silt that will be washed into the pond. It shortens pond life, and fish populations will be drastically reduced. Be aware of upstream uses by livestock, septic fields, and other factors that could introduce contamination to your pond.

Consider that your pond must have an adequate water supply and depth to sustain losses due to evaporation, seepage, and droughts. If your pond is to include stocked fish, it must be deep enough to assure their survival during the coldest winter months. This factor varies throughout the country, but your NRCS agent or the state department of fish and wildlife can give you good information on the water depths needed for a good fishery.

Unless your pond is fed by a spring or running stream, you should expect it to take 8 to 12 months to fill. During this time, you can place pilings for docks, grade and grass slopes above the waterline, apply fittings to pipes, and so on.

Dam

The dam should have a top that is at least 10 feet wide. This will help prevent damage from burrowing animals such as muskrats or groundhogs. If you plan to use the pond dam as a roadway, then it will need to be constructed even wider. Consult with the NRCS agent or your excavator to help determine the width to suit your particular needs.

Important features of a dam are the water outlets that control the flow of water from the pond. The primary outlet feature is the vertical pipe (riser) connected to a horizontal pipe (barrel) that actually passes through the dam. This primary outlet carries water during normal flows to maintain the pond water elevation. Pipes made of smooth metal, corrugated metal, or polyvinylchloride (PVC) plastic materials can be used. There are many different types and styles in use that can be tailored to your needs.

In addition, you will likely want to lay a pipe or two through the dam during its construction to supply farmstead water. These can be set in place during the construction phase and continued later to the various points on your place where you wish to utilize the water. I recommend a ¾-inch or 1-inch pipe running from the pond. You can later continue and branch off that to a livestock water tank, a household filter system, or other farm uses.

At one end of the pond dam, an emergency spillway is usually constructed. This feature is nothing more than a low spot in the dam itself to allow especially high water levels to run out of the pond without running over the top of the dam and jeopardizing the integrity of the dam itself. It acts as a sort of safety valve for your pond. There is no hard-and-fast rule for emergency spillway construction, but basically it needs to be

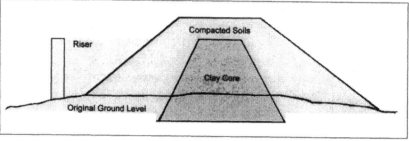

Cross-section of a pond dam. Note the clay core that not only makes up the core of the dam, but also extends downward into the original soil level.

large enough to adequately handle floodwaters. Its elevation should be set higher than the riser on the primary water outlet, and it should be about 2 feet lower than the top of the dam. Here again, your NRCS agent or contractor can help you with the design of the emergency spillway.

If necessary, the pond-side face of the dam can be protected from wind and wave action by riprapping it with rock. Riprap should extend several feet below the anticipated low-water level. This can become rather costly to install, and is more likely to be needed in shallower ponds in the more windswept parts of the country.

The pond dam should be seeded and strawed immediately after construction to prevent erosion. A permanent species of grass, suitable for your local area, should be used. A quality grass, properly fertilized, will quickly cover the site. It will prevent erosion and weed growth and will be easy to maintain.

Other Considerations

The pond bank should have a 2:1 slope to prevent excessive growth of rooted aquatic weeds such as cattails. Plan your pond to eliminate any wide shallow areas, unless you plan to maintain the spot as a beach or

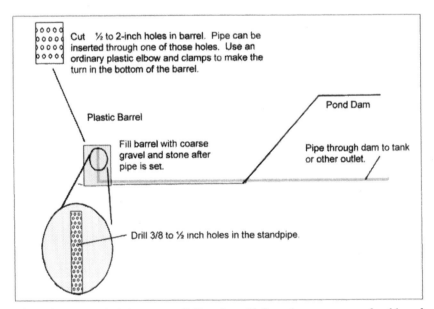

Cut ½ to 2-inch holes in barrel. Pipe can be inserted through one of those holes. Use an ordinary plastic elbow and clamps to make the turn in the bottom of the barrel.

Plastic Barrel

Pond Dam

Fill barrel with coarse gravel and stone after pipe is set.

Pipe through dam to tank or other outlet.

Drill 3/8 to ½ inch holes in the standpipe.

A good water intake is important. Follow the guidelines above to create a durable and functional intake for your pond.

swimming area. Shallow spots in ponds will soon become choked with cattails or other vegetation.

☞ Irregular-shaped ponds (noncircular) increase angler access by creating more shoreline and fish habitat. You can also increase fish habitat by placing a few old rooted stumps, large clay tiles, or other objects in the pond before it fills. These items will help create escape and nesting cover for the fish.

☞ Livestock should be excluded from ponds by fencing. Utilize a gravity-flow watering trough that can be installed below the dam for livestock water (see the illustration for an idea on constructing this water outlet). Provide for mowing of the pond banks and dam to control vegetation.

☞ Inspect and repair your pond periodically. Fill gullies, replant grass, and add riprap as needed. Mow pond edges to prevent woody plant growth and promote easy access.

☞ The pond should be cleared of trees and brush in a strip at least 20 to 30 feet around the shoreline. This will help minimize the number of leaves that fall into it. Excessive leaf fall into the pond will discolor the water and can encourage the growth of algae.

With some proper planning and construction, your dream of having farm pond on your own place can be realized. Ponds are an important asset to the country place, as well as being a source of recreation and relaxation. Once your pond is completed, you will see how well it fits into your homestead plan, adding convenience, enjoyment, and value to your place.

10

WELLS & WATER

Determining Water Needs

Wells

Cisterns

Springs

Public Water Supply

Pumping and Distribution

Filtering and Treating

A dependable supply of drinkable water is an absolute must for the farmstead. Sources usually include wells, cisterns, springs, ponds, and public water supplies. (Ponds are discussed in depth in chapter 9.) Even where public water supplies are available, some folks want the independence of utilizing their own private water system. More than 14 million households nationwide depend on their own well, spring, or cistern to supply water for home use. Important aspects of a home water supply are the quantity needed, pumping, distribution, and treatment.

Determining Water Needs

Before you consider what type of system is best, you need to determine just how much water you will likely be using. Likewise, when planning your water system, first determine your family's water needs. A conservative family will use about 50 gallons per person per day. A family of five would need a system that can produce and make available 250 gallons per day. Therefore, you will need a spring or well that can produce this kind of volume. If you're using a cistern system for storage, a 2,500-gallon cistern will provide only a 10-day supply using the above figures. Consider all this as you begin to assess your water system options.

Your home water system should be tested for bacteria at least once a year and after any repairs to the system have been performed. It is also important to assess the water quality if you suspect contamination due to a change in color or odor of the water, or due to continuing gastrointestinal illness. The quality of groundwater can be threatened by private sewage-disposal systems as well as past and present industrial, municipal, and agricultural practices.

Wells

Wells are probably the most common water source for independent country dwellers. A properly constructed well usually will provide a dependable supply of high-quality water for a long time with little maintenance.

Before contracting with a well driller, you may wish to become familiar with state regulations that apply to your area. Reputable and licensed well drillers know the proper procedures and techniques for drilling a safe and legal water well. Check with your county health department, county extension service, or state department of natural resources for information pertaining to the rules governing water usage in your area.

Modern wells are usually drilled by using mobile truck-mounted drilling rigs. In some areas, wells can produce good water at less than 100 feet. In others, including my own rocky corner of southern Indiana, you may have to sink a well more than 500 feet to reach good water. With well drillers charging from $10 to $15 or more per foot drilled, you can see that this can quickly add up. This makes site selection very important.

Modern wells are cased and grouted. Well casings keep the flow of water going and prevent caving in of the drilled well. Grouting is done to seal the well, to prevent contaminants from entering, and to protect your water system. Generally, a drilled well will utilize a submersible pump at the bottom of the casing to move the water to the point of use or storage.

MAINTAINING YOUR WELL

Early spring is a great time to test your well water and inspect your well. Another good time is the day after a heavy rainfall. Melting snow or running water transports a lot of material from the surface deep into the soil. This can cause material from the soil surface to move into your drinking water source. Testing your water at times when contamination is likely will provide you with the most accurate assessment of how safe your drinking water is.

PREVENTING BACTERIA FROM ENTERING YOUR WELL WATER

Treating contaminated well water is one way of ensuring your water is safe to drink. For a more long-term solution, the source of bacteria should be identified and, where possible, eliminated. If your water contains high levels of bacteria and nitrate, it is not wise to invest a lot of money in water treatment systems. These systems treat the water to eliminate contaminants, but they don't fix the problem, which is bacteria and nitrate entering your water supply. If possible, you should try to eliminate the source of contaminants entering the water or seek another source for your drinking water supply. This could mean drilling a new well, repairing your current well, or simply buying bottled water.

Cisterns

A cistern with enough capacity can provide water for domestic purposes, but it's usually not adequate for livestock.

Cistern construction, drainage surfaces, and filtering equipment are important considerations in preventing contamination of the water supply. A cistern must be large enough to provide water during periods of little or no rainfall, unless you can arrange to haul water to refill the cistern. Treatment of the water should be continuous to eliminate harmful bacteria.

Sometimes a rural water district is located in the area, but too often they are already operating at capacity. The only choices left are to develop a pond water system (chapter 9) or build a cistern. The cistern is usually lower in initial cost and maintenance. However, a properly designed cistern and its essential supply components are not inexpensive.

Cistern components include an adequate roof area, roof gutters, downspouts, downspout diverters, roof washer, water pump, and distribution pipe. A sand filter and chlorine treatment are wise investments in helping to guarantee safer water.

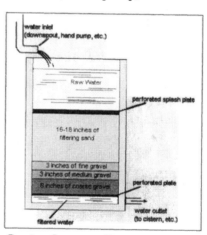

Gravity-flow water filter.

The downside of using cistern systems and water collectors is the area required to collect sufficient rainfall in many locales. For example, a family of five requires more than 5,000 square feet of roof area in many parts of the country to catch enough water to supply their annual needs. Obviously, most houses do not offer this type of surface area. Therefore, a large barn may be needed to supplement the house roof. If the cistern or collection roof is too small, the family will have to depend on hauled water during periods of low rainfall. I grew up in a home with this type of water system, and can remember those dry spells when we had to have water hauled and off-loaded into our cistern.

Sizing and placement of the roof gutters are very important to maximize the amount of rainfall caught for your cistern. Since you are using this as your domestic water, you will want to be vigilant in keeping the gutters clean and clear of debris. Gutter guards made of ¼-inch wire mesh help keep out leaves and trash. However, regular cleaning is still required. The downspout needs a diverter valve and waste pipe to drain roof water away from the cistern when it is full.

A device called roof washer is a very good investment, because it diverts contaminants washed off the roof before allowing the rainwater to enter the cistern. Between rains, drifting foreign materials such as sulfates and nitrates discharged into the atmosphere from power plants, highway vehicles, and other sources can contribute to roof sediment. Bird droppings and chimney smoke from wood fires can also contaminate the roof. It has been estimated that the first 0.01 inch of rainfall is adequate to wash foreign material off a roof. As an example, 15 gallons of wastewater would be adequate to wash a 2,400-square-foot roof.

Cistern water can only be as clean as the water that is allowed to enter it. You can make a sand-and-gravel filter to remove some contaminants. If the gravel is limestone rock, it will help neutralize the acidic rainwater.

Any filter must be maintained or it will slowly clog, resulting in ideal conditions for bacterial growth. Also, a mat can form from bacterial activity that will eventually plug the sand. The top 1 to 2 inches of sand become clogged with sediment and should periodically be removed and replaced with new washed, screened beach or quarried sand. Such a filter is very heavy (a cubic foot of rock and sand can weigh up to 150 pounds) and should not be placed on the cistern roof unless the roof was designed for such a load.

CISTERN MATERIALS

Cisterns can be made from reinforced poured concrete, reinforced concrete block, metal, or fiberglass. Because of the expected permanence of a cistern, reinforced concrete is usually the best investment. Concrete blocks have the potential for leakage at their many joints, metal has a tendency to rust, and fiberglass has strength problems when buried. A cistern built of concrete also helps neutralize water acidity.

The top, which can be poured separately with an opening for the roof water, should include a manhole for inspecting and cleaning. It should also incorporate a raised lip and heavy lid for cleanliness and safety. The cistern floor should have a light slope of about 1 inch for each 12 feet toward a small sump located under the manhole. This will allow for easy water removal when cleaning the cistern. Treat the inside with a quality masonry sealant, and treat the outside with good waterproof sealant below grade.

If possible, the cistern should be buried at least to the level of the overflow pipe for the following reasons:

☞ To give ample room to place a roof washer on top of the cistern.
☞ To make landscaping easier.
☞ To prevent cistern water from freezing.

Before a cistern is used, it should be cleaned and disinfected. After cleaning out any dirt and other debris accumulated during construction, scrub the interior with a solution of ¼ cup of 5 percent chlorine bleach mixed in 10 gallons of water. *Caution:* Make sure that there is ample ventilation for the workers inside the cistern. After this treatment, hose down the interior until the chlorine odor disappears and then drain. A cistern needs to be cleaned at least every five years, and perhaps more often where blowing dust, leaves, and fireplace or stove ash fall on the roof. Inspecting and cleaning the gutters, downspout, roof washer, and filter will help keep a cistern cleaner.

The following chart tells you how much of 5.25 percent solution of Clorox, Hilex, or Purex you'll need to disinfect your cistern.

CISTERN DISINFECTANTS

AMOUNT OF WATER	1 gallon	2 gallons	3 gallons	4 gallons	5 gallons
AMOUNT OF SOLUTION	3 drops	6 drops	9 drops	12 drops	15 drops

In addition, the University of Kentucky Extension Service recommends adding 1 ounce of regular 5 percent household bleach for each 200 gallons of water in your cistern, on a weekly basis.

Springs

A properly developed spring can provide water for domestic and farm use, if the amount of water available meets the needs through the year.

Springs do not necessarily provide safe water for drinking without treatment. Most states will not approve springwater supplies for domestic purposes unless the spring is properly improved and water tests are satisfactory. In many areas, groundwater may be inadequate, hard to find, or contaminated.

When an adequate supply of high-quality well or springwater is found nearby, this is the best system to develop. However, you must know the history of a spring before spending money on developing it into your primary water supply, because many springs are seasonal. That is, what may appear to be a gushing, rolling water supply in springtime may slow to a mere trickle come summer.

Public Water Supply

Many rural areas of the country have public water supplies available. Rural cooperatives similar to those that brought electricity to the countryside have been set up to help bring good water at a reasonable cost to areas where it was lacking. Where available, these systems provide a dependable water supply that is constantly monitored and treated. In some areas, they are the only practical means of supplying sufficient water to a family. We supply our household water with just this type of system and use pond water and an intermittent stream to water our livestock. We do, however, make some provisions for emergency water in the event that the public system is made nonfunctional.

When other options are available, evaluate the cost of water. This includes the cost of developing, managing, and maintaining a private system. There is no disgrace in hooking up to a public water system, particularly if you are working toward an independent system or can supplement it with other water for livestock and other agricultural uses to keep costs down.

Pumping and Distribution

Now that the water source is established, there still needs to be a delivery system for it to be utilized throughout your farmstead. With some ponds and springs, a gravity-flow system will suffice for supplying water, but in most cases you'll need to incorporate a pump.

For many wells and springs, the pump and an accompanying pressure tank can be neatly housed in a structure called a pump house. The pump simply moves the water from the water source into the pressurized tank. From there, the pressure moves the water through the supply lines to the respective water outlets as required. Locate the pump as close to the water source as possible. Remember, it is easier to push water than it is to pull it. Complete plans for a spring house and an insulated pump house are available from sources listed at the end of this chapter.

Delivery of the water to your house or to various spigots around the place can be done fairly simply. It will, however, require a lot of digging. This is a good reason to sit down and sketch a diagram of your proposed water system. You will be able to draw and redraw water lines in the locations where you will need to do the least amount of digging. This will save work and material when the actual installation begins.

When you are installing water lines on your place, be certain to place them deep enough to prevent freezing. This will save you a lot of headaches (and backaches) later on if you have to dig up and repair a burst line. The frost line in our area is about 16 to 18 inches, so I always try to put water lines at least 18 to 24 inches deep. When backfilling your water-line ditch, be mindful of any large or sharp rocks that could end up wearing a hole in your line. Try to fill directly around the line with fine, rock-free soil first.

It is a good idea to use a ¾-inch supply line on the place and branch off it with ½-inch line to spigots, valves, and so on. On any pressurized system, I recommend using only PVC hard plastic pipe for most applications, not the black roll plastic pipe. I have had far fewer problems (breaks) with the rigid PVC pipe. For gravity-flow systems, the less expensive black roll pipe should work acceptably. Your local hardware supplier can help you select all the pipe, fittings, and other hardware you will need as you plan your system.

Filtering and Treating

Technology for home water treatment has advanced considerably over the years. From basic sand-and-gravel filters to reverse osmosis models, a wide variety of purification products is available. Small charcoal filters are available that attach directly to the kitchen faucet as a final point-of-use filter. All these filters are good and do the job for which they are designed. You just have to decide on the level of treatment that you are comfortable with. Some folks firmly refuse to treat their water at all. Consult some of the informative booklets and Web sites listed at the end of this chapter to help you make this decision.

As I've noted, I grew up where the cistern water was caught from roof runoff and ran through a very crude sand-and-gravel filter. During some dry summer months, we had to have water hauled from town. A local water hauler had a truck set up for this purpose and could haul about 1,000 gallons at a time. As far as I can remember, the only chlorine or other treatment our water received was when the occasional "town water" was mixed with it.

The federal Environmental Protection Agency (EPA) has a very good descriptive Web site pertaining to treatment of home water systems. It can be found at http://www.epa.gov/seahome/private/src/ treat.htm.

A good water source will help you to achieve greater independence on your place. Refer to the sources listed in this chapter, check with materials suppliers, and use your own ingenuity to come up with the best system for you.

WATER SYSTEM RESOURCES

THE NATURAL RESOURCE, AGRICULTURE AND ENGINEERING SERVICE, Cooperative Extension, 152 Riley-Robb Hall Ithaca, NY 14853-5701, 1-607-255-7654, fax 1-607-254-8770, NRAES@cornell.edu.

This organization offers a helpful publication, *Private Drinking Water Supplies: Quality, Testing, and Options for Problem Waters*, NRAES-47. This will help those who supply their own water better understand the factors that affect quality. The 60-page bulletin provides up-to-date information on U.S. EPA drinking water standards, water testing, the impact of land use on water quality, and options for obtaining a safe drinking water supply. The three chapters are supplemented by nine tables and 16 figures. Three appendices provide listings of drinking water contaminants, along with their possible sources and chronic health effects. Information on livestock water quality is also included. It is a general reference that will be useful for people who supply their own water from wells, springs, ponds, or cisterns; people who are dissatisfied with the quality of water from their public water supplies; and cooperative extension and water treatment professionals. The publication is available for eight dollars (plus shipping and handling) from NRAES. The shipping and handling charge is $3.75 for a single copy within the continental United States. New York residents, add 8 percent sales tax (calculated on both the cost of publications and the shipping and handling charges).

Several plans are available for homeowners who want to construct their own private water system.

SPRINGWATER COLLECTION AND STORAGE #5197, North Dakota State University, P.O. Box 5626, Fargo, ND 58105. The cost is two dollars. This publication describes some details on building a spring house. Note that NDSU offers several good plans for this purpose; ask for a list of plans or check out http://www.ag.ndsu.nodak.edu/abeng/plans/index.htm.

MWPS. A nice plan for an insulated pump house is available at

http://www.public.iastate.edu/~mwps_dis/mwps_web//frame_p.html.
Or it can be ordered from MWPS, 122 Davidson Hall, Iowa State University, Ames, IA 50011-3080, mwps@iastate.edu, 1-800-562-3618, fax 1-515-294-9589. Ask for the plan: Insulated Pump House, MWPS-74001.

The following books also provide more detailed information on water sources:

PRIVATE WATER SYSTEMS HANDBOOK, Midwest Plan Service No. MWPS-14, available from Agricultural Engineering Extension, 205 Agricultural Engineering, University of Missouri, Columbia, MO 65211, 1-573-882-2731. The current price is $7 plus $1.83 for sales tax, postage, and handling.

PLANNING FOR AN INDIVIDUAL WATER SYSTEM, Catalog No. 600 is available from the American Association for Vocational Instructional Materials, 745 Gaines School Road, Athens, GA 30605, 1-800-228-4689. The current price is $13, plus $2.50 for postage and handling.

WATER SYSTEMS HANDBOOK (10th edition) is available from the Water Systems Council, 600 South Federal, Suite 400, Chicago, IL 60605, 1-312- 922-6222. The current price is $15, plus $1.50 for postage and handling.

MANUAL OF INDIVIDUAL AND NON-PUBLIC WATER SUPPLY SYSTEMS, Order No. PB-92-117944, is published by the EPA and available from the National Technical Information Service, 1-800-553-6847. The current price is $27, plus $3 for postage and handling.

I I

PASTIMES
& PURSUITS

Fun, Games, and Gifts

Fun, Games, and Gifts

In this chapter, you will find some good ideas for gifts and pastimes that you can create easily right at home. Even if you are not a skilled woodworker, you should find these projects pretty simple to complete.

These ideas are not something that I have just copied or dreamed up to fill space. Each is an item that I have made and have used, given as a gift, or sold. You can do the same. Doing so, you can make some neat gifts and sale items, save some too-scarce dollars, and enjoy the satisfaction of creating something tangible with your own hands. Oh yes, you will probably want to make extras for yourself, too.

THE MOUNTAIN CLIMBER

The first item is one that my son and I call "the mountain climber." These are easy to make, fun to demonstrate, and amazing to watch. I can tell you from experience that children and adults will have fun with one of these.

To make your mountain climber, start with a piece of wood measuring about 4 inches by 6 inches by ¼ inch thick, along with some light string (I used light nylon twine). On this piece, draw or trace the figure you wish to use for your mountain climber. I have made them in the shape of gingerbread men, teddy bears, and simple human-shaped figures. Once you get the figure outlined onto the wood, simply use a band saw, power jigsaw, or coping saw to cut the figure from the piece. Once sawn, sand and smooth the figure with some sandpaper.

Now comes the important part. Near the end of each arm, where a rope might pass through the fist when gripped, carefully drill a hole down through the arm. Note that this hole does not go front to back, but rather top to bottom. Take some care, and this small-diameter

A mountain climber. They can be made in any figure you desire.

265

hole should not be too difficult to make. A ¹/₁₆-inch hole should be large enough; just make sure that the string you are using will pass freely through it. The important thing to remember is that each hole should slope outward from top to bottom when you drill (see the diagram). Use your favorite paints and decorate the figure however you like.

Next, cut a small piece of wood measuring about 1 inch wide by ½ inch or so thick by about 4 inches long. Near each end of this piece, drill a small hole. These two holes should be approximately the same distance apart as the two holes in the figure's "hands." Drill another hole in the center of the piece. Cut two pieces of twine, each about 3 feet long. Take one piece of the twine, run one end through the hole on one end of the small piece of wood, and tie a bulky knot in the end of the string so that it will not pull through the hole. Repeat with the other piece of string on the other end of the wooden piece. Through the center hole, run a short piece of string and knot it on the bottom side. Tie a loop on the top end of the string. The toy will be suspended from this loop.

Next, take the painted figure and run one string through each of the "hands." If you have a couple of large beads, thread them onto the string and tie a good knot in the end of the string. If you lack the beads, just make do with the bulky knot, but the beads make it easy for young hands to grasp the ends of the strings.

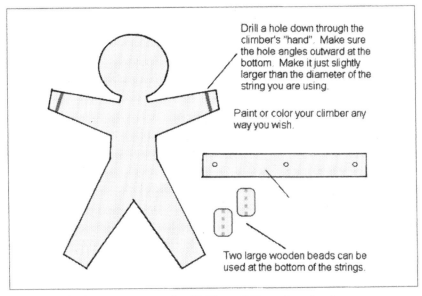

Drill a hole down through the climber's "hand". Make sure the hole angles outward at the bottom. Make it just slightly larger than the diameter of the string you are using.

Paint or color your climber any way you wish.

Two large wooden beads can be used at the bottom of the strings.

Mountain climbers are easy to make. Children of all ages love them!

Suspend the toy from a door-jamb, porch rafter, or similar elevated point. Grasp the ends of the strings firmly and alternately pull on them. First one, then the other, keeping tensions on them as you go. You should see the figure scamper right up the strings to the wooden cross-piece at the top. With a little practice, you can send the mountain climber all the way up the strings in a matter of seconds. Kids love this simple toy. I made one for my sons and soon had to make several more once their friends had seen them! These make really neat gifts, and best of all . . . they don't use batteries.

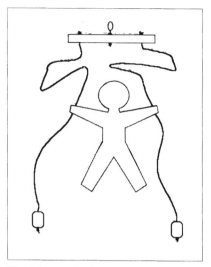

Here's how to rig the mountain climber toy.

HOMEY KNICKKNACKS

Most of us want our kids to pick up the desire and ability to make things in the workshop. Aside from aiding in motor skill development, working with Mom or Dad in the woodshop develops confidence as well as useful skills and abilities. Some of their work might appear to be rather freeform (!), but as the children mature, you will see the quality of their work improve. The important thing is to give them room, materials and the latitude to create . . . and to make mistakes. Let them "just do it." They will learn from it.

I used ordinary 1 x 2 furring strips to create these simple wooden ornaments or accents. Use lathe strips for the roof. Make B just longer by the thickness of the lathe strip, since it will lap over A at the peak of the roof. Paint, add a dot of black for the "opening", and add a screw eye to suspend it from.

With all that said, the next project is a simple one that the kids will enjoy helping on. These little house-shaped knickknacks make neat little ornaments for shelves and for Christmas trees. We made ours from small scraps of 1 x 2 pine. I allowed the kids to mark the simple 45-degree roof angle using a small carpenter's square. I then cut all the pieces on the band saw, ending up with a dozen or more, because we were just using up scraps. Next, I cut some ¼-inch by 1½-inch lath strips into small pieces to make the roof. One side must be cut about ¼ inch longer than the other piece to allow for lapping over at the peak. The measurements are not critical; just cut what looks good. We secured the roof pieces to the pine block using small nails and wire brads. To enable the little houses to be suspended on a Christmas tree, we used some light wire and just twisted up some small eyelets. The long ends of these small wires were forced into a tiny hole drilled into the center of the roof peak.

A coat of gold spray paint really made these little houses look neat. Finally, my son gently dipped the end of a ½-inch dowel rod into some black paint, then touched the front of each little house. The result was a neat round spot that gave the appearance of a hole in a birdhouse. My wife really liked these little houses and immediately suspended them from the Christmas tree. We had to make more to accompany them on nearby shelves. Additionally, my wife sold them for up to three dollars each at a local Christmas crafts fair. You might want to color coordinate them to your home's interior, paint them to match the outside of your house, or just let the kids paint them in bright and varied colors. With a fine brush and a steady hand, or with a paint pen, you can personalize these little ornaments as well.

SQUARE SNOWMEN

Another project that was made from scraps was square porch snowmen. Now, I can imagine most of you raising an eyebrow at this, but let me explain. These are wooden ornamental figures designed from 4 x 4 wood stock, and made to adorn the porch or other entryway of your home. They are painted up to resemble snowmen. Incidentally, when some of my wife's friends and customers saw these, I couldn't make them fast enough! They bought every one I could make.

To make these guys, simply cut a piece of 4 x 4 post into 16-inch lengths. The length is arbitrary, but 16 inches will allow you to cut six figures from one 8-foot length of 4 x 4. You may adjust the cuts to fit what you have. If you decide to sell them, you can adjust the selling price according to the length.

Using a couple of 3-inch deck screws, attach the 4 x 4 to a square piece of 2 x 8, which will become the base. Give the figure a good coat or two of white paint (it will probably take two coats to give a good white appearance). To make the "carrot" nose, whittle down 2 inches or so on the end of a ½-inch dowel rod. Then mark off another ½-inch and cut off the piece. The nose will go into a ½-inch hole that you can drill into the snowman later. Make as many of the noses as you have figures. Be sure to whittle them one at a time, and then cut them off. That's

The snowmen and the large Santa were made to sell or give as gifts.

much easier and safer than trying to whittle down a 2½-inch piece of dowel rod into a carrot shape. Paint each "carrot" with bright orange craft paint or model car enamel. I drove several small nails through a piece of scrap wood and pushed each "carrot" onto a nail. Then they were simple to paint.

At about this point (while all the paint is drying!), you will need to get your hand pruners and head out to the woods. Using your artful eye, select the appropriate pieces of small limbs that will become the arms of the snowman figure. Cut them off and trim them up to give two or three "fingers" per hand. Obviously, cut enough pairs of arms for the figures you are making. "Arms" of about ¼ to ⅜ inch at the base work well.

Once the white paint is dry on the figure's body, take another piece of ½-inch dowel rod and dip it into some black paint. Then gently dab the tip of the dowel straight down onto the spots where the eyes and the mouth are to be. Add three or four more down the front to resemble buttons. These spots will resemble the pieces of coal traditionally used when making snowmen.

After the paint dries, drill a ½-inch hole in the spot where the nose is to be. Drill it about ½-inch deep. Use a dab of wood glue and insert the orange nose into the hole. Next, using the appropriate-diameter drill bit, make one hole on either side of the body to accommodate the twig "arms." Use a dab of wood glue and insert each arm into a hole.

Now that the figure is nearly complete, you need only dress it up a bit. I went to the local Wally World and purchased several cheap sock top caps for 87 cents each. I topped off each snowman with one of the caps. Incidentally, dark green is a very popular color according to the womenfolk. A few in blue and others in dark red made a good variety. My wife supplied some strips of old blanket in complementary colors, and a neck scarf was tied snuggly around each figure's "neck." From this point, it was just a matter of letting customers see them and we sold them all.

We also made several of these as gifts for family and friends. One home nearby has three of them standing guard in front of their garage. Just as soon as I get done writing this, I'm heading to the scrap pile to rummage for materials to make this season's "square snowmen."

Yet another "snowman" figure was made in a similar, yet scaled-down version by using a 1 x 6 x 6 square base and a piece of 2 x 2 for the body. The figure is pretty much made just like the larger model, except for the "hat." Look at the accompanying photograph and you can see pretty much how they are put together. With these smaller figures, I cut the tip of the 2 x 2 at a bit of an angle. Next, I cut a scrap of thin board (I used a piece of luan paneling) in a generally square shape (about 4 x 4) and rounded the corners. Next, I measured the exact dimensions of the 2 x 2 body and marked the shape onto the luan paneling. Using a drill and electric saber saw, I then cut out the wood to make a snugly fitting hole. I worked this "hat brim" down over the 2 x 2 stock until I reached a point where I thought it looked like a slightly askew stovepipe hat. A light bead of wood glue secured the piece, and the whole hat was painted flat black. A touch of decorative spray "snow" added to the wintry look. These little rascals are selling very well, though they do require a bit more work per individual figure.

I have recently heard of jack-o'-lantern figures made from 4 x 4s cut to about 14 to 16 inches. They are painted orange; add a few black lines and the scary face of your choice. A piece of ½-inch dowel rod painted green and cut to about 4 inches can be glued into an appropriately sized hole drilled at a slight angle into the top of the figure. That makes the stem and completes the figure. Just set the wooden figure—or several of them—on your doorstep for a neat accent.

All these figures are easy sellers. I still must be charging too little for them! The small snowmen are selling for $10.95 to $12.95, and the larger ones are selling quickly for $16.95. We completely sold out of all of these in the first few hours of an annual Christmas crafts day. I have seen the small snowmen selling in fancy shops up north for $24.95 and the larger ones going for similarly higher prices, but I get a good return on my investment as it is. The main point is that these bring a really good monetary return for a very small investment in materials. It takes a bit of time to get them all put together, but even then most of the time is allowing the paint to dry!

FRONT-PORCH RING TOSS

For those of you who have a front porch, I'm certain that you know that it is an excellent place to laze away a Sunday afternoon. After a big Sunday dinner, the herd often moves outside to sip iced tea and sort of let everything settle. Good family, friends, and conversation often help.

Here's something that can be an interesting diversion for those front-porch sessions. It is a simple, yet captivating—sometimes nerve racking—game made for just a few cents.

On one of your front-porch posts—preferably one somewhat out of the way of heavy traffic—screw in a heavy hook at about waist level. On one of the adjacent porch roof rafters, screw in a stout screw-eye. Tie a length of sturdy string or twine to the eye and measure down to the hook. Allow a little extra to work with. Next, tie a 3-inch harness ring to the end of the string. Measure off when you tie so that the ring reaches and hooks easily over the hook in the post. Leave some of the string so that you can adjust the ring later if you need to.

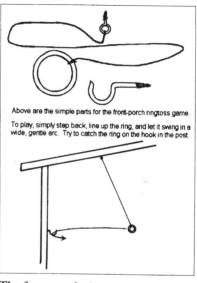

Above are the simple parts for the front-porch ringtoss game.

To play, simply step back, line up the ring, and let it swing in a wide, gentle arc. Try to catch the ring on the hook in the post.

The front-porch ring toss is a simple—and addicting—game.

Now all you have to do is sit back in your rocker and swing the ring and try to hook it over the hook in the post. Hold the ring way back and get a good smooth swing. Just let the ring go and let it arc around and click onto the hook. Sounds easy, doesn't it? Good luck!

GOLF TEE LEAPFROG

Another simple and fun game is golf tee leapfrog. This game was popular long before it became a dining table staple in one of the franchised country restaurants that appear along the interstates. With a scrap of wood, a drill, and a handful of golf tees, you can whip this one out in no time.

Begin by taking an ordinary 1 x 6 board (which is actually a bit less than 5¾ inches in width). Sketch onto the board, or onto a sheet of paper, an equilateral triangle the width of the board. Measure in from each edge of the triangle about ½ inch and make a light line. Lay out and mark your holes 1 inch apart. You should have five holes in the baseline, four in the next, and so on up to the top hole, all equally spaced on the board. Measure the depth of the hole needed— about ⅝ inch. Mark your drill bit with a wrap or two of tape ⅝ inch above the tip to make each hole uniform in depth and to help prevent drilling completely through the board. Drill a hole just slightly larger than the golf tee. You should end up with 15 holes on the board. Paint the board if you wish—the kids may want to pick their favorite color for this!

A simple and fun leapfrog game made with a scrap of wood and some golf tees.

To play, just start out with a golf tee in every hole but one. Leapfrog a golf tee to an empty hole and remove the one you jumped. Jump another and remove it. The idea is to keep going until you end up with only one tee on the board. A simple game, yes; a challenge, you bet!

MAKE YOUR OWN MUSIC WITH HOMEMADE WIND CHIMES

You know, there is something special about sitting out on the front porch, sipping a glass of tea, and enjoying a cool evening. That relaxing feeling is further complemented by the addition of simple yet melodious wind chimes.

The gentle melodies of wind chimes do, indeed, entertain and relax as the slightest breeze artfully plays a tune. My wife really enjoys hearing the wind chimes' melodies as she goes about her chores. Always different, the tunes play along with the whims of the breezes.

The first stop was for tubing for the chimes themselves. After some studying, I decided that I could recycle some old aluminum lawn chairs and utilize sections from the aluminum frame. With trusty hacksaw in hand, I proceeded to dismantle the chair, piece by piece. I cut every section a bit long, so that I could cut them to the proper length on the workbench. I got enough sections from one old chair to make a set of chimes with six pipes.

Another source for pipe is ordinary steel conduit, available at hardware stores.

Just what is the proper length for the tubes? That is a good question. And in doing some research for this, I learned that just as important as the length of the tube is the point at which the tube is suspended. Having studied radio and radio waves some, and being a student of the guitar, I realized that there are points on a sound wave, much like a radio wave, where the tone sounds "alive" and other points where it is a "dead" tone. So I located a chart that describes just where to hang the tube to get the best sound from it. In the table below, you can see the length of tube and the suspension point listed for several different diameters of tube.

The diameter of the clapper and the size of the paddlelike wind catcher will help determine just how much—or little—wind it will take to make your chimes . . . chime. If you want to hear music with the slightest breeze, then a

This wind chime was made using pieces cut from discarded aluminum lawn chairs. You may discover a variety of materials from which to make these.

larger clapper with very little clearance between it and the tubes will make music with just a wisp of wind. If you don't like the chimes to keep you awake all night, then consider a smaller clapper that requires more movement to strike the tubes. Similarly, a large wind catcher at the bottom of the set will get the tubes ringing more easily than a smaller one.

WIND CHIME TUBE LENGTHS

TUBE DIAMETER	NOTE	LENGTH (IN INCHES)	SUSPENSION POINT
1½ inches	Ab	29 $^{13}/_{16}$	6 $^{11}/_{16}$
	A	28 $^{15}/_{16}$	6 ½
	Bb	28 ⅛	6 $^{5}/_{16}$
	B	27 $^{5}/_{16}$	6 ⅛
	C	26 $^{9}/_{16}$	5 $^{15}/_{16}$
	Db	25 $^{13}/_{16}$	5 ¾

1 inch	Db	22 $^{9}/_{16}$	5 $^{1}/_{16}$
	D	21 $^{15}/_{16}$	4 $^{15}/_{16}$
	Eb	21 $^{5}/_{16}$	4 ¾
	E	20 $^{11}/_{16}$	4 ⅝
	F	20 ⅛	4 ½
	Gb	19 $^{9}/_{16}$	4 ⅜
¾ inch	F	17 ⅞	4
	Gb	17 ⅜	3 ⅞
	G	16 ⅞	3 ¾
	Ab	16 ⅜	3 $^{11}/_{16}$
	A	15 $^{15}/_{16}$	3 $^{9}/_{16}$
	Bb	15 $^{7}/_{16}$	3 $^{7}/_{16}$
½ inch	A#/Bb	13 ½	3
	B	13 ⅛	2 $^{15}/_{16}$
	C	12 ¾	2 ⅞
	Db	12 ⅜	2 ¾
	D	12	2 $^{11}/_{16}$
	D#/Eb	11 $^{11}/_{16}$	2 $^{9}/_{16}$

MAKE A STICK WHISTLE

Out here in the sticks, that is exactly what we use to make a neat toy whistle. Every spring when the sap starts flowing, the kids remember that it is time to make whistles and we journey out to get the proper wood. In addition to getting "whistle-makin's," the youngsters also receive some practical lessons in tree identification.

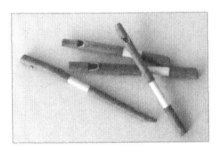

Some finished stick whistles.

To make your own whistle, you will need to select a sprout or sapling of one of the smooth-barked species of trees. In my area, tulip poplar and hickory are popular choices for making the little noisemakers. In other areas, I believe alder or willow is used. Basically, any species that can be made to slip easily from the bark will work. The important thing is to cut the wood in spring when the sap is running.

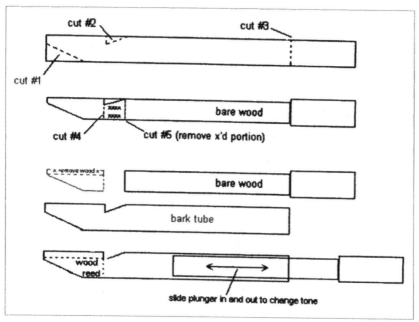

Construction details of a stick whistle.

Select a smooth section of young live wood about ½ inch or so in diameter and about 6 inches in length. I have made whistles up to nearly an inch, but the wood is much more difficult to work with. Try to pick the straightest piece you can find with no bud scars or knots. If you must select wood with scars or knots, cut the stick so they will be where the whistle notch will be located, or on the handle.

Now we're ready to start cutting. First, cut the angle at what will be the reed and mouthpiece. Start at a point about ¾ inch back from the end and cut up toward the opposite side, leaving about ⅛ inch inch of flat surface on the end. Cut number two is the notch cut into the stick as shown. Make the cut about a quarter to a third as deep as the diameter of the stick. Be sure to make the straight cut facing the mouthpiece end of the stick. Cut number three is just a bit different: Score through the bark all the way around the stick, cutting completely through the bark but just barely into the wood.

Now, with the smooth side of the handle of your pocketknife or a small hammer, commence rapping the bark of the stick all around the portion where you have cut the notches. Tap the bark lightly but firmly, not hard enough to split it. What you are doing here is loosening the bark from the woody stem inside. Take your time and tap the wood all over the stick above the line that you scored around the stick's diameter.

Now firmly wrap your hand around the loosened bark, and grasp the other end of the stick with your other hand. Gently but firmly twist the bark until it frees from the wood. If it hangs on a bit too much, just rap on it again until you are able to free it. Once the bark is loosened, slide the woody stem out of the bark.

Next, flatten the wood at what will become the reed. This is much easier to do while the piece is still attached to the "handle." Basically, you are flattening the "reed" to allow air to pass over it (remove the wood marked with the X's in the diagram).

Now make cut number four. Doing this will free the end of the woody stem from the rest. You will end up with the small wooden plug or reed. Shorten the plunger as shown and finish by whittling off the end to smooth it up.

All that is left is to insert the "reed" into the mouthpiece of the whistle as shown. Slide the plunger into the other end of the whistle and you are ready to go.

Now to piping! Slide the plunger in and out of the bark tube to vary the pitch of the tones produced. As a child, I'd apply a coating of shortening to the wood stem to keep the plunger operating smoothly. The whistle will last for many days, but after a day or so, you may notice the bark tube drying out and reducing the space over the reed. This will restrict the airflow over the reed and affect your whistling. To rejuvenate the bark tube and prolong the life of the whistle, just remove the plunger and soak the bark tube in a saucer of water overnight. In the morning, the whistle will be good as new.

This little whistle is simple and fun to make. Experiment with the length and diameter of wood that you use. You can amaze small children with your skill and know-how the first few times you create these simple, rustic music makers. After a few years, though, they will realize just how easy they are to reproduce and will begin to make their own!

Appendix

USEFUL TABLES, CHARTS, AND INFORMATION

Measurements, Weights, and Conversions

COMMON DRY MEASURES

2 pints = 1 quart
8 quarts = 1 peck
4 pecks = 1 bushel
1 bushel contains 2150.42 cubic inches or approximately 1¼ cubic feet.

COMMON LIQUID MEASURES

4 gills = 1 pint
2 pints = 1 quart
4 quarts = 1 gallon
1 gallon contains 231 cubic inches.
1 cubic foot equals 7½ gallons.

ITEM	MEASURE	APPROX. NET WT.
Alfalfa seed	Bushel	60
Apples	Bushel	48
	Northwest box	44
	Eastern box	54
Apricots Western	Lug (brentwood) 4-basket crate	24 24
Artichokes Globe	Box	40
Jerusalem	Bushel	50
Asparagus	Crate	30
Avocados	Lug	12-15
Bananas	Plywood box Fiber folding box	40 40
Barley	Bushel	48
Beans		
Lima, dry	Bushel	56
Others, dry	Bushel Sack	60 100
Lima, unshelled	Bushel	32
Snap	Bushel	30
Beets		
Without tops	Bushel	52
Bunched	Nailed crate	40
Berries, frozen pack		
Without sugar	50-gallon barrel	380
3+1 pack	50-gallon barrel	425
2+1 pack	50-gallon barrel	450

ITEM	MEASURE	APPROX. NET WT.
Blackberries	24-quart crate	36
Bluegrass seed	Bushel	14
Bran	Bushel	20
Bromegrass	Bushel	14
Broomcorn (6 bales per ton)	Bale	333
Broomcorn seed	Bushel	44-50
Buckwheat	Bushel	48-52
Cabbage	Open mesh bag Wire-bound crate Western crate	50 50 80
Cantaloupe	Jumbo crate	83
Carrots	Bushel	50
Without tops	Open-mesh bag	50
Bunched	Western crate	75
Castor beans	Bushel	46
Castor oil	Gallon	8
Cauliflower	1½ bushel crate	37
Celery	Crate	60
Cherry	Cherry lug	16
	4-quart climax basket	6
Clover seed	Bushel	60
Clover (sweet)	Bushel	60

ITEM	MEASURE	APPROX. NET WT.	ITEM	MEASURE	APPROX. NET WT.
Coal, hard	Bushel	80	Hungarian millet seed	Bushel	48-50
Corn			Kafir corn	Bushel	56
Ear, husked	Bushel	70	Kale	Bushel	18
Shelled	Bushel	56	Kapok seed	Bushel	35-40
Meal	Bushel	50	Lard	Tierce	375
Oil	Gallon	7.7	Lentils	Bushel	60
Syrup	Gallon	11.72	Lettuce	Western crate	70
Kafir	Bushel	56	Lime	Bushel	80
Cotton	Bale, gross	500	Limes (Florida)	Box	80
	Bale, net	480	Linseed oil	Gallon	7.5
Cottonseed	Bushel	32	Malt	Bushel	34
Cottonseed oil	Gallon	7.7	Maple syrup	Gallon	11.03
Cowpeas	Bushel	60	Meadow fescue seed	Bushel	24
Cranberries	Barrel	100	Milk	Gallon	8.6
	¼-barrel box	25	Millet	Bushel	48-50
Cream, 40%	Gallon butterfat	8.39	Molasses, edible	Gallon	11.72
Cucumbers	Bushel	48	Molasses, inedible	Gallon	11.77
Dewberries	24-quart crate	36	Mustard seed	Bushel	58-60
Eggplant	Bushel	33	Oats	Bushel	32
Eggs, average size	Case, 30 dozen	46.8	Olives	Lug	25-30
Escarole	Bushel	25	Olive oil	Gallon	7.6
Figs, fresh	Box, single layer	6	Onions	Bushel	57
Flaxseed	Bushel	56	Onions, dry	Sack	50
Flour, various	Bag	100	Onions, green		
Hempseed	Bushel	44	Bunched	Crate	50-55
Hickory nuts	Bushel	50	Onion sets	Bushel	28-32
Honey	Gallon	11.78	Orchard grass seed	Bushel	14
Honey ball melons	Crate	70	Palm oil	Gallon	7.5
Honeydew melons	Jumbo crate	44	Parsnips	Bushel	50
Hops	Bale, gross	200			
Horseradish roots	Bushel	35			
	Barrel	100			
Hubam seed	Bushel	60			

ITEM	MEASURE	APPROX. NET WT.
Peaches	Bushel	48
	Lug box	20
	California fruit box	18
Peas		
Green, unshelled	Bushel	20
Dry	Bushel	60
Peppers	Bushel	25
	Crate	50
Perilla seed	Bushel	37-40
Pineapples	Crate	70
Plums and prunes		
California	4-basket crate	20-29
Other	1/2-bushel basket	28
Popcorn		
On ear	Bushel	70
Shelled	Bushel	56
Poppy seed	Bushel	46
Potatoes	Bushel	60
	Barrel	165
	Bag	50
	Bag	100
Quinces	Bushel	48
Rapeseed	Bushel	50-60
Raspberries	24-quart crate	36
Redtop seed	Bushel	14
Refiner's syrup	Gallon	11.45
Rice		
Rough	Bushel	45
	Bag	100
	Barrel	162
Milled	Pocket or bag	100
Rosin	Drum, net	520
Rutabagas	Bushel	36
Rye	Bushel	56
Sesame seed	Bushel	46
Shallots	Crate (8 doz. bunches)	40
	Barrel (20 doz. bunches)	100

ITEM	MEASURE	APPROX. NET WT.
Sorgo		
Seed	Bushel	50
Syrup	Gallon	11.55
Sorghum grain	Bushel	56
Soybeans	Bushel	60
Soybean oil	Gallon	7.7
Spelt	Bushel	40
Spinach	Bushel	20
	L.A. crate	26-40
Strawberries	24-quart crate	36
Sudangrass seed	Bushel	40
Sugarcane syrup (sulfured or unsulfured)	Gallon	11.45
Sunflower seed	Bushel	24-32
Sweet potatoes	Bushel	55
	Crate	50
Tangerines, Florida	½-box	45
Timothy seed	Bushel	45
Tomatoes	Bushel	53
	Lug box	32
Tung oil	Gallon	7.8
Turnips		
Without tops	Bushel	54
Bunched	Crate	60-80
Turpentine	Gallon	7.23
Velvetbeans (hulled)	Bushel	60
Vetch	Bushel	60
Walnuts	Bushel	50
Water, H2O	Gallon	8.33
Watermelons	Average size	25
Wheat	Bushel	60

Gestation Periods for Common Livestock

DATE OF SERVICE	MARE	COW	EWE	SOW
01 January	06 December	10 October	30 May	22 April
01 February	06 January	10 November	30 June	23 May
01 March	03 February	08 December	30 July	22 June
01 April	06 March	08 January	28 August	21 July
01 May	05 April	07 February	27 September	21 August
01 June	06 May	10 March	28 October	20 September
01 July	05 June	09 April	27 November	20 October
01 August	06 July	10 May	27 December	20 November
01 September	06 August	10 June	26 January	21 December
01 October	05 September	10 July	25 February	20 January
01 November	06 October	10 August	27 March	20 February
01 December	05 November	09 September	26 April	21 March

Land Measurements

1 mile =	8 furlongs
1 link =	7.92 in.
1 foot =	12 in.
1 yard =	36 in. or 3 ft.
1 rod or pole =	16.5 ft.
	5.5 yds.
	25 links
1 chain =	66 ft.
	100 links
	4 rods
1 furlong =	40 rods
	660 ft.
1 mile =	5,280 ft.
	1,760 yds.
	320 rods
	80 chains
	8 furlongs
1 square foot =	144 sq. in.

1 square yard =	9 sq. ft.
1 square rod =	272.25 sq. ft.
	30.25 sq. yds.
1 acre =	43,560 sq. ft.
	160 sq. rods
	10 sq. chains

1 acre is about 208.7 sq. ft. or 8 rods wide by 20 rods long or any two numbers of rods whose product is 160 (25 x 125 ft.) = .0717 of an acre.

1 square mile or section =	640 acres
1 township =	36 sq. miles
	36 sections
1 township =	6 miles square

To find the number of acres in a body of land, multiply the length by the width (in rods) and divide the product by 160. When the opposite sides are unequal, add them, and take half the sum for the mean length or width.

Useful Information

STRAW IS A STRONG WATER ABSORBENT

Soil	40% absorbent
Wheat Straw	220%
Oat Straw	285%
Cut Straw	500%
Peat	600%

TO DETERMINE THE CAPACITY OF A CISTERN

A cistern 10 feet in diameter and 9 feet deep will hold 168 barrels.

A cistern 5 feet in diameter will hold 5 2/3 barrels for every foot in depth.

A cistern 6 feet in diameter will hold 6 3/4 barrels for every foot in depth.

A cistern 8 feet in diameter will hold nearly 12 barrels for every foot in depth.

A cistern 10 feet in diameter will hold 18 3/8 barrels for every foot in depth.

TO FIND THE CONTENTS OF SQUARE TANKS IN GALLONS

Multiply the area of the bottom by the height in order to secure the cubic feet. Multiply the cubic feet by 7½ (exact 7.48) and the result will be the number of gallons. For the contents in barrels, multiply the cubic feet by 0.2375.

TO FIND THE VALUE OF ARTICLES SOLD BY THE TON

Multiply the number of pounds by the price per ton, point off three places and divide by 2.

TO FIND THE CONTENTS OF BARRELS AND CASKS IN GALLONS

Multiply the square of the mean diameter in inches by the depth in inches and the product by 0.0034.

CIRCLES, SPHERES, AND OTHER GEOMETRIC FIGURES

To find the circumference of a circle, multiply the diameter by 3.1416.

To find the area of a circle, multiply the square of the diameter by 0.7854.

To find the surface of a sphere, multiply the square of the diameter by 3.1416.

To find the area of a sphere, multiply the cube of the diameter by 0.5236.

To find the area of a rectangle, multiply the length by the width.

To find the area of a triangle, multiply the base by the altitude by 0.5.

To find the area of a curved surface of a cylinder (like a silo), multiply 3.1416 by diameter by the height.

To find the volume of a sphere, multiply 0.5238 by the cube of the diameter.

To find the volume of a cylinder, multiply 0.7854 by the height by the square of the diameter.

To find the volume of a pyramid, multiply ⅓ by the area of the base by the altitude.

To find the volume of a cone (like a pile of grain), multiply 0.2618 by the square of the diameter.

CUBIC MEASURES

1728 cubic inches = 1 cubic foot

27 cubic feet = 1 cubic yard

128 cubic feet = 1 cord

COMMODITY WEIGHTS AND MEASURES

A pint is a pound—or very nearly—of each of the following:water, wheat, butter, sugar, and blackberries.

A gallon of milk weighs 8.6 pounds; cream, 8.4 pounds; 46½ quarts of milk weigh 100 pounds.

A keg of nails weighs 100 pounds

A barrel of flour weighs 196 pounds; of salt, 280 pounds; of beef, fish, or pork, 200 pounds; of cement (four bags), 376 pounds.

Cotton in a standard bale weighs 480 pounds.

A bushel of coal weighs 80 pounds.

A barrel of cement contains 3.8 cubic feet; of oil, 42 gallons.

A barrel of dry commodities contains 7,056 cubic inches, or 105 dry quarts.

A bushel, leveled, contains 2,150.42 cubic inches; a bushel heaped, 2,747.7 cubic inches. (Used to measure apples, potatoes, shelled corn in bin.)

A peck contains 537.605 cubic inches.

A dry quart contains 67.201 cubic inches.

A board foot = 144 cubic inches; a cord contains 128 cubic feet.

WEIGHTS AND VOLUMES OF WATER

One cubic inch of water weighs 0.036 pound.

One cubic foot weighs 62.5 pounds.

One cubic foot = 7.48 gallons.

One pint (liquid) weighs 1.04 pounds.

One gallon weighs 8.355 pounds.

One gallon = 231 cubic inches

One liquid quart = 57.75 cubic inches.

TABLES CONVENIENT FOR TAKING INSIDE DIMENSIONS

A box 24 x 24 x 14.7 inches will hold a barrel of 31½ gallons.

A box 15 x 14 x 11 inches will hold 10 gallons.

A box 8¼ x 7 x 4 inches will hold a gallon.

A box 4 x 4 x 3.6 inches will hold a quart.

A box 16 x 12 x 11.2 inches will hold a bushel.

A box 12 x 11.2 x 8 inches will hold ½ bushel.

A box 7 x 6.4 x 12 inches will hold a peck.

A box 8.4 x 8 x 4 inches will hold a beck, or 4 dry quarts.

A box 6 x 5.6 x 4 inches deep will hold ½ gallon.

CAPACITY OF SQUARE BOXES

A box with each side of the sizes listed below can contain the following amounts:

FEET	INCHES	BUSHELS
1	1	1
1	4½	2
1	6¾	3
1	8½	4
1	10¹/₁₆	5
1	11½	6
2	¾	7
2	2	8
2	3	9
2	4	10

TO FIND THE HEIGHT OF A TREE OR BUILDING

Set up a stick and measure its shadow. Measure the length of the shadow of the tree. The length of the shadow of the tree, times the height of the stick, divided by the length of the shadow of the stick equals the height of the tree.

SUITABLE DISTANCES FOR PLANTING

TYPE OF FRUIT	DISTANCE (FEET EACH WAY)
Apple, standard	30–40
Apple, dwarf	16–20
Pears, standard	16–20
Pears, dwarf	10
Cherries, standard	18–20
Plums, standard	16–20
Peaches	16–18
Apricots	16–18
Currants	3–4
Gooseberries	3–4
Raspberries	3–5
Grapes	8–12

To estimate the number of plants required for an acre, at any given distance, multiply the distance between the rows by the distance between the plants, which will give the number of square feet allotted to each plant, and divide the number of square feet in an acre (43,560) by this number. The quotient will be the number of plants required.

LUMBER MEASURE

To find the contents of boards, in square feet, multiply the length (in feet) by the width (in inches) and divide the product by 12.

Example: Find the contents of a 16-foot board, 9 inches wide.
9 x 16 = 144.144
divided by 12 = 12 square feet.

To find the contents of joists, etc., in square feet, multiply the length, thickness, and width together, and divide the product by 12.

Example: Find the contents of an 18-foot joist, 2 x 8.
2 x 2 x 18 = 288.288
divided by 12 = 24 square feet.

TO FIND THE NUMBER OF BOARD-FEET IN A LOG

Subtract 4 inches from the diameter and square the remainder. The result will be the number of board feet in a 16-foot log. Add an eighth for 18-foot logs, a quarter for 20-foot logs. Subtract an eighth for 14-foot logs, a quarter for 12-foot logs.

TO MEASURE CORN IN CRIBS

Corn in the ear of good quality, measured when settled, will hold out at 2½ cubic feet to the bushel. Inferior quality, 2⅜ to 2½ cubic feet.

At 2⅜ cubic feet to the bushel, divide the cubic feet in the crib by 2⅜ or multiply by 8 and divide by 19.

At 2½ cubic feet to the bushel, divide the cubic feet in the crib by 2½ or multiply by 2 and divide by 5.

TO FIND THE BUSHELS OF GRAIN OR SHELLED CORN IN A BIN OR WAGON BOX   Multiply the number of cubic feet by 0.8.

TO FIND THE NUMBER OF TONS OF HAY IN A MOW

Multiply the length by the width by the height (all in feet) and divide by 400 to 500, depending upon the kind of hay and how long it has been in the mow.

TO FIND THE NUMBER OF TONS OF HAY IN A STACK

Multiply the overthrow (the distance from the ground on one side over the top of the stack to the ground on the other side) by the length by the width (all in feet); multiply by 3; divide by 10; and then divide by 500 to 600, depending upon the length of time the hay has been in the stack.

MISCELLANEOUS INFORMATION

A gallon of water equals 231 cubic inches and weighs 8⅓ pounds. A cubic foot of water equals 7½ gallons and weighs 62½ pounds.

Water expands ¹/₁₁ of its bulk in freezing.

One cubic inch of water evaporates into a cubic foot of steam. To evaporate 1 cubic foot of water requires the consumption of 7½ pounds of coal, or about 1 pound of coal to a gallon of water. Each nominal horsepower of a boiler requires 30 to 35 pounds of water per hour.

One inch of rainfall means 100 tons of water on every acre.

A column of water 2³/₁₀ feet high equals 1 pound per square inch pressure. To find the pressure per square inch of a column of water, multiply the height of the column by the decimal 0.434.

Doubling the diameter of a pipe or cylindrical vessel increases its capacity four times.

Double-riveting is from 16 to 20 percent stronger than single-riveting.

To find the circumference of a circle, multiply the diameter by 3.1416.

To find the diameter of a circle, multiply the circumference by 0.31831.

To find the area of a circle, multiply the square of the diameter by 0.7854.

To find the sides of an equal square, multiply the diameter by 0.8862.

To find the capacity of cylindrical tanks, square the diameter inches, multiply by the height in inches, and this product by the decimal 0.34. Point off four decimals and you have the capacity in gallons.

To find the contents of a pile of cordwood, multiply the length, width, and height together and divide the product by 128. This will give you the number of cords.

AMOUNT OF PAINT REQUIRED FOR A GIVEN SURFACE

It is impossible to give a rule that will apply in all cases, as the amount varies with the kind and thickness of the paint, the kind of wood or other material to which it is applied, the age of the surface, and other factors. The following is an approximate rule: Divide the number of square feet of surface by 200. The result will be the number of gallons of liquid paint required to give two coats.

WORKING WITH BRICKS

Cubic yard—600 bricks in a wall

Perch (22 cubic feet)—500 bricks in a wall

To pave a square yard on the flat—41 bricks

To pave a square yard on its edge—68 bricks

A brick wall 8" thick requires 15 bricks per square foot

A brick wall 16" thick requires 30 bricks per square foot

A brick wall 24" thick requires 46 bricks per square foot

TO FIND THE INTEREST ON ANY SUM FOR ANY TIME

Point off two places to the left from the right of the principal and multiply by the number of months. This is the amount of interest at a rate of 12 percent per year. Deduct one-sixth for 10 percent; one-third for 8 percent; add one-sixth for 14 percent; one-third for 16 percent, et cetera.

Capacity of Corn Cribs
HEIGHT, 10 FEET; DRY CORN, BUSHELS

Width							LENGTH							
	½	1	12	14	16	18	20	22	24	28	32	36	48	64
6	13	27	320	373	427	480	533	587	640	747	853	960	1280	1707
6¼	13	28	333	389	444	500	556	611	667	778	889	1000	1333	1777
6½	14	29	347	404	462	520	578	636	693	809	924	1040	1387	1849
6¾	15	30	360	420	480	540	600	660	720	840	960	1080	1440	1920
7	16	31	373	436	498	560	622	684	747	871	996	1120	1493	1991
7¼	16	32	387	451	516	580	644	709	773	902	1031	1160	1547	2062
7½	17	32	400	467	533	600	667	733	800	933	1067	1200	1600	2133
7¾	17	34	413	482	551	620	689	758	827	964	1102	1240	1653	2204
8	18	36	427	498	569	640	711	782	853	996	1138	1280	1707	2276
8½	18	38	453	529	604	680	756	831	907	1058	1209	1360	1813	2418
9	20	40	480	560	640	720	800	880	960	1120	1280	1440	1920	2560
10	22	44	533	622	711	800	889	978	1067	1244	1422	1600	2133	2844

The length is found in the top line, the width in the left-hand column–the height being taken at 10 feet. Thus, a crib 24 feet long, 7½ feet wide, and 10 feet high will hold 800 bushels of ear corn, reckoning 2¼ cubic feet to a bushel. If not 10 feet high, multiply by the given height and cut off the right-hand figure. If the above crib were only 7 feet high, it would hold 800 x 7 = 560 (0 bushel, etc.). The same space will hold 1⁴/5 times as much grain as ear corn. Thus a crib that holds 800 bushels of ear corn will hold 800 x 1⁴/5, or 1,440 bushels of grain.

Capacity of Silo

A silo, properly filled—that is, if the contents are made compact throughout—contains 1 ton of silage for every 50 cubic feet of space. To illustrate the economy of a silo to store stock feed as compared with a barn, a ton of hay requires 400 cubic feet of space. A farmer can easily figure how much a silo will contain by the following rules.

Multiply the square of the diameter by 0.7854; this will be the area of the circular floor. Multiply the area of the floor by the height, which will give the number of cubic feet. One cubic foot of silage weighs 40 pounds. Multiply the cubic feet by 40, and the result is the number of pounds of silage the silo will contain. Divide that by 2,000 to find the number of tons.

DIAMETER	DEPTH	CAPACITY IN TONS	ACRES TO FILL 15 T/ACRE	COWS IT WILL FEED FOR 6 MONTHS AT 40 LBS./DAY
10	20	31	2⅓	8
12	20	45	3	12
12	24	54	3²/₅	15
12	28	63	4¹/₅	17
14	22	67	4½	18
14	24	74	5	20
14	28	87	5⅔	24
14	30	93	6	26
16	24	96	6²/₅	27
16	26	104	7	29
16	30	120	8	33
18	30	152	10¹/₅	42
18	36	183	12⅓	50

Miles Traveled in Plowing an Acre

WIDTH OF FURROW, INCHES	MILES
10	9⁹/₁₀
11	9
12	8¼
13	7½
14	7
15	6½
16	6¹/₆

Acreage per Mile of Various Widths

WIDTH	ACRES	WIDTH	ACRES
1 foot	0.121	15 feet	1.815
5 feet	0.605	16 feet	1.936
8 feet	0.968	18 feet	2.178
10 feet	1.21	20 feet	2.42
12 feet	1.452	24 feet	2.904
14 feet	1.694	25 feet	3.025

Miles Traveled in Planting an Acre— 3-Foot 6-Inch Rows

1-row planter	2.34 miles
2-row planter	1.17 miles
3-row planter	0.78 mile

There are 10,667 stalks in an acre planted in 3½-foot rows, three stalks to the hill, hills 3½ feet apart, or drilled one stalk every 14 inches.

There are 3,556 hills in an acre planted in 3½-foot rows, hills 3½ feet apart.

Plant Food Guide—Elements Available

AVAILABLE POUNDS OF: FERTILIZER OR MATERIAL	N	P2O5	K2O
Ammonia, anhydrous	82	0	0
Ammonium nitrate	33.5	0	0
Ammonium nitrate–limestone	20.5	0	0
Ammonium phosphate sulfate	13-16	20-39	0
Ammonium sulfate	21	0	0
Aqua ammonia	15-30	0	0
Calcium cyanimide	21	0	0
Calcium nitrate	15.5	0	0
Cottonseed meal	6-7	2.5	1.5
Diammonium phosphate	21	53	0
Manure salts	0	0	22-26
Monammonium phosphate	11	48	0
Nitrate of soda	16	0	0
Nitrogen solutions	37-47	0	0
Potash, muriate of	0	0	50-62.5
Potash, sulfate of	0	0	48-52
Rock phosphate	0	3	0
Sewage sludge	1.5-3	1-2	0
Sulfate of potash–magnesia	0	0	22
Superphosphate, concentrated	0	42-48	0
Superphosphate, normal	0	18-20	0
Urea	45	0	0
3-12-12	3	12	12
5-10-10	5	10	10

5-10-5	5	10	5
10-10-10	10	10	10
4-16-16	4	16	16
10-10-5	10	10	5

Plant Food Guide to Determine Fertilizer Needs

REMOVAL–POUNDS

CROP	YIELD	N	P205	K20
Alfalfa hay	4 tons	187	47	180
Apples	400 bu.	20	7	30
Asparagus	1 ton	64	32	80
Barley (grain)	60 bu.	53	23	15
Beans, snap (pods & vines)	2 tons	135	12	55
Beets, sugar (roots)	20 tons	73	29	71
Cabbage	15 tons	100	25	100
Celery	350 crates	80	65	235
Clover, red	2 tons	80	20	70
Corn (grain)	100 bu.	78	36	26
Corn (stover)	3½ tons	52	19	94
Corn (grain & stover)	100	130	55	120
Cotton (lint & seed)	1⅓ bales	57	27	21
Grapes	4 tons	10	6	20
Lespedeza hay	3 tons	130	30	70
Lettuce	8 tons	40	10	48
Oats (grain)	75 bu.	53	23	15
Onions, dry	10 tons	76	17	85
Oranges	600 boxes	65	23	105
Peaches	500 bu.	30	15	55
Peanuts (nuts)	1 ton	60	10	10
Peas, green (peas & vines)	1 ton	50	15	35
Potatoes, Irish (tubers)	500 bu.	108	42	192
Potatoes, sweet (roots)	500 bu.	75	25	125
Soybeans (beans)	40 bu.	176	56	64
Spinach	9 tons	90	30	45
Timothy hay	2 tons	53	20	60
Tobacco	2000 lbs.	73	13	106
Tomatoes	10 tons	60	20	80
Wheat (grain)	40 bu.	47	21	12

Reproductive Process in Farm Animals

SPECIES	AGE AT PUBERTY, MONTHS	NORMAL BREEDING SEASON	AGE AT FIRST BREEDING, MONTHS	LENGTH OF GESTATION OR INCUBATION, DAYS
MAMMALS				
Cat	12-15	Spring and fall	15	63
Cattle	6-9	Continuous	15-24	281
Dog	6-8	Spring and fall	12	58-68
Goat	6-8	Fall	18	151
Horse	10-12	Spring	20-30	336
Rabbit	4-6	Usually continuous	5-8	31
Sheep	4-8	Fall	15-18	149
Swine	5-8	Spring and fall	9	112
BIRDS				
Chicken	3-6	Winter and spring	6	21
Duck	3-6	Spring	9-12	30
Goose	9-12	Spring	9-12	30
Guinea	9-12	Spring	9-12	24
Turkey	9-12	Winter and spring	9-12	28

Rule-of-Thumb Guide to Metric Measurements

The following guide should prove sufficient for everyday measurement of metric units.

	NAME	SYMBOL	APPROXIMATE SIZE
LENGTH	Meter	m	39½ inches
	Kilometer	km	0.6 mile
	Centimeter	cm	Width of a paper clip
	Millimeter	mm	Thickness of a paper clip
AREA	Hectare	ha	2½ acres
WEIGHT	Gram	g	Weight of a paper clip
	Metric ton	t	Long ton (2,240 pounds)
VOLUME	Liter	L	1 quart and 2 ounces
	Milliter	mL	⅕ teaspoon
PRESSURE	Kilopascal	kPa	Atmospheric pressure is about 100 kPa

Units of time, money, and electricity will not change.

The Celsius temperature scale is used. Some common points are:

DEGREES C.	DEGREES F.	
0	32	Freezing point of water
100	212	Boiling point of water
37	98.6	Normal body temperature
20-25	68-77	Comfortable room temperature

Quantity of Seed Used per Acre

Alfalfa	8-15 lbs.
Buckwheat	50-60 lbs.
Bluegrass seed	25-40 lbs.
Barley	95-100 lbs.
Corn	8-11 lbs.
Clover seed, red	10-15 lbs.
Clover seed, sapling	10-15 lbs.
Clover seed, alfalfa	15-25 lbs.
Clover seed, white	6-8 lbs.
Clover seed, alsike	8-10 lbs.
Cane seed, in drills	20-30 lbs.
Hungarian grass seed	35-50 lbs.
Flax	55-80 lbs.
Hemp	40-60 lbs.
Kaffir corn	40-60 lbs.
Millet seed, Missouri	35-50 lbs.
Millet seed, German	35-50 lbs.
Millet seed, Siberian	20-25 lbs.
Oats	60-70 lbs.
Onion seed	10-12 lbs.
Onion sets	10-12 bu.
Orchard grass seed	25-35 lbs.
Potatoes, Irish	550-650 lbs.
Red top seed, in chaff	25-35 lbs.
Red top seed, fancy solid	10-12 lbs.
Rye	50-80 lbs.
Stock peas	50-80 lbs.
Sunflower	8-10 lbs.
Sweet clover	10-15 lbs.
Timothy seed	12-15 lbs.
Wheat	75-110 lbs.

Fruit Grower's Guide to Planting

| FRUIT | PLANTING DISTANCE | | | Years to full prod. | Life span of plant (in years) | Height of mature plant (in feet) | Est. # plants for family of five |
	Between rows (in feet)	Between plants (in feet)	Interval from planting to fruiting (in years)				
Asparagus	3	1	1	3	20+	4	25-50
Rhubarb	3-5	2	1	2	20+	3	4-6
Strawberry	3.5-4	1.5-2	1	1	3-8	1	100-200
Currants	6-8	4	2	4	12-15	3-4	4-6
Gooseberry	6-8	4	2	4	12-15	3-4	4-6
Raspberry, red	6-8	1-2	1	3	8-15	4-5	25-50
Raspberry, black	6-8	2.5	1	3	8-10	4-5	25-50
Blackberry, erect	6-8	3	1	2	10-12	4-5	25-50
Blackberry, trailing	6-8	6-10	1	2	8-10	6-8	8-10
Blueberry	8-10	6-8	2	5	20+	6-10	8-10
Grape	8-10	6-8	2	5	20+	6	5-10
Everbearing strawberry	1-1.5	1-1.5	60 days	1-3	1	100	
Everbearing raspberry	8	2-3	H	2	8-15	4-5	25-50

Index